A PLUME BOOK

LOVE IS A FOUR-LETTER WORD

Courtney Wilson

MICHAEL TAECKENS received his MFA from the Iowa Writers'
Workshop. He lives in Durham, North Carolina.

"These dispatches from the deep dark depths of romantic doom
will make you cringe, laugh, wince, sigh, laugh again, nod along
in I've-been-there empathy, and recoil in thank-Jesus-I-never-
went-*there* chagrin. Here's the end of love, or what sometimes
passes for it, in all its many forms: wistful, bitter, confused,
tender, regret strewn, and sometimes freakin' deranged.
—Jonathan Miles, author of *Dear American Airlines*

"The song says breaking up is hard to do, but the superb writers in *Love Is a Four-Letter Word* say heartbreak is just a little more complex. These hilarious, poignant, and insightful stories trace the oft-inescapable journey from love's bliss to its brutal undoing and somehow, miraculously, back again. Read these tales to be moved, surprised, healed, and, most of all, transported from the wreck of your own heart."

—Jennifer Gilmore, author of *Golden Country*

"It is a truth universally acknowledged that anyone who has ever ventured into a relationship has a messy breakup story to tell, and this anthology throbs with tales of heartbreak and woe by the best and brightest of today's literary scene. In these deft, funny, and honest tales you're apt to recognize yourself on the giving end, on the receiving end, and, God help you, on both ends."

—Mark Sarvas, author of *Harry, Revised*

"If I were able to write about my ex-girlfriends with this level of wit, passion, and insight, I probably would have a lot fewer of them!"

—Kevin Smokler, author of *Bookmark Now: Writing in Unreaderly Times*

"Love is laid bare in these absolutely human stories, and in so many different ways that I understood more about myself than I could have ever entertained. *Love Is a Four-Letter Word* is an exquisite glimpse into the heart, into romance, into love. These words hurt and shine as much as the tales' many landscapes, and I am left with a less-broken heart for having read them."

—Brad Land, author of *Goat: A Memoir* and
Pilgrims Upon the Earth

"An alluringly voyeuristic collection of romantic cautionary tales, without the predictable 'happily ever after' endings—at least fifty new ways to leave your lover."

—Amy Fine Collins, author of *The God of Driving*

LOVE IS A FOUR-LETTER WORD

 *True Tales of Breakups,
Bad Relationships,
and Broken Hearts*

Edited by Michael Taeckens

Introduction by Neal Pollack

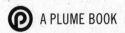 A PLUME BOOK

NOTE ON THE TEXT
Names and other pertinent details have been changed to protect the identities of those who broke our hearts and/or vice versa.

PLUME
Published by the Penguin Group
Penguin Group (USA) Inc., 375 Hudson Street, New York, New York 10014, USA • Penguin Group (Canada), 90 Eglinton Avenue East, Suite 700, Toronto, Ontario, Canada M4P 2Y3 (a division of Pearson Penguin Canada Inc.) • Penguin Books Ltd., 80 Strand, London WC2R 0RL, England • Penguin Ireland, 25 St. Stephen's Green, Dublin 2, Ireland (a division of Penguin Books Ltd.) • Penguin Group (Australia), 250 Camberwell Road, Camberwell, Victoria 3124, Australia (a division of Pearson Australia Group Pty. Ltd.) • Penguin Books India Pvt. Ltd., 11 Community Centre, Panchsheel Park, New Delhi – 110 017, India • Penguin Group (NZ), 67 Apollo Drive, Rosedale, North Shore 0632, New Zealand (a division of Pearson New Zealand Ltd.) • Penguin Books (South Africa) (Pty.) Ltd., 24 Sturdee Avenue, Rosebank, Johannesburg 2196, South Africa

Penguin Books Ltd., Registered Offices: 80 Strand, London WC2R 0RL, England

First published by Plume, a member of Penguin Group (USA) Inc.

First Printing, August 2009
10 9 8 7 6 5 4 3 2 1

"Homecoming, with Turtle." First published in the *New Yorker* and reprinted by permission of Junot Díaz and Aragi Inc. Copyright © 2004 by Junot Díaz; "Texas." First published in *Playboy*. Copyright © 2007 by Gary Shteyngart; "Head Lice and My Worst Boyfriend." First published in *One! Hundred! Demons!* by Lynda Barry. Copyright © 2002 by Lynda Barry; Lines from personal letters and recordings of James D. Shea reprinted by permission of the estate of James D. Shea. Grateful acknowledgment to Melodie Ranstrom Wallace for the use of this material.

Ⓟ REGISTERED TRADEMARK—MARCA REGISTRADA

LIBRARY OF CONGRESS CATALOGING-IN-PUBLICATION DATA

Love is a four-letter word : true tales of breakups, bad relationships, and broken hearts by American writers / edited by Michael Taeckens ; introduction by Neal Pollack.
    p. cm.
    Includes bibliographical references.
    ISBN 978-0-452-29550-6
1. Dating (Social customs) 2. Separation (Psychology) I. Taeckens, Michael.
HQ801.L654 2009
306.7—dc22   2008051022

Printed in the United States of America
Set in Fairfield Light

For T. A. S.

Contents

Acknowledgments

Thank you to:

Doug Stewart, my agent, for believing in this project from the outset; Signe Pike, for her enthusiasm and expert editorial eye; Nadia Kashper, Alexandra Ramstrum, Cristi Hall, and everyone else at Plume who has made this such a wonderful experience; David Cashion, for first seeing promise in this book.

All of the fine contributors—I feel humbled to be in your company.

Wendy McClure, for twenty amazing years of friendship and for being the first to say yes to contributing to this anthology. Her talent and wicked sense of humor never cease to amaze me.

Chuck Adams, whose sagacity, encouragement, and friendship meant everything.

Wendy Brenner, whose all-around awesomeness makes me feel blessed just to know her.

Pamela Strauss, a significant friend in every way, who said exactly the right thing to get me started on this book; and Patty Van Norman, dear friend and contributor, who is not fat and ugly and dumb, but thin and pretty and smart.

Michelle Green, Maud Newton, and Amanda Stern, for their advice, suggestions, and overall support.

All of the great people at Algonquin and Workman, past and present, who I feel very fortunate to know and work with.

And to Patty Berg, Nicki Clendening, Katie Courtland, Diane Daniel, Marianne Drysdale, Amy Forstadt, Antonia Fusco, Rebecca Gimenez, Shelly Goodin, Carla Gray, Kim Hicks, Lou Jobst, Geoff Kessell, Kevin Kopelson, Lance Luckow, Mark Lazenby, Mickey Madden, Kristin Matthews, Sue Meyer, Beth and Javier Parada, Shannon Ravenel, Aimee Rodriguez, Leslie Rossman, Thomas Sherratt, Kim Small, Bruce Staska, Jenny, Jon, and Sterling Whaley, and Jesse Wilbur.

The heart was made to be broken.
                    —Oscar Wilde

Introduction

Neal Pollack

ADVICE TO READER
Be forewarned & SPARE yourself!!

WEARISOME! TEDIOUS

REDUNDANCY AHEAD!

(except for Linda Barry)

SHINE

tion, and its shoals have
being romantic and often
anyone; stories of ruined or
since the dawn of storytell-
and, by association, dating)
may not penetrate the fog
there for us to read when
ature, or at least good litera-
hopeless, sad waste of time.
"The Lady with the Dog."
at the theater, this goes
clearly that for him there
so near, so precious, and so
oman, in no way remarkable,
vulgar lorgnette in her hand,
sorrow and his joy, the one
happiness that he now desired for himself, and to the sounds
of the inferior orchestra, of the wretched provincial violins, he

thought how lovely she was. He thought and dreamed." Though the story doesn't end with a breakup, per se, it does end with the protagonist clutching his hair in his hands and moaning, "How? How? How?"

Hey, pal, we've all been there, and many of us have written about it.

Those of you who have been left sobbing on a subway platform, or have suffered the indignity of sitting in a bar waiting for a love who won't ever arrive, would have done well to remember your forebears. *Romeo and Juliet* may be an overly referenced, obvious, or extreme example, but it's endured for a reason. Minus the swordplay, its themes of heartbreak and sexual frustration would be plenty at home in a *Nerve* cover story. Goethe's Werther kills himself because of unrequited sexual passion. Frédéric Moreau, the protagonist of Flaubert's *Sentimental Education*, spends an entire revolution pining desperately after a married older woman (while quoting Goethe), only to conclude, later in life, that his one true passion is, in fact, a pretty ordinary woman. My point is, all this might make getting dumped over e-mail look like a good day.

Then again, it may be just a little unfair to compare the contemporary torrent of nonfiction relationship writing to the best work of the greatest novelist of all time. What if Flaubert had to resort to hackery of our specific kind? Imagine if, hard up for cash, he'd written a true-life essay version of *Madame Bovary*: "I was a good-for-nothing layabout. She was a bored provincial housewife with misguided notions about romantic love. It couldn't end well."

Alternately, I could see F. Scott Fitzgerald doing this

kind of work: "Sometimes, Zelda and I think we should stop drinking."

In our era of optionable true-life tales, of incessantly candid blogging and downtown reading series, the relationship essay seems to have become a self-sustaining genre. To say that I speak from experience somewhat diminishes people who have *actual* experience in the world, but I did spend years making car payments by churning out my own monthly variations on the destructive relationship theme. For Cupid's sake, I wrote a column called "Bad Sex with Neal Pollack." When my term ended, the magazine kept the column going and never wanted for contributions.

So what makes this writing collection different? The many excellent pieces are by turns sad, funny, and revelatory, the best possible examples of the form; they read like carefully composed diary entries. They're sad and wistful and a little Chekhovian and do, in the end, what good relationship writing should do: illuminate larger truths about the human condition, about our foibles, fears, weaknesses, insecurities, and passions.

Our current human situation has produced an abundance of breakup literature. I could give credit to the fact that we live in a fragmented society where it's hard to come by actual connections with people with whom we might consider building a life, or to a world where alienation and misunderstanding are the norms. But that would make me a sociologist, and I hold no such degree. Besides, the human heart has been continually broken since the first one began beating. Instead, I'll credit it to the blossoming of a generational point of view.

It's no accident that most of the stories in this volume are written by people in their early thirties and above. They no longer feel the first sting of discarded love, but the disastrous events still seem fresh. In later years, love-related memories tend to wrap themselves in a gauzy mist. Heartbreak stories written by people in their early twenties generally lack depth, not to mention a sense of humor. If I'd written about my bad sex experiences just after they happened, they would have been mopey, self-absorbed, raw, and melodramatic. A decade, or even a half decade later, I was able to see my own culpability in the disasters. Sometimes they were partially my fault, or at least half my fault, even *mostly* my fault. That was hard to see when I was missing a certain smell of hair or a particular desirous glance.

The stories in this book have perspective, knowledge, wisdom, and a general understanding that young people are largely foolish morons and that their relationships are bound to fail. When you're young, you screw up because you think things are going to turn out differently. When you're older, you do it because you know they're not.

Whether in fiction or non-, disappointment is the common thread that moves throughout all this literature. We're disappointed at ourselves for having had such mediocre judgment; we're disappointed at other people for being so cruel and mediocre; and, most of all, we're disappointed at the world for not caring enough, for not giving us better options, for leaving us to ponder the void with only a string of disastrously dead "relationships" to show for our troubles on Earth.

From there, the common thread unravels. The stories in this

volume follow two different paths toward catharsis. There's relief, and there's regret.

The "relief" essays tend toward the comic. They say: However complicated my current life, at least I'm not dating that painter I met at some long-forgotten party twenty years ago. At least I didn't permanently give over my soul to a crazy person. My life is better and calmer now, and I'm a wiser person with a more developed sense of humor.

Regret, on the other hand, leans toward the wistful, even the tragic. It goes much further than moping about the one who got away. I should have handled this situation differently, the writer thinks. My life would have moved in another direction, possibly better, probably worse, but I'd like to have the do-over anyway, because at least I'd still be young and have the energy and hope of youth.

Bad relationships have such a totemic power over us because they represent a time of life before possibilities begin to narrow and fade, before the thrills of self-creation give way to the mire of midlife and the inevitable contractions of age. Here, while there are some exceptions, my generation falters. If early life disappointment is sad, midlife disappointment is downright tragic. You can recover from bad choices made in your twenties, but if you make bad choices after that, you're stuck. Sometimes those bad choices are Andre Dubus–like, full of neuroses and little cataclysms, and sometimes they are small, almost imperceptible, or even unavoidable. Like the characters in Tom Perrotta's *Little Children*, those choices end up in affairs, or the decision to skateboard long after your body has told you to stop, or both.

We'll have to wait a decade, or at least half of one, before the rest of us start reading and writing juicy Cheeveresque tales of divorce and regret, about how our children disappointed us and how we disappointed our children. As that happens, our children will begin to write their own breakup literature, and the cycle of navel-gazing will continue. At that point, we'll miss our youthful heartbreaks. We used to get laid, we'll say. We used to do stupid things. Compared to the slow, sad burn we face going down, it will all seem like lost playtime. At least we'll have something spicy to think about. This anthology isn't going to help you solve your own relationship problems—anyone who considers taking romantic advice from a bunch of writers is beyond help anyway. But, at the very least, it will give us plenty of retroactive gossip material as we drift toward cultural irrelevance. It's always nice to know that no matter how badly you've screwed up your love life, someone else has done far, far worse.

LOVE IS A
FOUR-LETTER WORD

Homecoming, with Turtle

Junot Díaz

That summer! Eleven years ago, and I still remember every bit of it. Me and the girlfriend had decided to spend our vacation in Santo Domingo, a big milestone for me, one of the biggest, really: my first time "home" in nearly twenty years. (Blame it on certain "irregularities" in paperwork, blame it on my threadbare finances, blame it on me.) The trip was to accomplish many things. It would end my exile—what Salman Rushdie has famously called one's dreams of glorious return; it would plug me back into that island world, which I'd almost forgotten, closing a circle that had opened with my family's immigration to New Jersey, when I was six years old; and it would improve my Spanish. As in Tom Wait's song "Step Right Up," this trip would be and would fix everything.

Maybe if I hadn't had such high expectations everything would have turned out better. Who knows? What I can say is that the bad luck started early. Two weeks before the departure date, my novia found out that I'd cheated on her a couple of months earlier. Apparently, my ex-sucia had heard about our planned trip from a mutual friend and decided in a fit of vengeance, jealousy, justice, cruelty, transparency (please pick one) to give us an early bon-voyage gift: an "anonymous" letter to my novia that revealed my infidelities in excruciating detail (where do women get these memories?). I won't describe the lío me and the novia got into over that letter, or the crusade I had to launch to keep her from dumping me and the trip altogether. In brief, I begged and promised and wheedled, and two weeks later we were touching down on the island of Hispaniola. What do I remember? Holding hands awkwardly while everybody else clapped and the fields outside La Capital burned. How did I feel? All I will say is that if you fused the instant when heartbreak occurs to the instant when one falls in love and shot that concoction straight into your brain stem you might have a sense of what it felt like for me to be back "home."

As for me and the novia, our first week wasn't too bad. In one of those weird details that you just couldn't make up, before leaving the States we had volunteered to spend a week in the Dominican Republic helping a group of American dentists who were on a good-will mission. We would be translating for them and handing them elevators and forceps and generally making ourselves useful. Even with the advantage of hindsight, I can't figure out why I thought this was a good way to kick off a homecoming, but that's just how we thought back then. We were young. We had ideals.

Our group of five dentists and five assistants treated roughly fourteen hundred kids from some of the poorest barrios in the city of La Romana (which is, ironically, the sugar capital of the

D.R.). We weren't practicing the kind of dentistry that First Worlders with insurance are accustomed to, either; this was no-joke Third World care. No time or materials for fillings. If a tooth had a cavity, it would be numbed and pulled, and that was that. Nothing else we can do, our chief explained. That week, I learned more about bombed-out sixes, elevators, and cow-horns than a layperson should ever have to know. Of our group, only me and the novia could be said to speak any Spanish. We worked triage, calming the kids, translating for everybody, and still we had it easy, compared with the dentists. These guys were animals; they worked so hard you would have thought they were in a competition, but by the thousandth patient even their hands started to fail. On the last day, our chief, an im-mensely compassionate Chinese-American with the forearms of a major-league shortstop, was confronted with one extrac-tion he just couldn't finish. He tried everything to coax that kid's stubborn molar out of its socket, and finally he had to call over another dentist, and together they pulled out a long bloody scimitar of a six. During the ordeal the twelve-year-old patient never complained. *¿Te duele?* we asked every couple of minutes, but he would shake his head fiercely, as though the question annoyed him.

Tu eres fuerte, I said, and that might have been the first sen-tence I had conjugated correctly all week.

No, he said, shaking his beautiful head, *no soy*.

Of course, we fought, me and the novia—I mean, the needs of the pueblo aside, I had just been bagged fucking some other girl—but it was nothing too outrageous. For one thing, we were too busy wrenching teeth. It wasn't until the mission was over and the dentists had packed their bags and we had headed out into the rest of the island that our real troubles began.

I don't know what I was thinking. Traveling the Third World is challenging enough as it is, but try it with a girlfriend who is only just realizing how badly she's been hurt and a boyfriend who is so worried that he no longer "fits in" at "home" that every little incident and interaction is sifted for rejection, for approval—a boyfriend who is so worried about his busted-up Spanish that he fucks up even more than normal. What I wanted more than anything was to be recognized as the long-lost son I was, but that wasn't going to happen. Not after nearly twenty years. Nobody believed I was Dominican! You? one cab-driver said incredulously, and then turned and laughed. That's doubtful. Instead of being welcomed with open arms, I was overcharged for everything and called un americano. I put us on all the wrong buses. If there was money to lose, I lost it; if there was a bus to catch, I made us miss it, and through some twist of bad luck all my relatives were in the States for the summer. The one relative we did manage to locate, a great-aunt, had been feuding with my moms since 1951, when Mami had accidentally broken her only vase, and my arrival signaled a new stage in the age-old conflict: each morning, she blithely served me and the novia sandwiches completely covered in fire ants.

Now that we didn't have the dentists to hold us back, we basically went off the deep end. We fought about everything: where to eat, what town we should visit, how to pronounce certain words in Spanish. We fought our way across the country: from La Capital to San Cristóbal to Santiago to Puerto Plata and back. It was miserable. If one of us wasn't storming off down the road with a backpack, the other one was trying to hitch a ride to the airport with strangers. Our craziness culminated one night in a hotel in Puerto Plata when the novia woke up and cried out, *There's someone in the room!* If you've never heard those words being shouted into your dreams, then yours has been a blessed life. I woke in a terrible fright and there he was—the intruder we'd all been waiting for.

It's at a crossroads like this that you really learn something about yourself. There was someone in the room with us, and I could have done any number of things. I could have frozen, I could have screamed for help, I could have fled, but instead I did what my military father had beaten into us during his weekend toughening-up exercises: no matter what the situation, always attack. So I attacked. I threw myself with a roar at the intruder.

It wasn't a person, of course. The intruder was a sea-turtle shell that had been cured and waxed and mounted on the wall. For the sake of national honor, I can say that I acquitted myself well in the battle. I smashed my head clean through the shell, struck the concrete wall, and bounced back to the floor. But instead of staying down I went back at him again, and only then did I realize I was punching decor.

That was the end. A couple of days later, we returned home, defeated, she to New Jersey, me to upstate New York. There was no miracle reconciliation. For a couple of lousy months, the relationship dragged on to its inevitable conclusion, like the heat death of a universe, until finally, having had enough of me, she found herself a new man who she claimed spent more money on her than I did. You're cheap, she asserted, even though I'd used a travel grant and all my savings to pay for our trip. She broke my heart, that girl did, which was a fair trade, considering that I'd broken hers first. But in the end none of it mattered. Even though a dead turtle had kicked my ass, even though my girlfriend had dumped me and a family member had tried to poison me with fire ants, even though I was not granted a glorious return by my homeland, I wasn't entirely crushed. Turned out I wasn't all that easy to crumb; before the year was out, I was back in the D.R., trying again. I kept going back too. I had committed myself to the lucha, much as I had committed myself to that fight with the damned turtle.

These days, I get around Santo Domingo pretty easily (Los Tres Brazos? La Pintura? Katanga? Capotillo? No sweat), and most people will at least concede that I have some Dominican in me. My Spanish has improved to the point where I can hold forth on any subject—animal, vegetable, mineral—with only one major fuckup per sentence. I'm sure if you'd shown me that future during those last days of my trip with the novia I would have laughed at you. But even in the midst of the rubble there were signs; even on that last day, at the airport, I was still trying to pick my stupid self off the floor. My head was throbbing from the tortugal beat-down, and my nose felt as if it had only recently been reattached. (When I got home, my roommate blurted out, without so much as a hello, *Fool, what the hell happened to you?*) I was beat, truly beat, and, just in case I hadn't got the point, there was nothing cold to drink at the airport. But that didn't stop me from engaging in the debates that were going on all around me regarding the recent election and

Santo Domingo's eternal President Balaguer—blind, deaf, and dumb but still jodiendo el pueblo. A present that the United States gave our country after its last military occupation, in 1965—God bless them all! Just before our flight was called, I was asked by a group of locals what I thought of Balaguer. I went into fulmination mode, and said he was a murderer, an election thief, an apologist of genocide, and, of course, a U.S. stooge of the Hosni Mubarak variety.

See, the newspaper seller announced triumphantly. Even the gringo knows.

The Last Man on Earth

Wendy McClure

When I was a kid I daydreamed about love at the end of the world. This is probably because I grew up in the early eighties, during the years of Reagan and the late cold war anxiety that manifested itself in dozens of film plots involving nuclear war or Russian invasion or, really, any kind of fictional apocalypse, as long as it left at least a few attractive and relatively unmangled survivors. I watched *The Day After* and *Red Dawn* and parts of the Mad Max trilogy and even *Night of the Comet*. I loved anything with baleful, mooing sirens heralding the coming disaster; movies in which all hell broke loose and martial law was enforced, and the old rules didn't mean anything anymore—which, of course, could only help with the romance part. I was a sucker for love among the ruins.

Love, or, um, something. In the movie *Testament*, which I have seen on cable numerous times, there is a scene toward the end where everyone is dying of radiation, and Jane Alexander's character numbly drags various expired family members to a mass grave, and the one clergyman left in town, a priest, is shuffling around having to mumble the burial rites, and Jane Alexander starts howling and shaking Father What's-His-Face by the shoulders, and then he grabs her, and then they smash their heads together and start sucking face. And *how cool was that?*

It's not that I didn't wish for world peace. But it was hard not to think of the apocalypse as kind of awesome, a panoramic realm of artfully torn clothes and special effects. Surely, a world war could transform any mumbling, indifferent seventh-grade guy into a road warrior with smudged biceps. At school I'd consider the possibilities while gazing across the lunchroom at my crush objects. *You ignore me now, Joshua Kroger,* I'd think, *but it would be different if we were stranded in an underground bunker.*

These fantasies might lead one to conclude the following:

a. That I longed for brave new vistas in which anything, including making out with priests, was possible.
b. I had about as much self-esteem as an orthopedic shoe.

. It seemed too much to ask for a relationship based on mutual attraction, but I would certainly settle for one that took place on a barren landscape of glowing rubble. Never mind that it was the sort of thing that had little chance for the long term, at least not without hazmat suits.

But years went by, and no End of Days came to pass. No cities had to be annihilated in order for me to hook up with a guy, though plenty of brain cells were annihilated one way or another. In my early thirties I decided I'd work on my self-worth issues and was attending weekly sessions with Catherine, my therapist. She'd been with me through the toxic personals dates, a radioactive crush, and now, we were carefully taking stock of my new relationship with Ben.

I'd met Ben partly through the online personals and partly through the fix-up efforts of a mutual friend who'd shown me Ben's Match.com profile. At the time, the only thing that appeared wrong with him was that his photo was sideways. I didn't get to see him properly vertical until our first meeting, where I promptly got drunk and went home with him. Now I was working with Catherine, trying to figure out how I felt about Ben. Or, at least, how I felt about the fact that he was still living with his ex-girlfriend Lisa.

"You know, I think it's okay," I told Catherine. "Like, they went through all the weird stuff a long time ago. They're done with the open relationship thing that they tried. He said so."

I didn't tell her exactly *what* he had said, which was that there were condiment jars in the back of the fridge he'd rather stick his dick in than sleep with Lisa again. "No offense to her or anything," he'd added.

"Do you believe him?" Catherine asked.

I did. Most kitchen stuff was pretty unfuckable by nature, but this was especially true of Ben's kitchen. I thought of his silverware drawer and how the spoons and forks lay under a sedimentary layer of cereal bits and cat hair.

"What else do you like about him?" Catherine asked.

"Oh, he's very funny," I said, because funny could explain a lot.

A week or two earlier I'd been in her office trying to decide whether I should let things continue further with Ben or else go on another date with Jacob, a guy I'd met through the online personals. Jacob wrote software manuals; he had an apartment facing Wicker Park and a very well-designed Web page where he published articulate "rants and musings." Ben, on the other hand, worked nights doing data entry. He had a tiny bedroom with a lumpy futon with ironically chosen Strawberry Shortcake sheets. But he also had ambitions: he'd been working on a novel for several years—he was getting ready to apply for a Guggenheim Fellowship—and he rode his bike long, impressive distances.

It might have just been a matter of physical attraction: Ben was tall and broad shouldered; he often asked me if I thought he looked like Vincent D'Onofrio (someone had told him that once), and he did, somewhat. I didn't think Jacob was quite as cute. But to be sure, I'd made a list of pros and cons with Catherine. The things wrong with Ben included: sort of broke, heavy smoker, living with ex-girlfriend, odd schedule. I couldn't put my finger on what I found wrong with Jacob other than the tattoo on his bicep. But then, I really wasn't sure about this tattoo. It was an abstract design he'd had copied from a Russian film poster, he'd said. But to me it just looked like a big blurry anvil rendered in thick black Sharpie and beet juice. It was big, almost as big as my foot.

"I don't know if I can stand to look at it all the time," I'd explained to Catherine. "Plus, I don't know, he's not that *funny.*"

"That can be important," she agreed.

I wound up canceling my date with Jacob. Apparently the feeling with Ben was mutual. One night, after we'd been sleeping together a couple of weeks, he said, "I want to show you something."

"What?" I asked.

He was calling up his Match.com profile. He clicked purposefully until he got to an administrative screen. *Delete profile now?* it said. Ben hovered the mouse over the box that said *Yes*.

"Look!" said Ben, as he clicked dramatically. "See?"

"Wow," I told him. I wasn't sure how impressed I should sound. Nobody had ever done something like that for me. Something so *demonstrative*. That was worth something.

"I'm going to save you from being a spinster," he said.

I stayed up until 4:00 a.m. with him and bummed his cigarettes while he showed me his favorite movies. We watched Jodorowsky's *El Topo* and Pasolini's *Salò*. He was nice enough to warn me when torture and/or shit-eating scenes were coming up. For my part I learned how to hold my hand up to the screen to cover everything but the subtitles.

Our first few weekends together were messy and exhilarating. I would wake up feeling like a horse had stomped on my chest from all the smoking. Then I'd look at the clock and see that it was two in the afternoon. Really, I told myself, I needed this. After all, maybe my career *was* too staid (my publishing job was "old lady work," he said), the neighborhood where I lived too twee. But Ben was the first boyfriend I'd had in a while; from what I remembered of relationships, I knew they shook you up, in good ways. In what *had* to be good ways.

I made more lists in my sessions with Catherine.

Things that indicated Ben cared:

1. Wanted to spend time with me, even if the quality time was often at 3:00 a.m. and involved watching "severely underrated" Ken Russell films.

2. Brought me books to read, mostly surrealist erotica, but also some pretty good stuff that *didn't* make me want to peel my skin off.

3. One night, he told me, he was having a beer after work and he decided to buy a cookie from Muffin Mary, the old lady who made the rounds of the bars selling marijuana-laced baked goods, and he went home and ate the cookie, and the THC was way stronger than he'd expected, and he couldn't sleep all night, and he started having all kinds of intense thoughts and realizations, and one of them was that I was really a great person and he needed to do more to show his appreciation, which was why he promised to take me out for dinner sometime, at a normal hour, and at a restaurant that wasn't a twenty-four-hour pancake house.

4. Definitely wasn't sleeping with roommate/ex-girlfriend. She was always at her boyfriend's place, but, still, that was a plus.

5. E-mailed me porn that he said reminded him of me. "The one bent over the scooter has an ass like yours," he'd write.

Things that indicated he wasn't quite what I thought he would be, but chose to ignore for the time being:

1. The Guggenheim thing clearly wasn't going to work out, considering the only thing he'd published had been

a Listmania! list he'd posted on Amazon.com, with his favorite books, mostly surrealist erotica. "Literary Journeys into the Dark Dreamworld of Sexuality," the list was called, "by Benjamin J. Gottlieb, Writer."

2. He couldn't show me his novel yet or say how long it was because it was still untyped. Like, all of it.

3. He only rode his bike when he couldn't depend on someone (like me) for a ride.

4. He had no driver's license.

5. Or bank account.

"You know, you can't fix him," Catherine told me.

"I know," I said. Still, I brought him my mom's old electric typewriter, hoping he would use it.

"Do you ever feel you deserve more?" Catherine asked me once, after I had been dating Ben for about six weeks.

"I don't know," I said. *Yes.* "I just feel like I want to *experience* this a little more." I couldn't explain it. There were times I'd wake up on Ben's futon among the usual debris—there were ashtrays and twisted towels and coffee mugs with their moldering contents and stacks of warped paperbacks and a broken VCR and a cat litter box—and yet I'd feel a deep satisfaction. I could survive that room; I could endure anything. With Ben, I felt like I was ready for whatever—an earthquake, a flood, a date night that revolved around finding a currency exchange that stayed open after midnight so that he could cash his paycheck. Sometimes it was rough, yes, but sometimes, it seemed, I thrived on this broken frontier where Ben had brought me. I could make it work.

* * *

The rest of my life, the luxuriously ordinary parts, continued in fits and starts. One Tuesday morning I called in late to work while I waited for a new mattress to be delivered. I was glad I had a legitimate excuse to be late—Ben's sleep schedule was starting to affect mine—as well as some time to myself. I sat in the kitchen waiting while I smoked and read. It was sunny and clear outside, and everything was very pleasant. Everything except the book, *Story of the Eye*, which Ben had insisted I read, and which made me wish I could cover parts of my brain the way I so successfully managed with the TV screen. All the same, it was a gorgeous day, and quiet. Sometime after 10:00 a.m. the buzzer rang; the mattress had arrived. I went out to the stairwell and watched the two delivery guys maneuver the new mattress and box spring up around the landing.

They seemed very excited about something.

"Are you watching the TV?" one of them called up.

No, I told them. I didn't watch TV in the mornings.

"There's all this crazy stuff going on all over the place," the other one said. "Like, all this *stuff!*" I couldn't tell if he was serious or not.

"You should turn on the TV," the first one said, as they guided the mattress through the front door. "Really. Now where does this go?"

I decided to indulge them and turn on the television, so they could watch whatever the hell it was they wanted to see.

The news was on. Some special kind of news—*breaking news,* and all kinds of banners and headlines cluttered the edges of the screen, which was split to show two video feeds:

New York. Washington, DC. Both showed smoldering things. There was something about the World Trade Center and something about planes and something about bombs and something about America, like they kept saying *America* and I kept saying *oh shit oh shit.*

The mattress guys had assembled the metal box-spring frame in no time. "Yeah," one of them kept saying, "it's crazy." They flipped up the old mattress and box spring and laid down the new; the huge slabs seemed to float in their hands as they worked.

"Oh shit," I said.

"They said there are three more planes still in the air," the first mattress guy said. "They said one is headed here to Chicago. To hit the John Hancock building." He held out a small clipboard. "Sign here." I did. Then they left.

Ben was actually awake when I called. "I'm watching the news," he said. He'd woken up when his boss had called to tell him not to bother coming downtown to work. "I guess the world is ending or something."

"I'm coming over," I said. I packed a bag. I didn't know when or if I'd be coming back to sleep on my new mattress.

I drove down Western Avenue, keeping an eye out for police barriers. I hadn't fully processed what happened yet, and I wondered if the city was now under martial law. Being a survivalist I stopped at a supermarket, figuring that I'd better stock up on *something*. As I wandered the aisles with my cart I felt, somehow, that I ought to buy things that I might conceivably need but that wouldn't convey how very flipped out I was. Now that there was a good chance that the end of the world could happen, I hesitated at the threshold of my old fantasy. So I held off on the bottled water and canned soup and batteries. I picked out pretzels; snacks seemed both necessary and safe. Bananas; also a comb. And cigarettes. I was secretly very glad I had a reason to smoke cigarettes. I made sure to throw in a pack of Marlboro Reds for Ben.

We spent the afternoon in Ben's living room, watching the news on TV and making phone calls to family members. We sat side by side on the floor and smoked and went through the food I'd brought. Outside, we could hear military jets zorching back and forth over downtown. The terrible news was relayed in constant loops, and we watched it for hours. It left me feeling sick and adrift. I tried to think grounding thoughts in order to return to myself: *This is me; this is now; this is September; this is my boyfriend's place; this is my boyfriend.* Some thoughts worked better than others.

Once, when Ben came back from the bathroom, I stood up. "Come here," I told him.

"What?" he said.

I stepped forward and hugged him. It seemed we should be holding each other more at a time like this. Maybe it would help.

"Oh, okay," he said. He hugged back. "You're not freaking out, are you?" he asked.

I considered which answer would be most conducive to continuing the hug. "No," I said.

"Good," he said. "You'll have to warn me if you're freaking out." He broke away and sat back down.

We decided to take a nap to get away from the TV. The

usual squalor of Ben's room had started to get to me in recent weeks but now it felt oddly comforting again. Ben spooned me; I savored the weight of his arm across my side. I lay there thinking that things were going to get better and that I was strong enough to get through this—no, to *do* this. I kept thinking, *here we go.* I was tired, but my heart was still faster than my breathing; it seemed I was waiting for something to begin, or rather, that I couldn't wait. I started taking the deepest breaths I could in order to slow my body down. I hoped to God the world wasn't ending but if it was, here we were: Ben and me. *Here we go,* I thought. *Here's where it might get good.*

The first couple weeks afterward were so woozy it was almost exquisite. It was Indian summer, an ideal environment to be floating around in on four hours' sleep. The days were brashly sunlit and cinematic (we drew the blinds). The nights were immense, and the TV in Ben's dark living room was our encampment. We watched as the president addressed press conferences and the girl in *The Texas Chainsaw Massacre* got impaled on a big hook.

When we went out, we went to diners. We sat at our booth at the Golden Angel for hours, as if it were our only refuge. Ben pointed out that there wasn't really a name yet for what had just happened in New York and Washington and the field in Pennsylvania; we just kept calling it "everything." We had outrun history; we were hovering outside it. I watched the way Ben held his coffee cup and wondered if I would live to remember the sight of his hands on the coffee cup, the cup that was constantly being topped off with coffee as hot as the urgency of the endless present moment, and would we be going back to my place after this? We were, right?

One night, after Ben got off his late shift and cashed his check, we wandered the deserted aisles of the twenty-four-hour Walgreens. He insisted I pick something out and that he would pay for it. "Daddy got paid," he said. "Daddy got scratch to help the economy." We set out to find the most ridiculous things in the store, much of it from the toy aisle: baffling little figurines of poodles wearing tutus, a tiara that said "Princess," American-flag stickers. "Go on, you can get more," he said. I got bags of candy and a big piña colada–scented candle; Ben got a creepy ski mask. We amassed a stockpile of stupid; we carried it all in our arms like looters, dumping all the crap on the checkout counter. Ben paid from a big wad of bills. *If there is another attack*, I thought, *who knows if ATMs will still work?* I was glad I was with someone like Ben, what with "everything."

"But tell me more about the panic attacks," Catherine said during one of our October sessions.

Oh, yeah: those.

They weren't full-blown but they were getting worse. They'd happen when I drove downtown to pick up Ben from work, on the nights when he was done at ten. I couldn't help it. The city had put up concrete barriers around the government building plazas to prevent car-bomb attacks. And the terrorist rumors were rampant. "Did you hear whether or not they found the truck yet?" the receptionist at my office had asked me one afternoon.

"What truck?" I didn't know what she was talking about.

"The missing truck. The truck full of twelve thousand pounds of explosives that disappeared from a construction site, and they're looking for it, and they say that it might be terrorists who are going to do another attack. It was on the news," she said. I knew this was the same woman who forwarded e-mails about the alleged dangers of shopping-mall rapists brandishing drugged perfume samples, but, still, I spent the two hours trying desperately (and in vain) to find the missing-truck story online, endlessly clicking away at links on the local TV news sites. *What truck?* my mind screamed. *What truck?!*

And now, every couple nights or so I had to make my way downtown, where I'd grip the wheel harder as I drove along Wabash under the elevated train tracks. The buildings looked like breathing things; their lit-up emptiness unnerved me. I was always relieved when I'd spot Ben standing at the curb waiting for me.

I told Catherine. "I guess that's why I panic. I don't want anything to happen to him."

"Of course," she said. "You care about him." She made everything sound like it made sense.

"Yeah," I said. It was true; I *cared* about Ben. It was all I could go on. But I didn't know what to do with it, this *care*: it was unmoored and purposeless. I'd given up on the notion of fixing him—was relieved to be free of it, really, now that we were in a time of much greater crisis. He had a broken living situation and broken credit, and that stupid night schedule he loved broke his days. And in those movies I loved, those apoca-lypse movies, broken things stayed broken and weathered the toxic future bravely. Or sometimes—especially in Ben's case—bitterly. But if I cared, that had to help.

One night when I went to pick him up he wasn't outside in his usual spot. I'd circled the block for half an hour, getting uneasier by the minute. The concrete barriers made the streets seem narrower; I tried to stay in the center lane, as far from them as possible. Something was going to happen; I had a feeling. I was tired of feelings.

Finally he materialized, waving his arms frantically.

"Sorry," he said when he got into the front seat. "I forgot you were coming."

"You mean you were just going to work until the middle of the night by accident?" I asked him.

"It's not by accident," he said. "Sometimes I just *like* to. Just like you like to work at that spinster job of yours." He loved to call it that. He also claimed it was my old lady existence that was making me paranoid about driving downtown lately. "What's wrong?" he asked. "You're not freaking out again, are you?"

"It's just my little panic thing," I told him. "It's fine."

"You're freaking out again," he said. Once he got started on this there was no convincing him otherwise.

I tried anyway. "What do you want to do?" I asked him. I was hoping we could go to a bar. Even after two months, our best dates still involved drinking.

"Well, seeing as how you're freaking out, we probably should just rent a movie," he said.

"No, we could do something else. I'm fine."

"The thing is," he said. "I'm really tired now."

We wound up at my place without a movie, because I lived in a spinster neighborhood where the video store closed at 11:00 p.m. At least I had beer.

We had sex, mostly because there was nothing else to do, and I thought about how much trouble we all were in—the world, I mean. I had mastered the art of bringing it to mind all at once—and with it a feeling that opened a pit in my stomach. It was terrible and yet reliable. And somehow Ben was a part of it too: it was how I got to him, how I'd experience the sensation of his hands and the weight of his shoulders and the smell of his skin. Or, I mean, it was how I tried.

"I'm freaking out," I said, a little later. He'd turned the light out afterward so we wouldn't have to talk, but I couldn't stand it.

He hesitated a moment. "Yeah?" he whispered.

"Yeah," I whispered back. "About everything. I'm so scared." I hated how this sounded. I wanted more words for this. Better words.

"I know," he said.

"And also, us," I said. I didn't know what I meant by that.

He didn't say anything. I waited a long time, a minute or more.

"I love you," I said. I wasn't sure if it was true. But I said it anyway because I wanted to see if it *needed* to be said. A time like this, the world exploding: you never know. Even though, deep down, I *did* know.

I felt him freeze; his shoulders tensed up. Okay, then. I figured as much.

*   *   *

Our doomsday was just a matter of time after that. We were at DEFCON 3 when I decided to return some of his things. It escalated when he admitted he was seeing a lot of one of his coworkers, a nineteen-year-old named Penny. But there was no final firestorm, just a long night of negotiations where we tried to get our old selves back, to disown who we'd been for the past three months, because we'd been the wrong people all along.

"So there was this one night a couple weeks ago," Ben said. "When you said this *thing*. You probably don't even remember it."

I was pretty sure I knew what he was talking about. "Go on," I told him.

"It was when we were going to sleep, and you said this *thing* when you were drunk, I guess."

"Oh yeah?" I said. "What about it?"

"Just that it freaked me out, and that was when I knew we had to end," he said. "God, I didn't think you'd remember."

But of course I remembered. There was a lot to remember. As soon as I'd said the words, I knew we *could* end, that it was allowed. I realized that I didn't have to keep this up to keep the world going. The night I said this incredibly wrong thing, the landscape of my mind began to change and its cities no longer burned the way they used to. As much as saying the *thing* stung, somehow I also felt better—safer—for the first time in weeks. The radiation of my anxiety was wearing off; the panic attack had stopped thrumming in my stomach, and the new mattress felt good. The end of all this would come to pass. And then, thank God, it did.

Trans

Jennifer Finney Boylan

With Maeve it ended with a big fight. This was back when I was still a man. "I never know what you're thinking," she said. We were at a bar in Baltimore, eating potato skins. "I mean, what the fuck. Who are you, anyway, when you're out of my sight?"

I waved my fingers in front of her eyes. "These aren't the droids you're looking for," I said.

She looked confused. *"What?"*

"You're free to go about your business," I said.

She sighed. "Fine," she said. "Whatever." Now she was sore.

Maeve was in my fiction workshop at Johns Hopkins. She owned a rabbit. It was becoming clear to me that Maeve was a realist, not only in her writing, which was fine, but in her life as well, which was where the trouble came in.

"So it's your theory," I said, "that we're going to get to the truth by having, like, some big conversation about it?" The truth didn't sound like much fun when you put it that way, at least I hoped not. I finished my pint. "Why can't the truth be about this, instead?"

"About what?"

"About making each other laugh. Telling stories. Singing songs. The *blarney*. That's so wrong?"

Her tears had stopped. She was looking around the bar, as if she'd already decided it wasn't too soon to start shopping around for another boyfriend. "You know, Obi-Wan," she said. "Sometimes you're a real asshole."

"Obi-Wan?" I said, surprised. "Now, that's a name I haven't heard in a *long* time."

Afterward, I went back to my apartment on the corner of Maryland and Twenty-ninth Street, locked the door, pulled down the shades. I got out the cardboard box that contained all my stuff, put on the bra and hose, the blue sweater, the black skirt. Did the makeup too, although I didn't like makeup. I thought it made me look fake.

The wig was last. It made me look kind of like a run-down Joni Mitchell. Then I walked back out to the living room and sat down on my black leather chair with a copy of an anthology entitled *The Major Poets*, edited by Coffin and Roelofs. I was reading a lot of Keats back then. It was our man's theory that truth was beauty; beauty, truth. It was nice to think this might be true.

I looked at myself in the mirror above the parlor fireplace. I didn't look so terrible. Most of the time, when I went out *en femme* in Baltimore, you wouldn't know I was reprehensible unless you looked real close.

I always passed well, maybe because of the slender bones. I could go from the world of men to the world of women at the drop of a hat, and no one was any the wiser, or for that matter, dumber. It was terrifying and amazing, having a secret identity. It was like I was Clark Kent and Lois Lane, all my own damned self, both the experiment and the control.

I thought about Maeve and the big fight we'd had in the bar. I felt bad for her. She wasn't wrong about me, either. Sometimes it *was* hard to know what I was thinking.

There were all sorts of ways of ending things. You'd have a big fight, one of those calls where you slam down the phone, and then it rings again three minutes later and you keep on like that all night long. A fight in a public place was more final than a fight on the phone, though. Because there were witnesses.

Or you could write a letter, saying you just weren't ready. You were too immature. Make it sound like you were doing her a favor. Which, of course, you were, but not because you weren't ready. It was because you and she were, you know, *same same*, not that you could possibly ever explain that.

It was tempting, of course, to try to put it all into words. Usually people assume that the reason you want to change genders is because you are, deep down, kind of an asshole, or that you hate yourself, or that you are actually gay and just don't know it, or that you can't figure out a way of being feminine in the culture while still being a man. None of that had anything to do with it, though. Even now, you occasionally meet trans people who say: *Oh I'm a woman too! I love to make cookies and play with dolls!* To which you want to wearily respond: *Jesus fuck, if you want to play with dolls, play with dolls. You don't need a vagina for that.*

But most of the time you just have to resign yourself to the fact that people who are not trans will never get it. Why should they? They've never had to think about what gender they are. If you're not trans, you're free from thinking about what gender you are in the same way that white people in America are generally free from having to think about what race they are.

The women you knew, for their part, liked the fact that you had a feminine streak, that you seemed to be sensitive and caring, that you didn't know the names of any NFL teams, that you could make a nice risotto. A lot of straight women love a female sensibility in a man, an enthusiasm that goes right up to, but unfortunately does not quite include, his being an actual woman.

The romances didn't last, of course. Because, let's face it: you were keeping the basic fact of yourself camouflaged. How are you supposed to fall in love when you're so frequently lying? How is it possible to be vulnerable with someone from whom you are, at that same moment, hiding?

The best strategy, actually, was no breakup at all. You'd just stop answering the phone, or you wouldn't hang around her part of town. By the time you did run into each other, on the street, she'd be in the arms of some other guy, and what could you do? Give her a peck on the cheek, wish her well. Think about her earrings, wonder where you could get some like that.

Tell her you were happy.

With Allison, I went home one day and just erased myself. It was the kind thing to do, I thought. I'd been living with her for three years, although the last year and a half we'd been losing steam. Quite frankly, I'd gone off to grad school in Baltimore partly so I could get away from her without having to have some whole big fight about it. The relationship had become like one of those balloons in the Macy's Thanksgiving parade that starts leaking helium, and the next thing you know Superman's collapsed on top of the guys holding the strings.

I did love her, though, for a little while anyhow. That was the thing: I still believed, on some fundamental level, that love would cure me. That if I were only loved deeply enough by someone else I could be content enough to stay a man. It wouldn't be my authentic life, but it would be all right. Anyhow, my authentic life meant coming out as transsexual and taking hormones and having some repulsive operation and walking around like one of those Herman Munster chicks you see on TV talk shows and please. My authentic life wasn't very appealing. And so I allowed myself to be lifted off the ground by the levitating properties of romantic love. It was a nice effect.

Of course, nobody really gets cured by love, but then transsexuals are hardly the only people who believe that romance will lead them outside their selves. We all believe this, at times, even if this belief turns out, in the long run, not to be true. You can't fault a person for hoping that love will make her into someone else, someone better. The world is full of false hopes, most of them dumber than the hope of being transformed by love.

I'd started messing around with this girl named Shrimp Cocktail that first week I'd left New York and moved into the apartment in Baltimore. Like me, she was incredibly flat chested. When Allison called on the phone, Shrimp Cocktail had to pretend she wasn't in the room. *Be vewwy quiet. I'm hunting wabbits.* Thank God they'd never brought out the Picturephone, was my conclusion. Then, after Shrimp Cocktail left, and I was finally off the phone, I pulled down the shades and got out the cardboard box with the wig in it. It was just one damn thing after another.

I was working on a novel. The name of the novel was *Invisible Woman*. It wasn't about transsexuals, though. It was about a woman who walks around wearing gauze bandages like Claude Rains. Why would she do this, you ask? Because she didn't want people to know who she really was.

Anyway, after that first year at Hopkins, it was clear enough Allison and I weren't getting back together. So I told her I was coming up to New York to get my stuff, and she said fine, whatever. It wasn't a surprise to her by that time. I drove to Manhattan in my Volkswagen Golf and 'loaded the last of my things into the hatchback while Allison was at work. There wasn't much—some posters, a box of books, an Autoharp. Then I put her apartment back the way it used to look before I'd moved in, three years before. She'd had a painting of *Girl with a Pearl Earring* by Vermeer over the fireplace, but I'd taken it down. That girl always gave me the creeps.

After I put Allison's stereo back where it used to be, after I took my books off the shelves, the last thing I did was put the Vermeer back above the fireplace. The girl in the painting looked at me with her accusing, liquid eyes, and said *Klootzak, je donder!* and I felt like a real heel. In Dutch this means "Bastard, you bastard!" She said it again as I left the keys on the kitchen table and then closed the door of the apartment for the last time. *Klootzak!*

And then, sometimes, the breakup would just be a complete bloodbath. Example: in high school I'd been in love with a girl named Willow. This was 1976, the year of the bicentennial. Willow was an actress, a tall, breathless girl whose parents were alcoholics, the both of them. They were like a perfect matching sweater set of dipsomania. I was drawn to Willow because of her high-strung energy, because of her quick comic mind, and also because, let's face it, if I'd been a girl all along I might have been someone like this. Although it wasn't her life I wanted, it was my own. Still, you know how it is. It's important to have role models.

I was crazy about Willow. I wrote a poem for her called "Kiwi," which used as its central metaphor the New Zealand bird that has no wings and cannot fly. It's also a brand of shoe polish.

Back then I was renowned for my imitations. Elvis: *Wella-wella-wella-wella*. Nixon: *I am not a crook*. Dylan: *Jeez. I can't find my knees*. I was very entertaining. For some reason I found it very easy to do Willow, to capture her breathless, effusive character. *Jaaames! How arrre you? I liiike you! Jaaames!* I used to do her all the time when she wasn't around. The imitation was so good that other people started doing it, although when they did it they weren't doing her, they were doing me doing her. Eventually this ninth grader, Scott Stein, whom everybody called Pink Lemonade, did his version of me doing her right to Willow's face. She didn't like it.

Later she called me up and asked why I was doing her.

"Jaaames," she said. "I thought you liiiiked me," she said. I wanted to explain that I *did* like her, that was the whole point. But it was impossible to explain. She sighed, and I said I was sorry. Then Willow said she had to get off the phone, because she had this big test the next day and she hadn't been able to study because her parents had been up all night again drinking and singing.

"Really, what's the test on?" I asked her.

"The Depression," she said.

A few months later, I asked her to the prom. She said no.

Just before graduation, Willow's school put on a talent show featuring a group called the Belles of Liberty. The Belles of Liberty was a group of twenty-five girls on roller skates, who wore red, white, and blue uniforms and sang while they skated. Willow asked if I'd play the piano for the show, and I said sure. I wasn't bad on stride piano. With my long, slender fingers, I could play walking tenths, could imitate Jelly Roll Morton. *I wonder what the poor people are doin' tonight!*

I went to the theoretically all-male Haverford School; Willow and her friends went to our sister institution, Shipley. This was on the Main Line, in the Philadelphia suburbs. I was the only boy in the show, if playing the piano counts as being in the show. There was Lisa Trousdale, who sang "Take Me Home Country Roads" on the guitar, and Shell Stockhausen, who had a ventriloquist's dummy named Corky Chorkles. *My dog has no nose!* No nose, Corky? Then how does he smell? *Terrible!*

The climax of the show was this: Two of my friends, Larry and Doober, who'd been planted in the audience, were supposed to start complaining about the program, and then I would get up off the piano bench and tell them to shut up. Then, all at once, I would throw a cream pie in Larry's face! After that, the Belles of Liberty would roll out on the stage, each one armed with a cream pie, and the girls would throw them at each other while singing "You're a grand old flag, you're a high flying flag, and forever in peace may you wave."

Maybe this sounds insane, like something out of a Thurber story, but believe me: all sorts of shit happened during the bicentennial. On this you're just going to have to trust me, which I hope isn't asking too much.

At the appointed hour I was sitting behind the keys of the baby grand piano in the auditorium of the Shipley School. Larry and Doober started up with their diversion, although at the last minute they cleverly changed the object of their derision from the talent show to its pianist, who was, of course, my own idiot self.

LARRY. What does he weigh, like eighty-two pounds?
DOOBER. And those television-tube glasses! I keep looking at them wondering, hey, man, is there anything else good on?
LARRY. You know what I think we should call him? Jimothy! He should go to school here, man! Be one of the girls!
DOOBER. Hey, that's pretty good! Hey, Jimothy! Where are you? Where's Jimothy?

I rose from the piano and said, "Hey, what's the big idea? You really have a lot of nerve. I think you owe everybody an apology!" This was supposed to be really funny, but in fact there were tears in my voice as I spoke the words.

Then Doober hit me with a pie. I was blinded by pie even before I reached center stage. He creamed me. My eyes brimmed with tears, and frosting.

And the Belles of Liberty rolled in from offstage. I couldn't see them, but I heard them. There were twenty-five girls onstage in roller skates, and everybody was throwing pies. "Should auld acquaintance be forgot?" the girls inquired. It was a fair question. "Keep your eye on that grand old flag!"

Larry had hit me so hard with the pie that my nose began to bleed. I stumbled around the stage, my arms outstretched, a blind thing oozing into my frosting.

I stood in the middle of the stage at an all-girls' school, in a spotlight, sightless. From my nose a bright red river of blood gushed into the white cream. All around me orbited two dozen girls on roller skates, including Willow, the girl for whom I'd written my first poem. The music of George M. Cohan rose toward the rafters.

Pies flew through the air. People screamed. I heard the sound of folding chairs overturning as the audience fled toward the exits. Some of the Belles of Liberty lost control and roller-skated off the edge of the stage and landed on the folding chairs. Others wiped out onstage and lay on their backs with the wheels of their skates still revolving. Someone else grabbed on to the curtain to keep from falling, and there was the sound of material ripping. Part of the curtain fell down. I took off my glasses to try to wipe my eyes again, and they slipped out of my hand and fell onto the floor.

There was the sound of glass breaking as Willow's friend Renee careened by on roller skates, screaming, "I can't stop! Help,

I can't stop!" an observation to which I could only bitterly reply, *I know exactly how you feel.*

Afterward we all went into the girls' gymnasium and took showers with our clothes on, washing off the pie. It was nice, showering with Willow and the girls. Later, I wrapped myself up in a towel and headed over to my friend Otto's house with Larry and Doober, where we changed clothes and listened to the Grateful Dead perform "Sugar Magnolia." *Sweet blossom come on, under the willow, we can have high times, if you'll abide.* We drank Pabst Blue Ribbon out of sixteen-ounce cans and had a good laugh about what had happened at the talent show. "Out of control!" said Otto. I didn't think it was all that funny, but I kept my comments to myself. If you were a boy, you couldn't just say, hey, you hurt my feelings. That wasn't the way it was done.

Twenty-five years later, after I became a woman, I wrote Willow a letter, letting her know about the recent presto chango. She hadn't heard from me in a long time, but I figured it was a good thing to keep her in the loop. Maybe now, I wrote her, some things about my younger self will make more sense to you.

A week later I got her reply: *You don't need to explain yourself to me Jennifer*, she wrote. *I never liked you anyway.*

Then there was Dora, who had a green streak in her hair. This was back at Johns Hopkins. I'd already moved on from Shrimp Cocktail. Dora was a writer too. She said she liked my prose. She said it had "a kind of felicity." This was funny, since Felicity was one of the names I privately used to describe myself, not that it ever really stuck. I kept thinking that if only I could find the perfect name for myself, my true name, I would somehow emerge from the shadows and be real. Jenny, for what it's worth, was a name I kept coming back to, then rejecting. It sounded like the name you'd give a donkey.

Dora and I made out a bunch of times but didn't get anywhere near actual sex. Most of the time, it wasn't actual sex I wanted. Like a lot of male-to-female TSs, I was attracted exclusively to women. But my desire was different from the majority of other bepenised individuals, I reckon. I was drawn to women sort of the way you'd be drawn to a fire in a very cold room. Mostly what I wanted to do was to lie beneath the covers and snuggle.

Women liked that, my concern with snuggling. But eventually the fact that the snuggling never went anywhere else just wore them down. *What's the matter with you?* they'd ask. *Don't you want me? I brought my diaphragm. C'mon, let's fuck!*

Of course I want you, I'd reply. *You're great.*

I reached this point with Dora fairly rapidly, a couple of weeks at most. Then, in order to shake her off the trail, I used a strategy I'd never employed before: pretending I wasn't home. The doorbell would ring, and I'd know it was her, just from the sound. I'd have to freeze there in my bra, even though the blinds were all down. I'd sit there in my big black chair and try to be completely silent. I figured she'd conclude I wasn't home and leave.

But instead she concluded that I *was* home and that I was just pretending I was out. So she rang the bell again. This pissed me off. How dare she assume that I was the kind of person who'd actually pretend he wasn't there? If that's the kind of person she thought I was, why was she so anxious to talk to me? Why would she keep ringing the bell at all? You'd think she'd just head off and find some other guy who, when he pretended he wasn't home, actually wasn't.

Sometimes I'd slowly creep out of my chair, hoping that she couldn't hear my footsteps as I moved through the living room and into my bedroom, where I could take off the wig and the skirt. I couldn't wash off the makeup, though, because then she'd hear the tap running.

When things got quiet, after a while, the hard thing was knowing the difference between the silence of her actually leaving and the silence of her waiting on the marble stoop, pretending to have left. She knew that two could play this game; if I could pretend I wasn't inside reading Keats while wearing a bra, she could pretend she wasn't on the front porch holding a bouquet of flowers and a little card that read *Let's never fight again*. The cards always annoyed me, because of course we hadn't really ever fought in the first place, not unless you consider sitting inside wearing Playtex products while reading Romantic poetry and not answering your doorbell a kind of fighting.

After a while, Dora stopped coming by to ring my doorbell, and I didn't see her anymore. Every now and then, when I was in boy mode, I'd look up from my chair and think I heard something. I'd open the front door and walk out on the stoop and look around. But she wasn't there.

Rose liked that I had a sense of humor. I met her at a model-rocket launch some poets were having. On the weekends, Rose transformed herself into an alternate personality by the name of Scarlett. Scarlett used a teasing comb and a can of hair spray to create Baltimore-style big hair. She wore spandex bustiers, rubber miniskirts, fishnet stockings. She had a pair of ruby slippers, like Dorothy in *The Wizard of Oz*. I wasn't crazy about this look. I thought it seemed unnatural.

Rose hung out in a bar called Club Charles, which was across the street from the art movie house, the Charles Theatre. It was a terrible dive, the kind of place where people got stabbed in the bathroom. It was very popular.

I liked the fact that Rose had another personality, although unlike me, hers wasn't some big state secret. "Why the Scarlett?" I asked her, not because I disapproved, but because if I could figure out why she needed to be Scarlett then maybe I could figure out why I needed to be Jennifer. Or Felicity.

"I don't know," she said. "It's fun being someone else, I guess."

I didn't really agree with her on this point. The someone else that I had to be was the person I was almost all the time, this James. I didn't find being someone else any fun at all.

Things got complicated with Rose because she had all these other boyfriends when she was Scarlett, guys whose names sounded like the names of amplifiers, like Peavey and Pignose. I felt jealous of them, even though Rose and I weren't actually sleeping together. She said it didn't matter what she did when she was Scarlett, because Scarlett wasn't her true self. "What matters, James," she said, "is who I am when I'm with you."

There were times when I felt that I really loved her.

One Friday afternoon in spring we had a fight about what I called her "split personality." If you really loved me, I said, you'd be just one person, instead of two. Why do you have to have this whole Scarlett thing? It's creepy. I was pretty rough on her, I guess. I made her cry.

What she should have said was, *hey, man, she who smelt it, dealt it.*

That night I put my girl self together and got into my car and drove down to Fell's Point, the part of Baltimore with the whores and the sailors. There were plenty of she-males on the street too, although I didn't think of myself that way. I just thought of myself as a woman with a *unique history*. Then I headed up to the Club Charles. There she was, at a corner table: Scarlett, her hair reaching halfway up to heaven. She didn't recognize me, which isn't really a surprise. When I was female, I wore contacts. So I sat down at the bar and had a glass of wine. After a while, I noticed that Scarlett was crying. Big mascara streaks trailed down her cheeks. Then she got up and went into the ladies' room.

"What's with Scarlett?" I asked the bartender.

"I don't know, sweetie," he said, shaking his head. "I think she had some big fight with her boyfriend."

Oh for God's sake, I thought, looking at myself in the mirror behind the bar. A run-down Joni Mitchell stared back. *I'm not her boyfriend.*

I went into the ladies' room. It had a cement floor and a broken window. On the wall were phone numbers, profanities, names of men and women enclosed with hearts. I saw the ruby slippers beneath a stall. I entered the one next to her.

For a while we sat there, on either side of the divider. I could hear her sobbing. "Hey," I said, in a voice that did not sound like the one she was used to. "You okay?"

"No," she said.

"What's wrong?"

"Oh, there's this guy . . . ," she said, then stopped to weep some more.

"Tell me about it," I said, but she didn't. She just sat there, behind the wall, weeping. Who knows? Maybe it wasn't even me Scarlett was weeping for. For all I knew it might have been Peavey that had her in tears, or Pignose. I wondered, as I sat there, what I could do for her, whether there were any words I could offer her as Jennifer that I could not speak as James.

"Listen," I said. "I'm sorry."

There was a loud snuff, followed by silence. After a while she said, "What's your name?"

I had never told anyone my real name before.

"Jenny," I said.

"You're nice, Jenny," she said. She snuffed some more, but it sounded like she was descending out of her crying jag now.

"It's going to be all right," I said. "Really."

"Listen, Jenny," she said. "Can you pass me some paper?"

I tore off some tissues from the roll and passed it to her, under the divider.

For a moment our fingers touched, as she took the paper from me. Then they weren't touching anymore.

Exactly like Liz Phair, Except Older. And with Hypochondria.

Dan Kennedy

I told myself she reminded me of Liz Phair, but without the marijuana-steeped tomboy, devil-may-care, laid-back attitude of Liz Phair. This is the type of thing you tell yourself when you're young, or at least when I was young. The point is, I was twenty-two and dating a thirty-two-year-old divorced hypochondriac who had a condo out by the freeway, made her living as an aerobics instructor, and who was convinced she and her love of self-help books could make a well-organized, ambitious, proactive, so-called normal man of me. The problem was that I felt perfectly happy being a college dropout who still had a shift at the college radio station and no big ideas. I figured this thing she called a "life's mission statement" would come to me when it came to me. If it came to me. After all, there didn't seem to be much sense in my chasing it, considering I was perfectly happy having my days free to hang out with my best friend Dave, drinking canned beer and having bottle-rocket wars in the yard of the small mother-in-law cottage he and I were renting. And in retrospect I was right to be wait-

ing instead of chasing a so-called Life Plan or making something she called my "List of Intentions." I wound up working
in New York advertising agencies and then writing books, two
careers you actually shouldn't rush into; as a matter of fact, two
things you will be better at the longer you wait to get started
doing them. And anyway, sometimes Dave and I would blow
up crab apples from the tree out front with firecrackers—huck
them like grenades and say what we thought the soldiers or the
Sandinistas in Clash songs said when they threw grenades. Or
sometimes we would try to surprise whichever one of us came
home late by jumping from the roof onto the latecomer as he
fumbled with keys at the front door in the dark. I loved Dave. I
don't know, maybe that was the problem: I liked my girlfriend
and I loved my best friend. Or maybe it was the age thing. At
least the sex was good. *Wait, please don't close this book, that's as
disturbing as I'll get, I swear.*

While my girlfriend was completely cool to be around when
she had been drinking, the rest of the time was a challenge, to
put it mildly. But I was young enough to think that there was
nothing wrong with having a two-year relationship with someone ten years older than me and spending eighteen months of
it in something called couple's counseling. And as we get a little
older and wiser, we ask ourselves why. But it's like asking somebody why they bought *Storm Front* by Billy Joel or why they
shaved their head on acid or wound up living with a cult in the
mountains outside Portland; sometimes shit just kind of happens. I agreed to go to couple's counseling with my decade-older
divorced girlfriend the way you might reluctantly say, "Sure . . .
I can be there on Thursday," if a good friend was asking you to

help them paint their living room. In the sessions she told her therapist—a forty-something man who smelled like a bottle of vitamins with a hint of hair tonic or aftershave—all about me and why I was frustrating. There were myriad reasons.

"How do I know he's not sleeping with other women? They all think he's funny; they all want to hug him when they see him. How can I be sure there isn't more to it? He needs to convince me I can trust him."

"Ah-ah-ah," he started to politely correct her.

Thank God.

"You *feel* like he needs to convince you that you can trust him."

"Yeah, I mean, I think that's just a feeling, honey. I mean, why would I be cheating on you? Sure, you *feel* like I need to convince you that . . ."

"Well, you do need to convince her."

"What?"

He continued, "Well, she's got a point. How do I know you're not cheating on me? How do I know these girls I've seen saying hello to you so exuberantly aren't lovers of yours?"

"How . . . do . . . you? Know?"

"I'm speaking as her. From her point of view."

"Uh, because I love . . . you? But I mean, obviously, her."

He took her side in everything. Jesus, seriously, it was creepy. It was like being framed in a bad television movie of the week, every single week. And it fueled her crazy possessive streak, which, I think, in retrospect, my ego must've loved. I mean, as I aged and—how do I put this gently—took another decade and change to end my prolonged adolescent slacker lifestyle, the women I found myself dating were not exactly concerned about the possibility of my cheating on them. I think they figured it was pretty safe to assume that other thirty-two-year-old women weren't exactly beating down the door for a chance to sleep with the beer-bloated unshaven guy who still thought bottle-rocket wars were awesome even though he was living alone now that his buddy Dave had long since moved out, started a successful career, and gotten married to a beautiful woman doing her premed schooling. At that point women were more like, "Look, Wayne, we can kind of be friends, and even more than friends sometimes . . . but you've got to face the fact that even Garth has moved on and grown up." So, I guess, at the time, having someone be possessive of me felt almost like hav-ing made something of myself, and something in me knew to enjoy it while it lasted because it was as close as I was going to get to making something of myself for a while—the next thirteen years, as it would turn out. My older possessive, di-vorced, hypochondriac girlfriend had a point though; girls hugged me sometimes—pretty often, really. But, I mean, we're talking about friends of mine, and we're talking about good old-fashioned everyday people like myself—in other words, it's not like I had hot young fashion model genetic freaks hanging on me like I was a pop star or drug dealer. We're talking about my heavyset small-town lesbian friend named Kim from the com-munity theater. Or my friend Alison from the comic book store who sounded ironically like Butt-Head from television's *Beavis and Butt-Head*. I'm not saying these people weren't beautiful, because they were and they are. I'm just saying you couldn't have picked worse culprits in trying to build a case for girls making sexual advances toward me in public; for that matter, you couldn't have picked a less likely guy to start with, but like I said, I wasn't about to end this before it ran its course—what was the point? It would be like the bassist of Counting Crows deciding to quit the band because people were treating him strangely now that they had a big hit single. So what? It'll be over soon enough, and it's probably never going to be like this again, so enjoy it while it lasts. I knew where I stood in the food chain of modern love: it ain't like I was the worst thing you've ever seen, but at the same time I was smart enough to know that this was probably my one big hit single; there'd likely be plenty of time in this life to *not* feel someone be possessive and jealous.

But then there was the painful evening when Kim was in Westside Espresso when my girlfriend and I walked in. Of course, she ran up to me and hugged me—partially because she's friendly, partially because she had just received some good news about a show of hers that she was hoping would get accepted at a theater downtown. And also partially because she was a big-boned twenty-something lesbian. I mean, find me a full-figured community theater lesbian in her twenties who *doesn't* hug her friends when she sees them in a café. But my girl wasn't having it. Homey didn't play that game.

I remember it mostly in a slow-motion blur. We walk into Westside Espresso. I hear Kim say, "Daaaaaaaaan!" She comes running toward me. I feel that weird mix of dead calm before disaster and total internal panic; I feel like I'm wearing a wire, like a man who knows there are rifle scopes trained on the people around him and that any one of them making a wrong move will be taken out in a silencer-hushed precision firestorm. Kim keeps advancing. I hear something in my earpiece from one of the SWAT team protecting me: "What? Oh my God, you have to be kidding me. Who is she? Damn it, this is exactly what I was talking about in therapy." Kim, of course, can't hear this. Kim, of course, knows nothing about the world I'm living in. Kim, of course, hugs me and asks how I am. Suddenly, I am shoved a bit to the side and there is someone wedged between us.

MY GIRLFRIEND: What you're doing is really inappropriate.

KIM: What?

ME, *thinking*: Jesus, which part of it is she talking about? Community theater? Being a lesbian?

MY GIRLFRIEND: Adults have certain boundaries. Certain behavior is acceptable and certain behavior is not. If you and I are lovers, then hugging is appropriate. (Kim and I both seem confused about this last line. Kim seems a bit unclear as to whether or not she's just met someone new, and I feel a weird excitement then shame wash over me, and then, finally, the dread of being only twenty-two years old and knowing this will all be rehashed in my couples therapy session.)

KIM: Um, okay. Dan is an old friend of mine. I'm saying hello to him. I didn't hug you. I won't hug you. I mean, I'm not trying to say . . . I mean, I'll obviously . . . Do you (*pause*) *want* a hug?

ME: (*I start cracking up*)

MY GIRLFRIEND: You actually think this is funny?

ME: No. I don't. It's just that none of us . . . Well, yes! It's
   funny.

KIM: (*Pointing at me and laughing.*)

The whole damn thing was so awash in the power of in-
nocence and honest-to-God confusion. If every tense moment
could be swept up in such an utter lack of agenda, wars would
cease to exist. It was beautiful and small, this moment where
Kim and I were so scared, then so confused, then laughing like
kids in the same family. We were so honestly powerless that
it became impossible to consume and defeat us, like we were
something as simple as rain and someone was trying with all
their might to get us to stop falling from the sky—the easiest
thing in the world for dumb little raindrops like us to do.

"Oh my God, I'm having a panic attack."

"Oh, gosh, here sit down," says Kim suddenly serious. "Do
you want some water?"

"Honey, just focus on your breathing," I say, all the levity
drained from the room.

"Does she get these often?" Kim asks.

A handful of big dumb innocent punch lines that Kim would
love race through my mind.

The modern reverse: "Only around completely inappropriate lesbians who have no boundaries."

The Marx Brothers twist: "How should I know, doctor, I've
never seen this woman before in my life!"

The Woody Allen lift: "Her analyst gave us his emergency
number to call if she *isn't* having them."

But of course I used none of them. And there wasn't any

laughing. There were glasses of water. There was controlled breathing. My girlfriend was silent. And I was calm, and maybe a little sad, only because I had been through a handful of these attacks, and somehow they felt like reminders that my girlfriend and I never laughed together. These panic attacks always seemed to happen in moments where levity was reminding us both that none of this was to be taken too seriously, and that none of it was even in our control, and that when it came to matters of the heart, everyone on earth was simply doing their best. These panic attacks even lead to regular emergency room visits, during which doctors would say that there was nothing abnormal about her blood pressure, that there was nothing abnormal about her breathing, and that there was nothing abnormal about her pulse. And, even, that everything seemed fine with her heart. Oddly enough, though, each time, when we were walking out of the emergency room and back into the night, mine felt a little heavier, like it was worried I would never learn that its purpose was not to fix the hearts of others.

Very shortly after this incident, life stepped in, as if we'd needed reminding that it was bigger than the both of us; things faded between the two of us, and she started dating a man her age who was a self-help author and who, like her, had also spent a lot of time as a fitness instructor. Somewhere in there I had to hope she was happier, and I got to thinking that maybe we just weren't that great together. Toward the end I was a jerk, she was a jerk, we were jerks to each other—nothing too terrible, but we were always punctuating a point by slamming a door. We were always raising our voices and feeling like we weren't heard. Maybe because we had to make it clear to ourselves why this couldn't work. And then, one random Tuesday or something, you both get tired of the smoke, and somebody finally yells fire, and its over. But it's funny how quickly you get to feeling better when you're twenty-two. Sure, it was still a breakup, but it was back when a breakup was marked by a lack of adult responsibility, by sleeping in and dealing with it by listening to songs on college radio that comfort the listener with big fat warm guitars and words about hearts, and by still feeling like a misfit. I'm not trying to say it was easy, I'm sure I was heartbroken, but from eighteen years down the road and looking back, it seems like it was that young version of heart-break that comes with the excitement of wondering what might be next—you stay awake nights smoking cigarettes that can't kill you yet, wondering who will be the next person to actually let you see them naked. You're made confident by nothing more than knowing that with so many years still in front of you, it is simply bound to happen again.

Shadow Dancing

Kate Christensen

The first time I ever got drunk was in the spring of 1978, in a hotel room in Mazatlán, Mexico. I was fifteen and with a thirty-six-year-old man who was perfectly frank about the fact that he wanted to seduce me. I wanted him to seduce me too, but I knew I was too young to sleep with him and that therefore no such thing was going to happen, if only because I wouldn't let it.

Tim and I were in Mazatlán with my high school Spanish club, on our yearly trip to Mexico, an annual trip intended to allow us to try out our supposed language skills in a natural setting and, incidentally, to drink all we wanted in a country without a minimum drinking age. Tim was, ha-ha, the chaperone. He was my younger sister's friend's father, some sort of pillar of the community. He was also tall, handsome, sexy, and very recently divorced. He also, my sister told me, had French-kissed his own thirteen-year-old daughter, claiming that he was just teaching her how to do it.

I was a skinny, opinionated, bookish sophomore with a

sleek feathered brunette bob, a cute butt, and green eyes. I had known Tim since last year's Spanish club trip to Puerto Peñasco, when he had also been the chaperone; I had bantered with him and challenged his opinions and discussed deep philosophical questions with him while stargazing on the beach. We were pals. I cracked him up; he made me feel smart and appreciated.

When, on our second evening in Mazatlán, he asked me to come to his room for a drink, I went, naively, without a clue.

Tim mixed me my first Tom Collins and handed it to me. While we drank out on his little balcony, we gossiped about all the other students on the trip: who had a crush on whom, mostly. The theme of sex having been established, he mixed us another round and then proceeded to find out about me.

"Have you done a lot of things with boys before?" he asked me.

Naively, without a clue, I answered honestly: "Not a thing."

It was time to go to dinner. We all climbed into the van, about twelve of us altogether, ten students along with Tim and our teacher, Mr. Schwarz. I sat in the back of the van by the window and looked drunkenly out at the nighttime Mexican resort city sliding by, leaning a thin, bare, suntanned arm on the windowsill, feeling alive and dreamy and festive. I loved being drunk.

At dinner, we sat at a long table. I acted exceedingly witty and sophisticated, making obscure, urbane jokes, flirting with the cutest guy on the trip, Hector, forcing him to notice me. I was heady with sexual power for the first time in my life.

After dinner, we all went to a disco near the beach. It was

the era of the Bee Gees; all the girls wore sundresses and wedge sandals. On the dance floor, Tim took my hand and put his arms around me, even though it wasn't technically a slow dance. When he kissed my neck, I looked him in the eye but didn't say anything. He didn't go any further.

Later, I watched him dance with Tammy. She was only one year older than me, but to me she seemed fully grown-up. She was a sexy, plump blonde girl with a wide, rapacious mouth, a smutty laugh, and a gap between her front teeth. She danced with Tim as if she were fucking him, her arms around his neck, laughing up at him as if she wanted to eat him alive, her body pliant and curvy against his. I felt no envy, only curiosity.

Falling asleep that night in a drunken haze, I fantasized about Tim. For the rest of the trip, he and I were inseparable. We hung out by the hotel pool together, sat together at meals. The sexual tension between us was shocking to me; I had never experienced the power of male desire before. He made me feel beautiful and hot. I felt no shyness with him at all; I zinged him with jokes and teased him and gazed blatantly into his eyes. I learned some of the rudiments of seduction by watching his responses.

We all drove home in the van at the end of the trip, starting out before dawn, back to Arizona. Just across the border, when we stopped to eat at an A&W, Tim asked if he could drive me home when we got back to the high school. I agreed. About an hour later, in the van, one of the other girls offered me a ride. Embarrassed to admit that Tim was driving me, not wanting to cause gossip, I kept my mouth shut. After a tense second, Tim said blandly, "I'm driving her home." I sensed a few people exchanging glances. Still, I didn't say a word or look at anyone.

We arrived in Cottonwood that evening, climbed out of the van with our backpacks, and began moving toward the various cars waiting in the Mingus Union High School parking lot. I went with Tim to his little green TR7: a midlife crisis car, I realize now. Without a word, we got in. We were silent on Highway 89A, through the Verde Valley to the switchbacks up Cleopatra Mountain to Jerome. The sexual tension had come with us from Mexico like a souvenir.

Just past the old high school, I said dramatically, like a soap opera heroine, "Can you please pull over? I have to say something to you."

Tim pulled the car onto the shoulder and turned off the engine. He looked at me. This should have been the moment I threw myself at him, the moment we began our unstoppably torrid, illegal, memorable, hot, educational, and ultimately heartbreaking affair, if only so I could write about that now instead of what really did happen.

I said in a heated voice, "You know, Tim, nothing can happen between us. It's inappropriate. I'm too young."

No doubt I had learned the word *inappropriate* from my mother, who had no doubt picked it up in her feminist consciousness-raising group in grad school in the early seventies.

"I really wish you were older," he said earnestly.

"Me too," I said.

Then he drove me home, all the way through town, up to the top of steep, cobblestoned Magnolia Road. We said good-bye, I got out, and that, I thought, was the end of that.

I lived with my mother and two younger sisters in the Tally House, a falling-down old mansion that had been the home of the Copper King when Jerome was a rich mining town, and which my mother now rented for twenty bucks a month from the historical society in exchange for doing renovations. It was a gorgeous ramshackle old wreck, heated by one sole woodstove in the living room in the cold winters, perfumed by honeysuckle vines in the summers. It had window seats and porches and a sunroom, a curving staircase with curlicues on the banisters. It also had a leaky roof, broken windows upstairs, and only one bathroom, but we had been raised to be stoic, romantic adventuresses; I don't remember minding the literally below-freezing temperatures upstairs in January.

But I didn't like living in Jerome, in general. My two younger sisters and I were city kids who'd grown up in Berkeley and Phoenix; we felt out of place and lonely in our schools there. The Tally House was only a way station; it wasn't ours. Staggering natural beauty aside, the Verde Valley was, at least back in those long-ago days, a backwater of fast-food chains, pickup trucks, ranch houses, and trailer parks down in the flats, and, up in Jerome and Sedona, clusters of weird, flaky hippies who made pottery or bad sculpture, talking about their past lives and smoking pot all day.

My mother, meanwhile, had a PhD in psychology and had studied the cello at Juilliard; she had grown up on the East Coast, in New York, where I already knew I was headed as soon as I was old enough. Solely because she'd had romantic ideas about the place, we'd moved up here from Phoenix just before I started high school. Then, a few months after we arrived, she announced that she was leaving our stepfather, who had adopted us and whom we called Dad. He stayed down in the place they'd bought together, and we moved again, up to the Tally House. And recently my sister Susan had left home, at thirteen, to live in Flagstaff and study ballet. Our family was falling apart, but we were all we had.

All through my sophomore year, as I wrote essays for my independent study on the short story, starred in all the high school plays, and lectured my English teacher on the subjunctive tense, I sent away for brochures from expensive, arty, faraway boarding schools, Putney and Interlochen and High Mowing, and pored over them with desperate concentration. I could see no way out. We were broke and had no connections.

After the Spanish club trip, I mooned around the Tally House daydreaming about Tim. My favorite fantasy was, unaccountably, one in which I arrived at his house in a rainstorm and he brought me into his kitchen, stripped me naked, toweled me off, then took me in his arms and led me to his bed to ravish me. I lost interest in the boys at school; they all suddenly seemed very young and boring.

One day about a week after the Mexico trip, Tim called me. "Hey, Katie," he said. "Want to go running?"

"Okay," I gulped. He was an avid long-distance runner, lean as a greyhound; I was a sprinter, but I was athletic, so I figured I could keep up. He drove up to my house with Carol, my twenty-five-year-old English teacher (but not the one who didn't know about the subjunctive), and the three of us set off jogging in our swishy shorts and Adidas along Perkinsville Road, the abandoned gravel road that led way back into the mountains to the old defunct, abandoned mine. I got a stitch in my side within minutes and was gasping for breath but refused to complain. I was fifteen; I could hack it.

As we trundled through the high mountain desert, it dawned on me that Tim and Carol were sleeping together. I don't know how I knew; they were very circumspect. But exactly like when I'd watched Tim dance with Tammy, I felt no envy, only curiosity. I knew he really loved only me. I knew I had the real power here. Women like Tammy and Carol, I thought arrogantly, were the ones he turned to because he couldn't have me.

As we looped around and headed back to the Tally House, Carol fell behind us for a while and then rejoined us and said something to Tim that I couldn't hear.

"She had a bout of diarrhea back there," Tim said to me under his breath as she fell back again. "Can she use your shower and borrow a pair of shorts?"

Back at the Tally House, no one was home. I led Carol upstairs to the white tiled shower with its window that looked out over the whole Verde Valley to the red rocks of Sedona in the east and up north to the snow-topped mountain peaks where Flagstaff was. "Enjoy the view," I said blithely, leaving her with a towel and a clean pair of shorts.

Downstairs, Tim and I sat comfortably on the side porch, drinking water, looking out at the view. Being with him felt beside the point: I preferred to think about him in bed at night. Then, at least, I could do whatever I wanted to him. Sitting next to him and not being able to touch him was just frustrating.

We went running together a few more times, with other students, with Carol, and once, in the early morning, alone. He never touched me, and constantly bemoaned the fact that he couldn't.

Early that summer, Tammy asked me out for lunch. She drove up to Jerome in her yellow Toyota Corolla and picked me up and drove me over to a restaurant in the Schoolhouse, a new artsy-crafty cluster of shops in the old elementary school building. The place she had chosen was chichi and touristy, the kind of place where middle-aged women went for lunch. There we sat, two teenagers, picking at our Caesar salads and sipping our iced tea. We weren't friends; I barely knew her. She seemed decades older than me; I was a goofy kid without a driver's license who daydreamed all day and wore bell-bottomed jeans, and she was like a grown woman in an imitation Chanel scarf, sophisticated perfume, and a pearl necklace. I didn't even feel shy with her, it was so surreal to be having this lunch.

"I want to talk about Tim Dell," said Tammy.

"Okay," I said cheerfully. "What about him?"

I don't remember what she said next, but I remember the distinct sense that she was trying to tell me something, or else she was trying, chummily, to bond with me about the fact that we were both in love with him.

At some point during the lunch I realized that she had slept with him in Mexico, that night after the disco, and maybe after that too. Maybe she wanted me to know this, and that was the real reason she had asked me to lunch. She seemed curious about him and me, but I betrayed nothing but amiable amusement; I didn't admit that I was in love with him, and I didn't satisfy her curiosity about what had or had not gone on between us. I would have told her everything if I'd had the presence of mind, but I was too naive, too arrogantly unthreatened by her.

In any case, she paid the bill and drove me home, and I never saw her again.

I left the Verde Valley about two weeks later. I went to spend the summer in Spring Valley, New York, my grandmother's community, to work as a waitress in the Guest House dining room at Threefold Farm. I lived in a room in the Summer Kitchen and waited tables; the rest of the time I fell in with the local high school kids, all of whom went to Green Meadow Waldorf School, which was just up Hungry Hollow Road from Three-fold Farm. With them, I ate meatball heros up at the Silo, went to Shakespeare in the Park in the city, swam in the local pond, got drunk at parties in the fields. They rightly thought I was provincial and full of myself, but they accepted me enough to urge me to apply for a scholarship to their school. I did so, and, to my surprise, I actually got one. Then I found free lodging with one of the high school English teachers in exchange for housework and babysitting. I presented this plan to my mother as a fait accompli: I had to get out of Dodge. I needed an edu-cation.

She had no choice; she let me go. That fall, I left Arizona for good.

Green Meadow was a total culture shock, both good and bad. For the first time in my life, I was in a school where all the other kids played instruments, read books, sang choral music, and spoke foreign languages; there was no Spanish class, so I took French. I felt as if I were finally among my own kind. My class had only thirteen kids in it. There were fewer than sixty kids altogether in the entire high school; it was a little hotbed of music, art, ideas, and idealism.

But still, I was as much of an outsider here as I had been in the Verde Valley, but for very different reasons. Some of these kids had known each other since kindergarten; they weren't overtly cliquish, but deep and ineradicable lines had been drawn in the sand long before I got there, lines I couldn't always read. I was far from home, the new kid, and suddenly I had to work for room and board instead of slouching off to my room after school and reading until dinnertime. Now I had to make the dinner and help the youngest daughter with her homework and answer to the demands of my hardworking, stressed-out teacher, who was a stranger, and now also my boss.

My math teacher, Willy, lived next door with his wife and three small sons. He was known for molesting all the teenage girls (he actually got one of them pregnant, a girl two years older than I was; she had a secret abortion and he went right on being a respected community member). Naturally, it didn't take long for him to suss me out as vulnerable prey: a fatherless girl, far from home. He started coming over and taking me on "walks" after dinner, ostensibly to give me guidance and sympathy because I seemed to be "having a hard time," but in fact to lead me into the deserted fields and rub his hard-on against me while trapping me in his arms as I struggled to break free. I disliked and feared him, but I had lost my nerve. I had been able to tell Tim, whom I loved and wanted, that I couldn't sleep with him; with Willy, I was mealymouthed and, with my silence, complicit somehow in his increasingly brazen maneuvers.

I still thought about Tim Dell during the first semester of my junior year. During the summer, while I was away, I had written him letters and sent him two short plays I'd written, and he had written back. Now that I knew I was gone for good, I stopped writing to him, but he was there in my mind as a kind of secret talisman, protecting me whenever I felt like a total loser, which was almost always.

To comfort myself during that terrifying and difficult first semester, I secretly gorged on bread and granola and gained about fifteen pounds; my butt was suddenly huge, for the first time in my life. I spent recesses and lunch breaks writing in my journal in an empty classroom, adolescent maunderings about loneliness and alienation. I listened to *Tapestry* on my eight-track over and over and over. In Spring Valley, I turned into someone I didn't recognize, someone shy and weird and furtive. I flew home for Christmas break feeling lost and lonely but determined not to let my mother know it; I had to prove that I had made the right decision to leave, not only out of pride, but also because she had been so heartbroken to see me go. I had to show her that it was all worth it, the sacrifices we'd both made. I pretended, when I got home, that Green Meadow was an academic and social idyll: rehearsing Mozart's *Requiem* and giving oral reports on Wordsworth and playing the violin in chamber orchestra, which, of course, technically it was, so I wasn't lying, but it made me feel even lonelier not to be able to confide in my mother and sisters how hard things were for me there.

One day toward the end of that winter break I took a walk through town for some fresh air and exercise. I strode down the mountain, swinging my arms, my face frozen and olive green and broken out, wearing too-tight jeans and a puffy down coat, my formerly sleek hair frizzy with an unfortunate perm. I rounded the corner past Main Street onto the series of switch-backs that led down to the gulch. As I approached the end of the first switchback, I glanced up at the house I was walking toward. There, framed in an upstairs window, was Tim Dell.

I waved; he looked puzzled and shook his head.

"Hi," I yelled, realizing he didn't recognize me. "It's Katie Christensen."

He opened the window and flinched in the sudden freezing air.

"Hey, Katie," he said.

There was something in his voice I didn't recognize at first, didn't identify until much later as disappointment and sur-prise.

We had a stilted, very brief conversation. The house he was standing in belonged to Carol, my former English teacher; they were living together. He asked how school was. I felt awkward and unhappy. There was no spark between us whatsoever any-more; it was gone, whatever it had been. I still viscerally re-member the hollowness in my chest as I realized that he didn't love me, this man I had had such power over, power I had taken for granted. Of course his lust for me had been contingent on my ability to provoke it; it did not exist independently of my ability to bewitch him with my ambitions and attitudes and brash, fierce confidence. Without that flashy armor, I was just another plain, lost, needy teenager.

We said good-bye, and I went on my way with my newly big ass and zitty face, no longer Lolita, no longer powerful, no longer fascinating.

I returned to Green Meadow at the end of the winter break, determined to regain my confidence and equilibrium, but presciently, painfully aware that it might be many years before I did. For the rest of that year, I went deeper and deeper into solitude and loneliness and alienation, excelling at my schoolwork, sustained by writing, reading, music, and, alas, a lot of alcohol. Needless to say, Tim no longer served as a protective mental good-luck charm of any kind. Willy kept pestering me.

I never saw Tim Dell again, but several years after our last meeting, on that winter afternoon, I found out that he had been a client of my mother's. She had been his shrink, briefly, in the aftermath of his divorce. When I told her about my nonrelationship with him, she laughed empathetically. "That makes perfect sense," she said. "He was a mixed-up guy . . . but so appealing, wasn't he?"

And that was the end of my first adult love affair.

Runaway Train
Saïd Sayrafiezadeh

I met Amy at a moment of desperation in my life. I was twenty-four years old and fully convinced that I would one day be a famous actor if I could only make it out of Pittsburgh, Pennsylvania. I knew I had no choice but to move to New York City if I was to have any chance at all at success, but New York City terrified me. From five hundred miles away it appeared large and angry and impenetrable, and every time I thought I was resolved enough to uproot myself and make the change, I would quickly retreat into the soft downy familiarity of my hometown. This indecisiveness had been going on for years, and soon I would be turning twenty-five, and after that twenty-six, and eventually I would become just like that forty-eight-year-old "actor" I knew who years earlier had moved to New York City only to return six months later to his old job selling insurance. "New York City's like a freight train hurtling down the rails," he had drunkenly confided one night. "It doesn't care if you hang on to its side, but if you fall off it'll run you right over." The image of my severed body on the tracks haunted me.

Then one spring a small theater company in Pittsburgh announced that they had somehow managed to get the rights to produce the American premiere of a new Ukrainian play by a famous Ukrainian playwright and that they were bringing in a very talented Ukrainian woman from New York City to direct it. Every actor and actress in Pittsburgh showed up for the audition—including me and the forty-eight-year-old insurance salesman—and when my turn came, I was ushered into the audition room, where I was shocked to see that the squat, elderly Ukrainian peasant I had been expecting to meet was actually a tall, statuesque blonde in her thirties.

"Hello, my name's Amy," she said without any trace of an accent. "I'm excited to see your work."

I was asked to read for the lead role, which I thought I was perfect for. The monologue was a complicated matter about a man looking for another man who may actually be himself. Throughout most of it I was confused about what I was talking about, but by the end I had grown so passionate that my voice wavered and my eyes filled with tears. When I was done I looked up and saw that Amy was staring at me with interest. Then she wrote something down in her notepad, stood up, walked around the director's table, and took my hand in hers. I saw that her eyes were green.

"You'll be hearing from me," she said with significance.

I ended up being cast in six small, thankless bit parts that infuriated me. During rehearsals I would sit among the props and watch sullenly as the actors pranced around onstage, feeling like I was acquiescing in my own burial. This gloominess remained constant and showed no sign of abating, until one evening about a week into rehearsal Amy happened to be standing next to me, casually pointing out something in my script, when I felt her breast pressing against my arm. I was certain she had done this on purpose, and I made no attempt to move my arm away, which was my signal to her that I was consenting. Yet as the moment grew longer and she continued to talk so animatedly about the play, I began to wonder if she was actually at all conscious of what was taking place. Could a woman really not know when her breast was pressing against a man's arm? When she had finished explaining what needed to be explained, she turned from me and resumed her seat behind the director's table, giving no indication that she had acted with intent.

After that I was invested in the play. I would sit patiently and contentedly in the wings, watching Amy, dressed so stylishly in overalls and a man's shirt, as she shaped the action on-stage with breezy confidence. "You should pause after your next line," she might say to an actor, her long blonde hair falling in front of her face as she spoke. And sure enough, that one small suggestion would open up the scene toward something new and unexpected.

When it was finally my turn to take the stage, I would enter with poise and professionalism, doing my best to access the underlying humanity of my six meaningless characters, while all the time studying Amy for a signal that she had known full well what had transpired between us. I read secret messages into everything she did. When she added a line for me, it was evidence. When she cut a line, it was evidence. When she cut me entirely from a scene—this was also evidence. In short, everything was the thing I wanted it to be.

And the thing that I wanted it to be was a very detailed fantasy I had mapped out in my mind, in which I am living in New York City with her in her apartment, and we have just had sex, and I am getting dressed to leave for the Broadway show that I am starring in and that she has directed. It was such a tantalizing fantasy that as the days passed it began to seem more and more real to me, more and more possible. I was sure I could imagine her apartment precisely as it was: small and charming with soft white carpeting, and illuminated by the blinking lights of a deli across the way. And the more real and possible this became in my mind, the less possible it became for me to take action. I could not bear the thought of losing what I felt I had already obtained.

The fact that the play would be opening soon, and that it would run for only fifteen performances, and that when it was all over Amy would be returning to New York City forever while I would be remaining in Pittsburgh forever, added a slow, agonizing ticking to my inertia. And beyond that ticking was the fear that all this great unspoken mystery between Amy and me was in my mind only, and that I was just a child to her, who she barely thought of or considered, or did not consider, romantically. And that I had embellished everything, beginning with the unconscious, inadvertent pressing of her breast against my arm, which only I remembered.

The play was a success, the reviews were good—"a deeply profound artistic vision"—and there were always at least twenty-five people in the audience each night. My role as the cobbler's son got laughs and made me confident that I was indeed an actor who was talented enough to make something out of noth-

ing. Meanwhile, the clock ticked. Soon there were twelve performances remaining. Then nine. Then Amy went back to New
York City to meet with a producer and had to miss two performances, but this only added to her allure and the allure of New
York City. When she returned with five performances to go, she
seemed taller and blonder and more sophisticated than she had
before. From the dressing room, I could hear her talking to the
patrons in the lobby, answering questions about the troubled
state of the Ukraine, which she had left when she was four.

"Theater in the Ukraine has always been a life-and-death
experience," she said to murmurs of assent.

Tonight, I thought, *tonight I must act*. But tonight disappeared,
and the next night, and then there were only three performances
left, and then two, and then it was all over and the show was
closed and the props were packed away and there was nothing
left but the final party to celebrate our accomplishment. Which
we all did—producer, director, actors—sitting around a long
table at a restaurant, toasting one another and laughing loudly
into the night. I watched her from across the table. I was sure
our eyes kept meeting expectantly, and I waited for a chance
when I could say something to her—what would I say?—but
she was surrounded by the others and no chance ever came.
And when the restaurant closed, all of us stood around outside in the warm spring air, saying that we didn't want to part
just yet and that we should go somewhere else to drink and
laugh. And so we divided up as we walked toward our cars,
and suddenly I found myself walking down a stretch of empty
Pittsburgh sidewalk, alone with her, just the two of us, and I
said, without thinking of what I was saying, "I'm going to miss

you, Amy." And in the darkness I could see her turn and smile at me sweetly, pitifully maybe, and she lifted her hand up and tugged gently on my earlobe like you would a pet. And then I pulled her against me and we kissed wildly on that Pittsburgh sidewalk.

Four months later I was living in New York City.

She nicknamed me Camel. A playful nod to my Middle Eastern heritage, my knobby knees, and some brooding quality she detected in me. When I would come out of the shower naked and damp she would say teasingly, "Has Camel been scrubbed and brushed?" In return I called her Giraffe. Tall, slender, self-possessed. As a joke she would put one leg out in front of her and bend stiffly from the waist in an almost perfect imitation of a giraffe nibbling at a bush. When we discovered later that the Latin name for giraffe was in fact *Giraffa cameleopardalis,* we saw it as some sort of divine confluence.

She had had difficult relationships with men. In bed with the lights out, she told me terrifying stories of her alcoholic father who had once chased her around the dining room table with a butcher knife when she was six years old. And then she'd tell me about her last boyfriend, "the pompous ass," who had promised to marry her before running off with someone else. And the one before that who was a fraud, and the one before that who was cheap, and the one before that who got her pregnant because he always came too quickly. And then she'd describe the guy on the subway last week who had said, "Let me lick it, baby." Which is why she made a point of dressing in shapeless pants and baggy shirts that accentuated nothing.

"Men are bastards," she'd say with frightening venom. And then she'd turn to me in the darkness and say sweetly, "Except you, Camel. You're different."

Through a friend of a friend I found an illegal sublet on the Upper East Side. For $412 a month I got two spacious rooms that had somehow passed undetected from one illegal subletter to the next for the last twenty years. It was filthy and unpainted, with a wooden floor that was so severely warped I could see light filtering in from below, but I saw it as a grand beginning to my life in New York City. An elegant claw-foot bathtub sat in the kitchen, next to the front door, equipped with a long metal hose that you attached to the faucet and then held over your head while trying to do everything else with your other hand. Next to the bathtub was a small sink that I used for both brushing my teeth and washing my dishes. When I was done I would stack the cups and bowls and silverware in the bottom of the bathtub to drip dry.

Through another friend of a friend I found a low-paying job working at an upscale art gallery in Midtown on Fifty-seventh Street. The owner was a jowly man who had worked in the art world for decades before hitting it big with a painter I had never heard of. I knew next to nothing about art, but it didn't matter because I was the receptionist and my responsibilities were to sit at the front desk, answer the phone, and greet people. For the most part, no one ever called or came in, and I would spend my eight hours swiveling back and forth in my soft swivel chair, while gazing at the wide white walls hung with paintings that sold for tens of thousands of dollars, thinking that I had become a part of this glamour, or that I would soon become a part of it.

At six o'clock each night I would pencil into a giant notebook the names of whoever had called that day, generally no one, and then walk out into the warm air and over to Lexington Avenue to catch the 6 train home. The subway was always filled to overflowing, and I would have to wedge myself into an opening and then keep from falling as it hurtled uptown at breakneck speed. Everyone on the subway had a bored, tired, disinterested attitude, apparently unfazed by the fact that they were living in New York City. I saw this as being impossibly chic and sophisticated. I knew it was the attitude of a true New Yorker and I tried to affect it for myself, standing casually, pretending to be indifferent, incurious, meanwhile marveling at how my life had changed in so short a time. At Eighty-sixth Street I would exit, imagining myself having been transformed.

Other nights I would go to Amy's apartment on West Forty-first Street. I always made a point of walking through Broadway so I could pass the marquees that I was sure would one day display my name. *Saïd Sayrafiezadeh is Hamlet.* And then I would walk by the fancy restaurants that were too expensive for me, and past the peep shows with posters of pretty blondes in bikinis, and past more modest restaurants that were also too expensive.

"Hello, Camel," Amy would say, opening the door, kissing me on the lips.

"Hello, Giraffe."

I would put my arms around her waist and pull her against me and we would hold each other for a moment in the open doorway. Then my hands would slide down and cup her ass and she'd let out a gasp of surprise. Lying on her futon in the evening light I'd unbutton her baggy shirt.

Her apartment was not quite how I had envisioned it when I was in Pittsburgh. It was just a small, charmless room on the sixth floor of an unswept walk-up. Ukrainian tchotchkes were everywhere and bad blue carpeting covered the floor. A photograph of her and her mother first arriving in the United States sat on the edge of a dresser, both of them looking sad. Taking up an entire wall was an enormous ill-conceived bookcase that made the place feel even tighter and more claustrophobic. The bookcase had been built by a previous boyfriend of hers. "Right before the coward broke up with me," she had told me ruefully. There was no deli next door to illuminate us romantically when we had sex. Instead there was Seventh Avenue, which roiled beneath us constantly. In the middle of the night I would wake to the sound of cars honking and people screaming as if they were being murdered.

There was a proper bathroom with a working shower. And there was a proper kitchen too, with cupboards and countertops, but there was never much food in it, being that she was between directing jobs and was low on money.

"What should we eat tonight?" I'd ask after sex.

"Oh, I don't know," she'd say. "I have some crackers and cheese."

She would try to say it simply, without worry, but it sounded poignant and sad and I would picture her as the little Ukrainian girl in the photo.

"Hey, let's go get some groceries," I'd say sprightly. "It'll be my treat."

And so we'd get dressed and walk down six flights to the filthy Fine Fare supermarket around the corner, where I'd buy her a week's worth of pasta and bread and Prego and grated Parmesan cheese. Back in her kitchen we'd set about making dinner, moving around in the tiny space as we boiled water and toasted bread, until my hands would slip down and cup her ass and she'd let out a gasp of surprise.

One of the first things I did after arriving in New York City was to send out a hundred head shots and résumés to agents and casting directors. I was sure that the combination of my exotic name and dark looks would easily set me apart me from the multitudes. Two months later, though, the only person who had called me was someone looking for an acrobat who could speak fluent Punjabi. So I sent out more head shots and résumés. And I waited.

It was November now. It was getting cooler. When I left the art gallery in the evening it was already dark. I would catch the subway home, wedged in painfully, hurtling northward. I'd make myself dinner and then get into the claw-foot bathtub and wrestle with the metal hose. Through the thin walls I could hear my invalid neighbor yelling at the basketball game. "Come on, bum!"

Amy was still without a directing job, and I had begun to realize unhappily that she was not as successful as I had first thought. In fact, she was something of a complete failure. And she was a failure precisely because she thought of herself as having already achieved success. This perspective placed her in the unfortunate position of refusing work that she saw as being beneath her, while at the same time being unable to obtain work that was really above her. So she drifted in a sort of snobbish unemployed artistic limbo that she blamed on sexism.

"It's disgusting the way female artists are treated in this country," she'd say.

She did have connections, however, and she was able to put me in touch with a friend of a friend who was in a bind and needed to cast the lead role for a staged reading of a new script. It was one night only at a community center on the Lower East Side, and it was really just to give the author an opportunity to hear his play aloud, but I was ecstatic nonetheless. I saw it as my break or my chance or at least a step forward. A week before the performance I stayed late at work and mailed out five hundred fliers with my photograph and the words *Saïd Sayrafiezadeh is Patrick Madden*. Only fifteen people showed up, and it seemed depressingly reminiscent of everything I had experienced in Pittsburgh. Amy said I was great, though, and that it was a great start, and that it was a shame that no one from the industry had been there to see me. And the director said that he would definitely keep me in mind for something else he might be doing.

And then I waited. And then another month passed. And then it was winter and I turned twenty-five.

One Friday night after work, while I was walking over to Amy's house, I found myself passing by the large window of a hotel bar that I had passed many times before. It was cold outside and the window was partially fogged, but I could still see men and women in fancy dress reclining in chairs. A pretty female bartender with blonde hair was mixing a cocktail. She was wearing a low-cut top that showed off her large breasts, and when she leaned over to pour the drink her breasts tumbled forward temptingly. It was just a brief moment, but after

I had passed the window I stopped, considered, and then returned. I watched myself return, then watched myself watching the bartender, who was now laughing with a customer. And as I stood there in the cold street, peering through the window, hoping to glimpse her breasts one more time, I suddenly saw that there was nothing at all glamorous about my life. I might have made it to New York City but that was all I had made. I was still as desperate as ever. No. I had become more desperate. I was just one of a million others who had come here trying to do the thing that was nearly impossible. There was nothing to distinguish me. Nothing that would ever distinguish me. It was true that success existed, but there were so many obstacles to that success. So many obstacles that had to be overcome, conquered, vanquished.

And then the terrifying thought entered my head that the first and foremost obstacle was Amy.

I felt a flash of panic and I pushed the thought from my head. But as I did it roared back. I could picture her so clearly in those shapeless pants and baggy shirts. Her disappointingly small breasts. Her disappointingly hairy and ungroomed pussy. There was a homeliness to her that I had never noticed before. Why hadn't I noticed that? I felt suddenly lightheaded from embarrassment. As if a joke had been played on me in front of lots of people.

I have to get out of this relationship, I thought. That's what I have to do. It's the only way.

I turned from the window and through the streets I walked. Now with dread and purpose.

"We need to talk," I would say. I would say it tonight. Why

delay? "We need to talk, Amy." That's how I would begin. "Just talk." Just a listing of the details of our relationship, an objective listing, which, once listed, would make it apparent to both of us that something was unresolvable, that we had always known something was unresolvable, and that it had of course come time to move on. It would be sad, but it would also be hopeful, optimistic. An opening out into new beginnings. For both of us. Yes. An opening. And then I thought about how I would now become one of those old boyfriends she would one day mock and belittle. What would she say about me to someone I didn't know? And then I also thought of *Saïd Sayrafiezadeh is Patrick Madden,* and how the director said he'd call me. Would he call me now? And what if Amy suddenly landed a directing job somehow, somewhere? Would she call me even if we were no longer together? But she wouldn't land a directing job, I knew, so cozy she was in her failure, in her anger over her failure, blaming everyone for her own shortcomings. And so I came back to the starting place, which was, "We need to talk."

When I arrived at her building I walked the six flights with sadness. The last time I would walk these six flights.

I knocked on her door.

"It's open," she called out spryly.

Inside she was lying on her futon with a book of poetry.

"Hi, Camel," she said. The word *camel* disheartened me.

"Hi," I said. My voice was heavy, cumbersome. Then I remembered that this was supposed to be an optimistic time for us, an *opening* for us, and I said loudly, "How was your day, Amy?"

"I have a surprise for you," she said.

A surprise?

"Turn around."

I turned and saw a plastic bag sitting in the middle of her kitchen table.

"No, Amy," I said with friendship, "I don't want a surprise."

"Go ahead and open it," she teased.

I felt my face go hot. "Come on, Amy," I said scoldingly, with a touch of reproach in my voice.

But she heard the reproach as feigned reproach.

"Go ahead, Camel," she said.

For a moment I thought I might be ill. Then I thought about pounding my fists on something, rending something. My clothes maybe.

The bag stared at me. I picked it up. I heard her giggle.

I opened it and slowly withdrew a stuffed camel about a foot tall. It was light brown and it was very soft and it had cloven hooves and two humps.

"It's a Bactrian," Amy said, and now she was standing next to me, her arm encircling my waist, taking the camel from me and putting its snout against my nose.

"Camel, meet Camel."

I dreamed I broke up. I was hanging from her windowsill. Down below me Seventh Avenue churned and boiled. Oh my God! I thought. I won't survive the fall! And then I thought with such sweet dream relief, why not just walk down the stairs?

Another time I dreamed that she was hit by a subway and died. And that was also with sweet dream relief.

In my waking life I concealed my treacherous thoughts. I was like a thief casing a store, waiting for that moment, that perfect moment, when I would be able to say, "We need to talk." But that perfect moment never seemed to come. And in the meantime we went to the Cloisters and to the Museum of Modern Art and once to Coney Island, where in the biting February air we walked down the beach bundled up against each other.

"Let's stay a little longer, Camel. Let's watch the sunset."

"Okay, Giraffe."

And then spring arrived. And then Amy turned thirty-four. And then she said we should think about having a baby.

We were sitting at her table eating pasta.

"Can I think about it?" I said jokingly.

"How long do you need to think about it?" she said. She wasn't joking.

"We have time, don't we?"

"I'm thirty-four," she said soberly.

"That's young," I said.

"No, it's not," she said.

"Yes, it is."

"No," she said, "it's not." And there was a sharpness in her voice that alarmed me. I stuck a forkful of pasta into my mouth and chewed and thought.

Finally I said, "I'm not ready to get married, Amy." And then I put my hand over hers, "I'm sorry."

"Who said you have to be married?" she said, and she pulled her hand away.

"Well, shouldn't we be living together at least?" I asked.

"No way!" she said, dropping her fork on her plate as if I were actually suggesting it at that moment. "I'm not living with you unless you're ready to settle down and have a baby!"

And before I could scarcely think of what I was saying, I blurted out, "Well, I'm not having a baby with you unless we're living together!"

Then we said nothing for a long time. This was our impasse. It was a good impasse to have. I was safe. Nothing would happen unless one of us gave in, and I would never give in. And soon she would grow tired of waiting and she would be the one to say to me, "We need to talk."

She's right, I thought to myself, *thirty-four is old. And twenty-five is young.*

After a while, as a peace offering, I said softly, "I'll think about it."

"I'm giving you one year," she said.

That April there was an opening at the art gallery, and part of my job description as the gallery receptionist was to work the bar. So after I had spent eight hours on the swivel chair I stood for another four hours popping open bottle after bottle of white wine while listening to praise bestowed upon a handsome young man who was just slightly older than myself. "Make sure to keep the cups filled," the owner said to me. At around ten o'clock the party broke up. I was starving but there was nothing to eat except some celery sticks, which I consumed along with three plastic cups of white wine. The wine went to my head. Then I called Amy on a whim.

"Can I come over?" I said. "I don't feel like being alone tonight."

"Of course," she said with sweet pity. "You can always come over."

"Do you have anything to eat?" I asked.

"They didn't feed you? Poor Camel! Well, I have lots of pasta and tomato sauce for you."

It was warm outside and I unzipped my jacket and took it off. On Forty-ninth Street a play had just let out and I was swept up by a crowd talking excitedly. Homeless men waving paper cups followed along clinging to the sides like barnacles. When I arrived at her apartment, huffing and puffing up the six flights, she was lying on her futon happily chatting away on the phone. She waved at me. I went into the kitchen and opened the refrigerator, where I found a jar of Prego that contained about a spoonful of tomato sauce.

"You call this tomato sauce?" I said rhetorically.

"Can I call you back?" I heard her say. Then the phone clicked and she appeared in the kitchen. "Let me tell you something," she said, "I'm not your fucking wife."

"You told me you had something to eat!"

"I'm not your wife!" she repeated.

"I'm hungry, goddamn it!"

In a blur I kicked her kitchen chair and one of its legs popped out.

"That's on loan from Susan!" she screamed in anguish.

"Get a fucking job and you wouldn't have to borrow things!"

The admission was inadvertent. She looked at me in shock and then she snorted as if she'd known it all along.

I saw suddenly that here was the moment I had been waiting for, the opportunity. It had arisen just like that. Of its own accord almost. All I had to do now was just say it. *We need to talk.* And everything would unfold from that.

I watched her kneel down beside the chair as if it were an injured pet that I had run over with my car. She worked on it for a while, trying to get the leg back in. I could see she had no idea what she was doing. I started to feel guilty, and then sad, and I wanted to help, but I couldn't bring myself to make an offer. Plus I didn't want to be the one to break the silence and have it be construed as an act of contrition. Finally she gave up on the chair and pushed it into the corner, where it sat hobbled and uneven. I toasted some bread, buttered it, and ate it standing up in the kitchen, pondering. Then I toasted another slice of bread. The perfect moment seemed to have passed. I went to the bathroom and ran the shower and got in. I stood for a long time under the hot water, letting it cascade over me. When I got out I could hear her talking on the phone in low, muffled tones, like a conspiracy. I thought about eating another slice of bread but decided against it and brushed my teeth. When I came out of the bathroom she was pretending to be asleep and I took out a pair of my underwear from her dresser and then crawled into bed without saying a word. The stuffed camel was under my legs and I kicked it to the side. I lay awake for a while, angrily enjoying the feeling of being hungry and victimized, and imagining that she was racked with sadness and remorse for me. I wondered if I'd have to pay for the chair.

The next morning I woke up at seven o'clock and without a word headed back to the art gallery. On Fifty-first Street I passed a peep show with a poster that read "Live College Girls Inside," with a picture of a pretty woman in a blue nightie, inexplicably holding a baby's bottle. I deliberated for a moment and then rushed inside. Three minutes later I was in a dark video

booth with eight dollars in tokens, masturbating to a woman
with a perfect pussy. She was wearing a pink tiara and giving
a faceless man a blow job. The perspective of the camera was
such that when the actress looked up at the guy it appeared she
was looking right at me. By the time I came I had mapped out
in complete detail how I was going to break up with Amy that
weekend.

Instead we went to the Guggenheim. And the weekend after
that we went to the Botanic Garden. And after that the Bronx
Zoo, where we oohed and aahed at the camels and giraffes.

That summer an up-and-coming theater company in SoHo
cast me as the Second Jew in Oscar Wilde's *Salome*. It was a
thankless role and I played it like it was a thankless role. No
one came anyway. Amy said I was great and that it was a great
start, but I was past starts. By the end of the run I had alienated
myself from everyone in the cast.

After that I turned twenty-six. Is twenty-six young? I could
see the time ticking away slowly. We were in a holding pattern,
Amy and I, neither one of us saying anything, just waiting, waiting for the other to finally come to a decision. Soon, I thought,
soon she will grow tired, anguished. How could she not? "I
can't wait for you any longer," she will say. I saw it so clearly
from her perspective that I also began to feel it from her perspective. It was true that there would come a point in her life
when it would be too late for her to have a baby. How horrible!
That something in life could ever be behind us, irretrievable.
That something could be *too late*. And after that there would be
no going back for her. And it would all be my fault. And I would

be the worst of all her boyfriends. The one who had made her wait for nothing.

And then I would remember so vividly those days in Pittsburgh that now seemed like they were from someone else's life. How I had longed so desperately for her. How I would have given everything for one thing. When had that changed? And the worst of all thoughts would come into my head, obliterating all other thoughts, that perhaps I was still in love with her.

It was true that from time to time I would slip and say something foolhardy and misleading. Once, walking past Macy's, she had stopped for a moment to admire a set of pink dinner dishes.

"Look how pretty those are," she had said.

"You'll see," I replied. "We'll have those one day."

"Oh," she had said, hugging me, "do you mean it? Do you really mean it?"

No, I thought, *I don't really mean it.* Or had I meant it? I could no longer tell.

"Of course I mean it."

That fall she got a job as an administrative assistant at an architectural firm. She hated it. She had to wear skirts.

"It's disgusting the way female artists are treated in this country," she said.

The pay was good, though, and shortly after she started she took me out for dinner at a nice little restaurant right around the corner from her apartment. I had a hamburger and a glass of red wine. The television was on loud and a group of girls with nice asses were standing around watching it. I kept looking over at them until Amy said, "Would you rather be over there?"

"What do you mean?" I said. "With those idiots watching television?"

She smiled at me.

When we were done, Amy paid the bill with a flourish and we walked back to her place, past the Fine Fare supermarket, and up the six flights of stairs.

"I'm going to take a shower," she said.

"Okay," I said.

I got undressed and lay under the covers looking up at the ceiling. And then I looked at the million Ukrainian tchotchkes. And then at the sad photo of her and her mother arriving in the United States.

She was naked when she came out of the bathroom and I avoided looking at her body. She lingered in the kitchen, putting some things away, and then she turned out the light and got into bed. I felt her snuggle up against me, her long blonde hair tickling my chest. I wanted to brush it way.

"I've been thinking about it, Camel," she said in a girlish voice. "I'm ready to live with you."

I felt my mouth go dry. I said nothing. She took my silence as speechless assent. She curled against me tighter. "I'm ready, Camel."

It was very quiet in the apartment. And very dark. I could only make out the outline of her body beneath the sheet.

Finally I said, "I'm not happy, Amy."

She giggled. Then she was silent. Then she said, "Are you kidding?"

I didn't respond.

I felt her body go rigid and she suddenly sat bolt upright in bed as if someone had called out *Fire!* the sheet falling away from her shoulders. Her posture frightened me. I tried to soften the blow.

"I'm not happy *now*," I said, meaning that it was only temporary and that of course it would be possible to be happy again, but even as I said it I could hear in my voice that it was not possible.

"Are you kidding?" she said again. Now her voice was loud, plaintive, desperate. "Are you kidding me?"

Yes, I'm kidding. Ha ha. "No," I said, "I'm not kidding."

And then without warning, though her posture should have been warning enough, she yelled out at the top her lungs, "I did it again!"

The hair on my arms stood up and I flinched from her as though she might turn and attack me.

"I did it again!" she shouted, calling out to everyone. "I did it again!"

I thought of the neighbors and what they would think. And now she slapped her hands hard against her thighs, stinging slaps, and her mouth opened, its gape adding to her silhouette, and a deep sob choked her.

"Amy," I said consolingly. "Amy." And I thought that I should touch her, hold her—*just kidding, just kidding*—but I stayed where I was.

Now there were no words, only tears and hands slapping legs.

"Amy," I said. "Amy, listen to me."

"I did it again," she said, but it was a whisper this time. She was telling herself that she had done it again.

"Amy," I said, "you didn't do it again." But she had.

After a while she became still. Just her labored breathing. And we sat there, neither one of us saying anything. I kept thinking of what should be done next. What was that next thing to do?

Eventually I got up from the futon and started to dress. Pants, shirt, shoes. My limbs felt heavy. She stayed where she was, sitting, facing forward, staring at something in a daze. And then I collected my underwear and socks from her dresser. Done with remorse. And then I remembered and I went into the bathroom and got my toothbrush. After that I took out a Fine Fare plastic bag from the kitchen and put everything inside.

Then I turned to the door. The doorknob glowed.

"Wait," she said, and she felt around underneath the covers, looking for something.

"Take this," she said. "It's yours." And she pulled out the stuffed camel.

I didn't want it. I took it. I put it in the bag. The bag rustled.

"Thanks," I said.

Then I walked down six flights of stairs and out into New York City.

Conversations You Have at Twenty

Maud Newton

Jake and I would have sex anywhere: golf courses, libraries, busy parking lots, other peoples' closets, driving down the highway. Once we did it in a hotel room while his mother was awake and lying in the next bed. I guess I must have gotten some physical pleasure from our escapades, but in hindsight I remember only an urge to impress him—the boy who at seventeen had enjoyed a ménage à trois with Swedish twins and by twenty-one had laid a total of forty-three women—and a mutual callousness that bordered on violence. He moved me around like a rag doll, twisted me like a flex toy. I handled him like I was taking revenge on everyone who'd ever wronged me.

When I tell stories now about our relationship, *he's* the crazy one who drove the wrong way down roads with his lights off, the asshole who berated me at public gatherings, the monster who gave me an STD and then insinuated that I'd given it to him. I leave out all the events that implicate me in the madness. The day I ripped my glasses from my face, twisted them until they broke, and flung them out of his speeding truck onto the highway. All the nights I fled our apartment in my nightgown to lie in the bushes and weep. The crazed summer afternoon that I brandished a kitchen knife at him, then at myself, then threatened to jump from the window.

We were living in the Gainesville student ghetto with my previous boyfriend, Todd. Being a sane boy, he had more or less stopped speaking to us about anything except who would buy the next round of toilet paper. When the phone rang, he didn't pick up. It was too likely to be Jake's mother, Mindy.

"Hi, kids," she would say, on the answering machine. "I've been in the hospital again, but don't worry. You're busy. You have more important things on your mind. And the doctor says it's not fatal—not yet, anyway. Speak with you when you have a moment."

Mindy feathered her hair back in a style ten years out of vogue. She kept it a purplish red that drained all the warmth from her already wan complexion. Her eyes were dark brown, almost black, and there was something dead in her gaze—maybe only a reflection of the gray half-moons that lay beneath her eyes like an accusation. As far as I could tell, she didn't sleep. She stayed up all night, worrying and starving herself.

It was 1991, the era of aerobics and bicycle shorts, of frozen yogurt and rice cakes and baked potatoes as health food. Mindy's larder was stocked with fat-free pudding, fat-free butter substitute, fat-free cheese product, fat-free wheat bread, fat-free frozen waffles, and bananas. She said she'd once gone two years without eating solid food. "I lived on laxatives and fruit juice," she told me, "and I annihilated my colon." Perhaps this explained her enthusiasm for enemas. Her bag hung by its tubing from a hook in the bathroom, right above the basket of *Playboy*s that, within an hour of my meeting her, she chastised Jake for hiding from me in the closet.

"Where are my naked girls?" she called from the hallway, where her robe had fallen open to reveal a lacy black bra and underwear. "Where did you put my magazines?"

"Why are you such a disgusting pervert?" Jake said. "And put your fucking clothes on. Did you forget you're meeting my girlfriend?"

Mindy led me by the hand to the magazines and opened one. A University of Georgia coed who professed to enjoy "a whole lot of sugar in my black coffee" lay back on brownish pink satin sheets exactly the same shade as her nail polish and her nipples. "It's nice to look at other women's tits," Mindy told me. "It makes you feel sexy." She worked as a junketeer, organizing gambling trips to Vegas, the islands, and Atlantic City. Sometimes a high roller gave her money to stay in his room for the weekend. Between trips she supplemented her income by blowing her boss at fifty dollars a pop.

I was a Docs-wearing, Shulamith Firestone–reading, porn-hating feminist, but as I leafed through the magazines later, I could see her point. I practiced sucking in my stomach, pursing my lips, lounging back on the sofa pillows as though I had no ambitions other than to have sex and be an ornament. That night Jake and I screwed on the beach. Then we did it on a lounge chair by the apartment pool. In the night, he reached for me and took off my clothes and said my name. His eyes were black and glittering. He pushed inside of me and then jolted awake. "Oh my God," he said. "Did I start this? I'm exhausted." He disengaged and rolled over.

I was sore. It burned when I peed, and I didn't know why. But this was a triumph: even in his sleep, I was the one he wanted to fuck.

On first meeting, Jake repulsed me. He was dark haired and lanky, with a rock star sneer and long legs to match, but I'd never been into tall guys. And between his hair—short on the sides, cascading between his shoulder blades in back—and tight white jeans, he looked like he'd just been beamed out of a South Florida mall and into my friend Matt's apartment.

Matt, a sweet, long-eyelashed Catholic boy who'd vowed chastity until marriage but had a crush on me, had invited me over for dinner. I was mooning over a breakup, writing furious and interminable poems in my journals, too bereft to feed myself.

The hallway of Matt's building smelled of garlic and marinara and melted cheese. His hand trembled slightly as he turned the key in the lock, and I was touched by his awkwardness, by all the trouble he'd gone to. Maybe tonight I would kiss him. His hands would slide up my shirt; he'd know intuitively how to touch me. By morning I'd be cleansed of my ex, and Matt and I would realize how much time we'd lost.

And then he opened the door to reveal Jake sprawled across the couch, drinking a Heineken. "Hey." He toasted the air with his beer. "I see we're having lasagna."

He turned to me. "I'm Jake," he said.

*   *   *

Jake was just out of a relationship too. His girlfriend of four years had left him, and he was drinking and fucking his way through the resulting heartbreak. "The only bad thing about sleeping with four different girls is how fast the sheets get dirty," he told me, while Matt set the dishes on the table. "Good thing I have lots of sheets."

Matt sat down, put his napkin in his lap. "Don't you want to settle down again?"

"With who? I like that girl Cara, but her pus—"

Matt cleared his throat. "There's a lady present," he said.

"Vagina makes this loud farting noise no matter what position I try." Jake turned to me. "Have you ever heard of anything like that?"

"No," I said, daintily patting lasagna from my lips with my napkin. "No, I have not."

After dinner and a six-pack, Jake stumbled off to find the blonde-haired girl who'd just moved into the apartment downstairs.

Matt raised his eyebrows. "She's seventeen, man."

"Who cares?" Jake turned in the doorway, mimed breasts. "Like a couple of grapefruits," he said.

Soon we heard him joking with the girl in the hall. "So I ask the waitress, does it matter who pays the check? 'No,' she says, 'I don't care.' So I say, 'Okay, then why don't you pay it?' " His laugh sounded like a tin can falling down stairs.

My own experience was essentially limited to three relationships. I wasn't prim so much as picky—and prone to serial monogamy. There was my devoted, car-obsessed high school boyfriend. We'd been together for three years, until just after graduation. Then I'd fallen for Nelson, a sweet-talking boy who'd enlisted and been shipped to Kuwait but still sent letters that turned my life upside down. And finally there was my most recent ex, Todd. He was clever and handsome, with black architect glasses, a bowler hat, and a collection of Elvis Costello posters, and, in the midst of our relationship, he admitted that he was attracted to my mind but not my body. I dated him for another four hopeless months after that. Hard as it is to fathom now, ours was the breakup I was still reeling from.

But after I cruelly raised Matt's hopes one February night by rolling around with him on the couch, convincing him that sex before marriage might, after all, be desirable, and then deciding I wasn't interested, it did occur to me that a quick fling might finally get Todd out of my system. Maybe I didn't need to fall for every guy whose bed I woke up in.

Whenever my thoughts drifted in this direction over the next few months, I considered calling Jake. True, he wasn't my type, but that was a bonus: there would be no danger of love, no talk of commitment. And with all that practice, he had to be good. Surely he would disprove my friend Rick's axiom: "No penis is a love-removal machine (thank you, Ian Astbury)." Late one afternoon I actually picked up the phone and dialed Jake's number, but his laugh came rattling out before I explained what I wanted, and I invented some other reason for phoning him.

"Matt's still all fucked-up about the breakup," he said.

I sighed. "What 'breakup'? We were hardly even dating."

"To him, you were practically married."

*   *   *

After that I avoided Matt, Jake, and the rest of their gang till the start of summer, when we all drove to Tampa for a Yes reunion concert we'd bought tickets to months in advance. Between Jon Anderson straining at the high notes and Matt gazing misty-eyed at me for the duration of "Owner of a Lonely Heart," the show was a letdown from start to finish. That night we crashed at Matt's folks' place in the suburbs. I lay beneath a frilly bedspread, surrounded by Madonna posters, in his little sister's bedroom. His mother, impeccably but frostily polite, had ushered me there and handed me a towel and washcloth. "Use these in the morning," she said.

Jake was to sleep on the floor of the same room. Matt and the other two guys we'd driven down with were next door. We could hear the rumble of their conversation through the wall. From time to time, Matt lumbered to and from the bathroom, hovering a little too long in the hallway on each trip. His nearness—or rather, my confinement in his child-hood home—felt like an indictment.

As Matt's step creaked down the hallway yet again, Jake looked at me and raised an eyebrow.

"Look, I said I was a bitch, okay? I shouldn't have kissed him. I shouldn't have let him reach up my shirt. But I've already apologized up, down, and sideways. I won't spend the rest of my life feeling guilty."

"Shhh," Jake whispered. "He might hear you."

I fluffed the pillow, turned on my side, pulled the covers up to my neck. "I don't care anymore. He needs to fucking grow up and get over it."

"It's hard, though. Love can make you crazy." Jake sat up in his sleeping bag, reached for the door and closed it. He rested his back against the wall. "Look at *me*—"

"What? Trying to cram as many lays as possible into twenty-four hours?"

"You didn't know me when I was with Ellen. I helped her quit coke. She slept with someone else, and I stayed with her anyway. We told everyone we were married. I used to put in her tampons."

Her *tampons*? "Jesus, that sucks."

"When she left me, I sat in her parking space and cried."

"Man." I propped my head on my hand. "How come she left?"

"I was an asshole."

I smiled. "So nothing's changed, then."

"No, really, I was."

"Oh, I believe you," I said.

It was one of those conversations you have when you're twenty years old. You're crashed out in an unfamiliar place with somebody you don't know too well and never liked all that much, and there, exposed in your nightclothes, the dark hours until sunrise stretched out before you, you discover an uncanny affinity. Naturally I opened up about my own exes. Six months after the fact, there was still the drama of the breakup with Todd to be rehashed. There were many angles from which to examine the question of whether the new mix tape and letters from Nelson—who was still in the army but safely in Germany now—proved he was my soul mate. No doubt we also discussed the guy in my Spanish class who liked the Replacements or the boy one floor up at my dorm who'd stopped me in the hall to ask for my number.

Jake had a way of listening without judging. I soon discovered that people were always telling him their secrets. They'd spent their tuition money on two days with a prostitute, maybe, or accidentally hit a neighbor's dog with their car and been so horrified and ashamed they'd left it there in the street to die. One guy confessed to taping a girl's wrists, stuffing a sock in her mouth, and raping her.

Things I never told anyone came tumbling out of my mouth that night. The church my mom had pastored in a warehouse, a strip mall, and then in a warehouse again. The drug addicts and prostitutes I'd known there. My stepfather, her copreacher, who did nauseating things to me in a bed one afternoon.

Toward dawn Jake brought out his own skeletons. There was an eight-year-old roommate in a home for asthmatic children who brutalized Jake when he was four. There was Mr. Nitzblum, the second-grade teacher who used to keep him in at recess, fondle him in a closet. And later, when Jake was in high school, there was the Haitian tennis coach his mom had dated. Jake had sex with the man but was confused afterward: he didn't exactly consent, he said, but neither did he object.

As the first rays of daylight shone through the blinds, the air was electric with confidences. My head was light—from excitement or lack of sleep or some giddy combination of the two. I noticed for the first time that Jake had a striking jaw, nice high cheekbones, beguiling dark eyes. Something was different.

"Hey, when did you cut your hair?"

"About a month ago," he said. "It was too Miami before, don't you think?"

Though we didn't consummate the attraction for another week, our launch into a poisonous three-year love affair was now inevitable. At breakfast Jake and I were exhausted and aglow, barely able to string words into sentences. Matt glumly pushed his eggs around on his plate.

"It doesn't have to be a big deal," I told Jake, after he and I first slept together. "I might be in love with that guy in the army who's getting out soon anyway."

Was it my indifference that inspired him to cut things off with the other girls? To wrap his gold chain-link bracelet around my wrist and tell me that he loved me? At first I said I didn't feel the same way, but he was so interested in me, so solicitous, I convinced myself I'd been wrong.

We had sex in the campus music-listening room, and we had sex out on Cedar Key. I never said no. I made a point of being ready. One night I led him to a porch swing in front of a doctor's office. We were absolutely shitfaced. Cars whizzed by, up and down University Avenue, but he sat, and I straddled him and held on to the back of the swing. It was over fast. "Jesus Christ," he said. "I saw stars."

I didn't trust Jake's compliments. He'd probably seemed euphoric to the girl with the farting vagina too. I needed independent verification, and eventually I got it—from his mother. On a visit she left her journal lying out, open to a page with my name on it. "I thought Ellen was hot stuff," the entry said. "But he tells me Maud is better."

* * *

We'd been together a month or two when I came home from the student infirmary with a prescription. "The nurse says this should clear it up," I said. "You'd better go talk to her."

"Thanks a fucking lot," he said.

"Don't look at *me*. I'm practically a virgin next to you. Go talk to Grapefruit Tits or Farting Pus—"

"I'll make an appointment," he said. "You don't have to be such a bitch about it."

We fought about the STD, and we fought about our parents. We fought about my writing, his music, and his motorcycle. If I hung out with other guys, he paced and stewed until I got home, then sat me down and quizzed me. If he ran into one of the girls he'd slept with, I feigned disinterest and then flew into a rage about the volume of his guitar, the way he swept the floor, how he failed to appreciate my attempts at baking. "Sorry, but your cookies just aren't very good," he said.

When Nelson was discharged from the service and came to visit, Jake followed us around campus. He roared up and down University Avenue on his Kawasaki while we sat in Joe's Deli eating sandwiches. "What did you tell him?" he asked me that night. "Does he know we're together?"

"Of course."

"But you'd rather be with *him*, wouldn't you?"

"Of course not," I lied. Anyway, it didn't matter who I might, theoretically, prefer. I was with Jake, and with Jake I would stay.

"Don't give me tomatoes," he would say to restaurant servers. "If there's a tomato on my plate, you're not getting a tip."

I would stare out the window. "Can't you just say you're allergic?"

"But I'm not."

"Who cares? That way you're not an asshole. And that way they won't spit in our food."

Once he propositioned a department store mannequin. I took offense.

"It's *plastic*," he said. "I was kidding."

I stood in the mall parking lot, ten feet from his truck, arms crossed, refusing to move. "It just shows me how you really think about women."

"Spare me your feminist diatribe," he said, "and just get in the fucking car."

We tried to change the subject, the mood, the setting. He took me out for pad thai, but the base was made with pork, and I was a vegetarian. I made him a pound cake. It turned out so dense that he suggested we use it to solve his roach problem. We drove around town, yelling at each other till our voices were hoarse. Then we had sex in some new and twisted locale. The afterglow upon us as we hitched up our pants and drove home, we laughed about the fighting and tried to blame it on something. It wasn't us, it was the weather, our classes, living too far apart.

Yes, we decided, that was it: Jake should live closer to campus. And how convenient: my ex-boyfriend Todd and I were becoming friends again, and he had an empty room to rent! Jake moved in. Soon I was living with them too. Strangely, this arrangement did not end up being the panacea we had counted on.

*   *   *

It was only December, just four or five months into our relationship, when Jake and I shacked up with Todd. That was also around the time I helped Mindy plan a surprise birthday party for Jake down at her place. She invited one ex-husband, all three of her sisters, and a handful of distant, wealthy relatives who were visiting from New York for the winter.

Jake's truck broke down en route to Miami, so we showed up late, dressed in old T-shirts and cutoffs, toting our laundry in trash bags through a lobby newly decked out in art deco pinks and blues. Two years after the end of *Miami Vice,* the rest of the country had moved on, but South Florida was still colored with the same palette, its reliance on Nagel prints, track lighting, and mirrored walls unwavering as ever.

The small living room was filled with people I'd never met. Cousin Marly, who answered the door, eyed our outfits disapprovingly. Everyone else embraced us. "Eat," they said, handing us plates. Dill pickles, pastrami, fresh rye bread, and every other offering from the nearby kosher deli were laid out on the table.

We'd been there maybe forty-five minutes when Mindy called us into her bedroom. She reached into her nightstand and pulled out a box. "Let me show you what my boss gave me for Hanukkah," she said, laughing. She held up a piece of gold jewelry the size of one of Run-DMC's nameplates. "HEAD," it read at the bottom, in diamond-encrusted letters. Above that was a carved-out etching of a woman bending down in front of a man, her mouth down deep between his legs, his testicles jammed between her lower lip and chin.

"Sue for harassment," said one of Mindy's sisters. "But your son's party, is this really the place?"

"What?" Mindy said. "I like it. If I had a thick enough chain, I would wear it around my neck."

"Of course you would," Jake said. "Because you're a fucking slut." He stalked out of the room, slammed the door. A few seconds later the front door slammed too. The elevator door dinged shut before I could catch up.

I found him standing beside the pool. I put my arms around his waist, and we stared at the water. "She can't help it, you know," I said. "She's trying to prove to herself that someone wants her."

"To herself? Or to all of Miami?"

"Let's go back upstairs. There are presents. People are waiting."

"Screw the presents." He led me to a place next to the Coke machines where two people could fit, and if they were quick about it, no one could see. He reached to unfasten my shorts.

"Seriously," I said. "Your family wants you to open the things they brought."

Leaning back against a cigarette dispenser, he sighed and looked at me. "Some birthday."

When we went upstairs, he opened my present first. I'd spent weeks looking for a sweater just the right shade of blue, in a loose-knit style I thought he'd like. His face fell as he lifted it from the box. "I'm allergic to wool," he said.

"That's okay," I said. "We'll exchange it."

But he pulled the soft crewneck over his head. He wore it until his eyes turned red and he started to wheeze.

Mindy smiled, gestured grandly in his direction. "See how much he loves her?"

"Who buys wool for an asthmatic?" Cousin Marly muttered into her wineglass.

"It's a metaphor for our relationship," I told him later. We were parked next to the Ft. Lauderdale airport, looking out at the runway as planes took off and landed. "Even when we try to do nice things, we make each other sick."

"Life isn't a novel, Maud. We're not in one of your stories."

"But why are we so sad? Why do we fight so much?"

He held me close against him. His breathing was shallow. "I don't know," he said. "I don't know, but we have to stop."

Through the winter and the spring and the summer we fought, and then we moved again, into a two-bedroom place with dark blue carpet that quickly became infested with fleas. My legs and ankles were riddled with bites. I kept a glass of water beside me to drown the bugs I caught. That autumn Jake and I were always setting off bug bombs and taking the dog out for four-hour walks. When we returned, the apartment was hazy with sweet-smelling poison.

I wish I could recall how our worst fights got started, how they built to a blind and furious crescendo that had him pushing me into walls and me brandishing knives, but the truth is, I look back on those days and nights, and all I remember clearly is the rage and the hurt.

When my parents argued, my mother cried and screamed and threw things. She opened the kitchen cabinets, hurled dishes and condiments and cutlery into the middle of the floor, and left. I carried this conflict-resolution strategy into adulthood. I followed Jake from room to room, crying and accusing, until he yelled at me, laughed at me, pushed me. Then I broke figurines, ripped dresses, tore up books. Some nights the apartment seemed too small to hold my grief, and I wandered outside, half-dressed, and cried there.

Every couple of months I packed up my things, planning to leave for good.

I would check myself into a hotel, but Jake would track me down and bring me flowers. "I've been emotionally abusive to you," he would say. "I'm going to change."

But was he the abusive one, or was I?

The night before his brother's wedding, I ran down the hall of the Charleston Marriott, sobbing, in sheer pink pajamas, while Mindy yelled at Jake in the room we were all sharing. "*This* is how you treat your girlfriend? *These* are the things you say to the woman you love? She's like a daughter to me. And you, my son, are a stranger. I blame myself, staying with your father when you were a baby. From your crib, you watched as he hit me."

The insults, the shouting, the utterly unhinged theatrics: so much grief, and I have no idea what set us off that time. Conflict was routine by then, as was making up. Mindy lay awake watching MTV as we writhed under the covers in the room's other double bed. I like to think we were at least quiet about it.

All the drama exacted a toll. My hair began to fall out in clumps. My eyes bulged, giving the constant impression of rage or insanity, or both. My hands shook so furiously I couldn't hold a piece of paper without it rattling. When I lay down to sleep at night, my heart pumped like a broken water main. I believed I was losing my mind.

In desperation I moved back home, into my mom's house in the Kendall section of Miami. Mom had fourteen dogs and a couple hundred birds. The kitchen was infested with rats. When I went swimming, my stepdad watched me inappropriately. But, I reasoned, I'd only be there for four months. In January, for want of a better plan, I'd be starting law school. Meanwhile, maybe the distance would take me far enough out of Jake's orbit that I'd be able to quit him. But no: we pressed on. He drove down every few weekends. I would meet him at Mindy's.

"What's wrong?" he would say. "Why are you shaking? Why do your eyes look like that?"

My thyroid had gone haywire. It was Mindy who figured that out; the doctor just confirmed it: Graves' disease. When at rest my heart was beating 127 times a minute. I was put on a beta-blocker and told to stay in bed. The hospital flew in a radioactive pill that I had to wear protective gear to take. Soon I was sluggish and chunky, no longer interested in manic sex and rabid fights and, consequently, in Jake.

I returned to Gainesville just as he took a job in South Florida. This was convenient: I kept his dog and his desk and moved into the place he was vacating—a studio in a converted motel adjoining a trailer park. The apartment featured a wall-mounted air conditioner/heater that could be set to "lo" or "hi" with little discernible cooling effect but a significant increase in clattering. A Texas-like shape repeated several times on each slat of the faux-wood paneling that covered the walls, and the bathroom cabinets were sticky and yellowed from the cigarette smoke of some prior occupant.

Law school started, but after the first week I attended only sporadically. Mostly I lay around petting the dog and eating candy and luxuriating in my solitude. It dawned on me that I was getting fat, so I adopted a tried-and-true weight-loss regimen: cigarettes.

When Jake called to pick a fight with me one afternoon in late January, I dumped him. "I can't do this anymore," I said, exhaling loudly. "I need to concentrate on my health and my schooling."

"Are you *smoking*?" His voice rose into a familiar quavery tenor. "You know I'm asthmatic."

"Really, it's over," I said. "And please don't call me. We need some time, and I'm busy with classes."

For the next few weeks, my days were so aimless and relaxed, I felt stoned. From time to time I thought vaguely of making my way to the registrar's office and dropping out. Mostly, though, I walked the dog and sat out in front of my apartment, smoking cigarettes and reading magazines and shooting the shit with the neighbors.

Next door was Kenny, who worked nights as a janitor at the university hospital and slept days. Despite his penchant for watching porno flicks at top volume on his nights off, he was sweet, always inviting me over for dinner (although he couldn't seem to understand why I declined every time, that being a vegetarian, I would never want to join him for pork chops). Occasionally Kenny seemed twitchy and agitated—months later, he confessed to smoking crack regularly—but so far he'd lost his temper with me only once, when my dog spent an afternoon barking at a telephone repairman through the window. I'd opened the door to find him, red-faced with anger. As he'd yelled, he'd banged his palms on both sides of the door frame.

Out across the way was Felipe, a self-proclaimed alcoholic and dishonorably discharged ex-con who worked on his ancient Camaro in the parking lot. He was smart and funny and doted on his grizzled collie. But he liked to joke about watching me undress through the blinds. When he really got going in that vein, I took my ashtray indoors.

I didn't hear from Jake again until Valentine's Day. Breaking with recent tradition, I picked up the phone. I was awaiting a call from some old friends about a single-girl-empowerment dinner we'd planned for that night and were all secretly dreading.

"How's it going?" Jake said, in lieu of hello. "Been on lots of dates?"

"No," I said, reaching for my smokes and lighter. "It's only been three weeks."

"Well, I thought you should know that I'm sleeping with someone else." His voice was chirpy and gloating.

Blood rushed into my face. My heart leapt back into the crazed, thumping rhythm I'd come to know so well. I banged down the receiver. The dog shrank against the wall, then trotted into the other room.

I opened the front door, went outside, and slammed it as hard as I could. Then I slammed it again. I did it another twenty or so times, stopping only when it wouldn't open anymore. I stood on the step, pulling at the knob. The door was so stuck, it didn't even creak.

Kenny pulled open his door and stuck his head out. His face was blotchy, his hair wild.

"Sorry." I smoothed my skirt and tried to assume the pose of a sensible girl. "I was—uh—just kind of pissed off."

He stalked out onto the sidewalk. I could see that he'd been sleeping in his clothes. "Kind of?"

"Actually, I was really fucking pissed off. Had a call from my ex."

I heard a light step behind me, and then Felipe said, "So no free sex show tonight, Ken."

Kenny chuckled, his lips a little too tight. At this range—a couple of feet—he was larger than I remembered. He smelled of sweat and chili and something faintly metallic. "You're a cute girl, Maud. But we can't have this door slamming."

He raised his hand, and I wondered if he was going to slap me. Instead he patted my head.

I nodded. "Right. No more slamming doors."

I stood there, smiling and nodding, until Kenny went back inside. Felipe returned to his Camaro. I waited for him to slide underneath the car, for the sound of his tools clanging, but he sat on top of it and watched me instead.

I pulled the screen from my window and climbed inside.

Then I closed the window and locked it. I realized that the phone was, and had been, ringing. I unplugged it.

When my friends came to pick me up, I didn't try to open the door. Afraid that they, like Felipe, would see me moving around inside, I slunk into the bathroom and sat on the floor.

The girls knocked and called to me until Kenny went out and yelled at them. "Shut up, you crazy bitches," he said. "All y'all crazy like that Maud."

As their car drove off, my heart was still hammering madly. I stood to get my cigarettes and caught sight of my bulging eyes in the mirror. They looked strange and robotic, as lifeless in their glassy protuberance as Mindy's grim black ones. I didn't see how I would find my way back.

Twenty-five to One Odds

Josh Kilmer-Purcell

Not having had much—actually, any—experience with breaking and entering, it wasn't surprising that I'd sliced my pinkie finger down to the bone on my first attempt. I'd cut it as I put my fist through a pane of glass in the back porch's French doors.

"You're supposed to wrap your shirt or something around your fist first," #25 pointed out helpfully, if a little belatedly.

I immediately realized I'd put my fist through the wrong pane—one that was nowhere near the dead bolt I needed to unlatch. I'd literally added insult to injury. My poor aim was doubly embarrassing, considering it was my own apartment I was attempting to break into. So not only had I cased the joint, I'd been living in it for almost a year.

I'd been unable to enter my apartment in my usual, less criminal manner since I'd left my keys behind with someone at the nightclub. I was far too drunk to drive, which may also have contributed to my poor cat-burgling skills.

With the clattering of a second pane of glass, I finally succeeded in forcibly gaining entrance to my home.

"Come on in," I said cheerily to #25, stepping over the strewn bits of broken glass and waving my arm in a gesture of hospitality, which sent an arc of blood across the dining room floor.

"Um, you gonna put a bandage on that or something?" #25 asked.

"This?" I asked bravely, looking down at the loose skin dangling from my finger, "*Nah.* It's nothing. Flesh wound. Let's fuck."

This is where, as a writer, I'd like to include a description of #25. I realize it might help complete the scene. Even something as simple as a name. But I can't. However, if I remember my taste in men correctly, #25 was probably taller than me. And blond. Or African American. Or short but cute. Probably on the heavy side. Unless he was rail thin. Hairy. Or smooth. Or smart or dumb or young or old.

The only thing I can be truly certain of is that he had a penis.

But an accurate description really doesn't matter nowadays any more than it did at the time. He was, simply, #25. All that mattered was that I was minutes away from having sex with magical Mr. #25, and I wasn't going to let something as flimsy as a pane of glass (or two) stand in my way. I had a goal to reach.

I was twenty-five years old. And up until that year, with the exception of one exploratory boyfriend whose idea of sex was closing our eyes and hoping for the best, I had yet to experience all the joys of gay sex I'd furtively imagined throughout my closeted teen years. My propriety, I believe, was the natural outcome of dozens of 1980s after-school specials. I'd been indoctrinated to believe that if I were to touch another nude body before marriage I would either find myself hooked on drugs, pregnant with crack babies, or dead of AIDS. In the Reagan era, it didn't as much matter if one went through puberty gay or straight, as long as you went through it fearing for your life.

But even from my limited exposure to what TV evangelists called my "lifestyle," I knew that I should be having a lot more sex. As a gay man, the world was supposed to be my prurient playground. What was I doing wrong? How was I going to become a good gay? Having grown up in a stolid midwestern environment, I considered every failure to be the result of simply not trying hard enough. Which is why, at the stroke of midnight on August 28, 1994, my twenty-fifth birthday, I decided to fuck my age in strangers.

The first two people I told about my resolution were my two closest friends at the advertising agency where I worked at the time—Pamela and James. Together, the three of us were assigned to create all the advertising for the Marine Corps. Our favorite in-joke was: How "few good men" does it take to make an ad for the Marines? Answer: None. Just two fags and a hag.

I honestly think they were happy for me and my new hobby. Or at least they were happy that I might begin to contribute something more exciting to our lunchtime conversations. They both led much more colorful lives than I. James had come out of the closet early, at sixteen. He regaled us with stories of past nocturnal escapades—silently rolling his parents' car down the driveway in neutral in order to drive into the city for nights of underage debauchery.

I sensed Pamela too had a past—if only because she shared so little of it. Neither James nor I knew her true age. She could have been anywhere from thirty to fifty. But her stiletto boots, husky menthol voice, and inappropriate-for-the-office clothing signaled a history, if not checkered, at least more interesting than mine. Plus her husband was blue collar. That alone, in my sheltered middle-class world, meant that she was rough around the edges.

So with their blessing, I embarked on my new odyssey with the enthusiasm of a hooker with OCD.

Most of those hapless twenty-five dalliances are a blur to me now, fifteen years later. Truthfully, many of them were a blur then—thanks to my other newest friend, vodka. But I do remember #1.

Like any good athlete, I started my quest by warming up. Taking it slow. Which meant that I made #1 take me to dinner before our sexual congress. I can't quite picture what he looked like, but I do remember that he owned a chain of driving schools. I remember this because, as I blew him in his car on the drive home from the restaurant, I wondered how many points this would cost him if he were pulled over.

Numbers 2 to 6 I don't remember at all. Nothing. Nada. I suspect that these men were unmemorable less because of anything they did, or did not do, but more because I was simply overwhelmed. I was experiencing too many back-to-back sexual firsts. And back-to-front sexual firsts. And front-to-front sexual firsts. My erogenous zones were being discovered more often than I changed outfits. I'm not exaggerating.

It's sad to me now to think of how quickly I sped through these early physical discoveries. I was in a drunken race to the finish, abandoning all pretense of romance for the sake of becoming a "good" gay. But if there is an upside to the speed at which I became numb to the physical side of sex, it's that I also quickly discovered how boring the mechanics of sex can be. And how, sometimes, after finding myself in bed with someone, I needed to put my imagination to work in order to finish the job at hand.

To this day, I'm proud that I can make a fantasy out of most anyone. I don't have a "type." I've slept with everyone from leather daddies to drag queens and had a blast with them all, even if I don't remember the particulars anymore. The danger of inflexibility was taught to me by #7.

He was a model. Probably the most classically beautiful man I've slept with. I needed no fantasies to enjoy myself with him. He was so beautiful that, unlike the others up to that point, I interrupted my breakneck pace to sleep with him several times in a row. I couldn't help it. It was like costarring in a porn movie.

The first time I went home with #7, we spent that awkward time between "Can I come in?" and "Can I come now?" watching a videotape of the television show *Wonder Woman*. I thought this was charmingly camp, and frankly it was the most interesting thing about #7 other than his chiseled cheekbones and six-pack abs.

The second time I went home with #7, we watched another episode of *Wonder Woman*.

By the third time I had an orgasm with Lynda Carter in the room, I realized what was going on.

"You can't have sex without watching *Wonder Woman*, can you?" I asked.

"Um, no," he answered sheepishly.

"Why not?" I asked, intrigued why this gay god needed to watch a cheaply produced 1970s television show in order to get an erection. I realized that I was probably not the best-looking person he'd ever slept with, but I had the distinct advantage, I thought, of being nonfictional.

"Um, I don't know" was his answer.

It's possible I overthink things, but if I had *that* specific a fetish, I'd probably have put a little thought into its origin. Then again, not being a model gives me the luxury of having thoughts in the first place.

That was the last time I saw #7. I was tired of playing an extra in a scene. If I wasn't the star, then I wasn't staying in the picture.

James and Pamela got a kick out #7's story. As they did with most all of them. They would look up quizzically from their newspapers on Monday mornings when I came in and regaled them with my weekend conquests.

"Numbers 9, 10, 11 . . . an orgy on the roof of my apartment building," I would announce, proudly.

They would burst into mock applause, and we would spend the rest of the morning discussing and laughing about my latest escapade. They were my best friends in the world. At the time, they were my only friends. While I was meeting dozens of new people each weekend, I only saw them as potential sexual victims. I had no idea that it was possible to be friends with someone you'd seen naked.

Until I met #17 and #18. Both were nice enough guys: #17 was stunningly handsome, #18 wasn't.

The two were regulars at the club James and Pamela were beginning to call "Josh's antechamber." They were roughly my age and had begun dating in high school. *High school.* The idea that two guys were senior sweethearts at the same time I was self-loathing myself into awkward heterosexual prom fumblings was mind-boggling. In their early twenties they'd bought a home together in the suburbs, complete with dog and matching place settings. Their life was a fantasy as remote to me as the suburbs themselves. I was curious. I wanted to try what they had. Which meant, of course, that I had to break them up so that I could move in on #17. The cute one.

I decided on a strategy of proposing a three-way to begin with. I'd learned enough to know that three-ways were the most dangerous threat facing gay couples. Global warming is nothing compared to the chill that descends over couples after their first ménage à trois.

I was a little surprised when they said yes. They seemed so perfect together. I accepted the fact that I was going to have to touch the less cute #18 naked in order to have my way with #17. It was a worthy sacrifice, I felt, and I undertook the task with my usual can-do attitude.

It was worth it: #17 was hotter in bed than any of my experiences to date. He was so good, in fact, that we started seeing each other clandestinely at my apartment every morning on his way into work in the city.

I had no shame about this. Theirs was not my marriage. Whatever #17 did behind #18's back was not my problem.

When I would inevitably run into them as a couple at the club every Friday night, we'd have a couple of drinks together and chat about the week gone by. Both #17 and I pretended to be surprised by topics we'd already chatted over earlier in the week, postcoitally.

While I had no sexual attraction to #18, I had to admit that he was as funny in conversation as I wanted to be and as generous as I'd never be. I found myself beginning to grow fond of him. He was an amateur home DJ and would bring me, each week, a CD of the music I'd liked from the club the week before. He also never failed to make sure that I was safely in a cab at the end of the night and to help screen my potential victims for me, knowing that I was unfailingly too drunk to make smart decisions.

During the time I was fucking his partner of eight years, #18 and I became great friends—better friends than I was with his partner, who, frankly, was beginning to get a little predictable in the sack. I realized how odd our secretive three-way relationship had become when one morning, with #17 still in my bed, I raced to call to #18 because our favorite singer was on the *Today* show.

I had no idea how to extricate myself from the situation. It turned out that I wanted to keep my newfound friendship with #18 intact while breaking up with his partner. James and Pamela were not much help with this particular dilemma, either. It seemed like a conundrum of biblical proportions. I was sure that I was going to have to cut someone in half by the time it was all over.

Luckily and unluckily, #17 gave me a quick, terse call at my office one morning, telling me that the jig was up. He'd spilled the beans after a particularly bad argument, and they both decided that it would be better if none of us kept in touch with one another. I knew that it would be strange at the club the following Friday and secretly hoped that they might not show up. My wish was granted, and while I was a little sad at what had transpired, I was also relieved to finally get back to my sexual conquest tally. I'd been out of the game for far too long.

I forget what number victim I left the club with that night. My erstwhile friend #18 wasn't there to vet him and put me into a cab safely. While I don't remember the number of this particular trick, I *do*, for a change, remember what he looked like. Down to the tiniest detail.

He was only about an inch or so taller than me but probably had at least forty more pounds than my skinny 135-pound frame. I knew this because I'd been feeling him up on the dance floor. He was wearing one of the more popular club uniforms of the time, jean overalls, with absolutely nothing underneath.

His hair was the kind of jet-black that reflected blue highlights under the parking lot street lamps. He had nice features. His eyes were small and squinty. He laughed a lot—too much, really. I wasn't at all sure what he was finding funny, but he repeatedly broke into unprovoked laughter as he drove us to my place. I'd obviously been missing a lot of humor during the eight-minute drive from the club to my apartment.

Looking back, I think what he must have found so funny was my utter stupidity in leaving with him.

As soon as I unlocked my door and let him in, he slammed it behind me and pushed me back against the door frame, pressing his mouth against mine. By this time I'd been involved in all sorts of scenes and figured that this guy, number whatever, liked it rough. Fine. I could do rough. I'd wrestle around for a half hour or so, get him out the door, and get some sleep.

We did wrestle around, nakedly, for a half hour or so. Satisfied with my latest bedpost notch, I uttered what was quickly becoming my signature line: "Would you like some water before you go?"

Before you go *now*, was the implied takeaway message. But my latest victim had no intention of leaving.

"No, I'm going to stay right here for a while," he said, still lying on the floor, staring up at the ceiling.

"Um, okay. But I have to be up early," I lied.

"Why? You have to go to *church*?" He found this to be even more uproarious than any of his other nonsensical jokes. His laughter must have lasted a full minute.

"Really, I have stuff I need to do," I said, picking my naked self up off the living room rug and collecting his overalls and socks.

He reached out from his prone position, grabbed my ankle, and twisted it until I had no choice but to collapse back down on the ground.

"Ow. If there's nothing else, you really should leave," I said firmly. It probably didn't sound that firm, however, since I'd started trembling a little.

"*Should* leave?!" he said, incredulously. "*Should* leave?! Tell me, exactly, why I *should* leave?"

I didn't answer. I didn't need to. He proceeded to speak and rant and laugh manically for the next four hours. Much of it didn't make any sense at all. But during the few moments he wasn't talking about who was trying to kill him and which branches of the government were colluding with people who lived in the core of the earth, I learned that he was homeless, having been thrown out of his parents' house in his teens.

I didn't interrupt much. I only spoke when he asked me to agree with him. If I hesitated or tried to change the subject to something like "I have 911 on speed dial," he grew even more agitated. I only tried to get up off the floor once more. This time he grabbed my neck and held it firmly against the rug as he explained why, exactly, he slept across the backseat of his car, underneath a blanket adorned with secret Native American symbols.

I was petrified. My mind raced back to when I was a child, lying in the dark, unable to sleep at night. I used to plot out multiple escape routes from my bedroom for various potential catastrophes. If a fire broke out across the hall, I could jump out my window, run across the porch roof, and climb down the downspout. If someone was breaking into my window, I could run into the hall, shimmy into the laundry chute, and slide to safety in the basement.

As I lay on the floor next to my psychotic one-very-long-night stand, I came up with multiple scenarios for escape. None of which he ever gave me the opportunity to put in place.

And then, just as the pink sun began to brush across the floor, he stood up.

"Is there a Krispy Kreme nearby?" he asked. "They owe me money. Lots of money."

"Uh, yeah. There's one right down the street on Ponce de León," I answered, sensing an end to my ordeal.

"Cool," he said. "Do you want anything while I'm out?"

Now it was my time to laugh. I laughed out of utter exhaustion, fear, and disbelief at the absurdity of it all. *Sure,* I thought to myself, *pick me up a cruller. Hurry back!*

"No, I'm good," I answered instead. And with that, he walked out the door completely naked—with his overalls, socks, and boots tucked under his arm.

I pulled on the outfit I'd worn the night before and ran the mile and a half to James's house, ducking down side streets and looking over my shoulder just in case I spotted a green Volvo racing up behind me with someone maniacally waving a powdered doughnut out the window.

I lived at James's for two weeks before I had the courage to go home again, and by then the fun was over.

While I do remember finishing up my resolution, I don't remember anyone who followed the psychotic trick except, of course, magic #25, for whom I broke into my own home, excited and weary at the finish line of my quest.

Except that the "immoral" of my story is that I didn't stop at #25.

I had several more years of getting myself into stupid and

dangerous situations. Whatever I'd started I couldn't stop. After moving to New York a few years later, I put myself in even increasingly stupider and more dangerous situations. I did it until I met the man I'm with today.

Then I stopped.

Only four years after I raced through my infamous group of anonymous numbers, I received a call that James was dying.

He'd been secretly living with HIV the entire time I'd known him. It was only on my final trip to visit him, on his deathbed set up in his parents' living room, that he told me that he was fairly certain he'd contracted the disease from his very first sexual encounter. It happened on one of those nights when he'd climbed out his bedroom window, jumped off the porch, and silently rolled the car down the driveway to escape into the wild and dangerously fun city.

Pamela didn't go to James's funeral. She was, I eventually pieced together, agoraphobic—only leaving the house to drive to work and back. More and more frequently she'd become unable to accomplish even that. Years later she looked me up in New York and called asking for money. Her husband was out of work, and they were days away from being foreclosed upon. An agoraphobic who was about to be evicted. I couldn't think of a worse fate. I gave her a month's payment and never heard from her again.

I don't know what happened to a single one of those first twenty-five men. Or the many that continued to come afterward. How many? Who knows? I long ago lost count. The number is insignificant. All that's important to me now is that I've been on the same number for over eight years. Whatever number he is, it is my lucky number. Of that much I'm certain.

I think of James and Pamela. Sometimes you leave home and bad things happen. Sometimes you stay home and bad things happen. I went out to dangerous places and brought home dangerous men, and I got away with murder. Or at least breaking and entering.

So, I guess, in the end, they were all lucky numbers.

I can forget a lot, but I mustn't forget that.

The First Time

Margaret Sartor

I was at home, reading a book with my feet propped up, when my best friend Tommy walked in the back door and asked me if I wanted to go and get saved. Since I had nothing else to do, I went. After all, I was fourteen, bored, and desperate for anything that might rescue me from my lackluster life and parents' rules.

The house where the meeting was stood on a corner with a screen porch, and though it was February, it was also Louisiana, so it was warm outside. Through the open door I could see Tommy's older sister, a handful of adults, and all these kids I didn't know—some were in college.

"This is weird," I said to Tommy, which was a good thing.

There were about thirty of us, and we sat in as much of a circle as was possible. We sang songs that were familiar and sweet and blended one into the other ("Jesus Loves Me," "Kumbaya"), while a guy with a guitar led us in rounds, like at summer camp. Then a girl by the name of Andrea took me into a side room, where she sat us down on the carpet and held my two hands and asked, "Margaret, do you know how very beautiful it is to be a loved child of God?"

"Not really."

"Would you like to?"

I was puzzled a little, because I didn't understand what she expected me to do exactly, but *yes*, I thought, *I want to be loved*. I was near to bursting with wanting to be loved.

Andrea led me back to the group and into the middle of the circle, where people stood with their arms around one another, heads bowed, and I closed my eyes. Right away there were hands touching me—my head, my shoulders, my sides, and my back— and I heard murmurings all around. "Thank you, Lord. Bless you, Jesus." Then my stomach began to churn like an ice cream maker, it was turning over and over, and my head felt dense but also bright and filled with sparks or fireworks. Some kind of cele- bration was happening inside me. I swayed, but someone caught me, who turned out to be Tommy, and it was strange but good and happy. I felt so happy. Tears were pouring down my face. I opened my eyes and saw Tommy, who had his arms around me, and he was crying too. It seemed everyone was crying.

People called us freaks, Jesus freaks, but I didn't mind. Nei- ther did Tommy. My chief sins at the time were:

1. Pride
2. Impatience
3. A growing aggravation with my inability to attract boys

Giving these up seemed a small price to pay for a meaning- ful life. Besides, being teased just gave me one more reason to avoid PE, which was all but unbearable, and skip French, which was a complete waste of time. To my classmates, in most ways, I remained the kid I'd always been, only happier and without the cussing.

Tommy suffered no uncommon sins, except maybe his over-attachment to Barbra Streisand and an annoying tendency to hum, but anything, we were told by born-again kids way older than we were, could be used by the devil to try to win us back, so we had to be on our guard. I liked this. It gave me a sense of purpose and had the truly miraculous power to quiet, though not entirely silence, those inner voices that told me I would never fit in or be asked to the homecoming dance. Being a Christian helped me figure out that I probably wasn't meant to date in high school. I didn't seem to have the personality for it.

Then I met Jackson.

On Jackson Bishop, Christian jewelry was sexy. He wore a wooden cross on a leather thong that swung gently or pounded on his football player's chest when he strummed the guitar or played the piano. Until he was saved, he'd committed loads of sins. He'd had lots of girlfriends too. He was two years older than I was. He had a Great Dane, wild hair, and the blazing look of a seer. (This last quality he lost, in my opinion, when he cut his hair and put on a cassock or a hassock or whatever it is you call those robes clergymen wear. But in 1974 he was startling.) Already, he could hold an audience rapt and preach a crowd to tears. His friendship with Tommy, me, and the other marginalized and hopelessly religious kids helped fend off bullies, and for this, Tommy thought of Jackson as a kind of savior. I thought of him too. Constantly.

I'd been born again for maybe two months when I first knew, a realization I noted, duly and without evident anxiety, in my daily diary: "I think I'm going to fall in love with Jackson Bishop." It was spring, late afternoon, and we'd gathered, a bunch of us, at the levee, to eat pizza and talk about creation. We discussed the end of the world, which we all knew would be soon, and I remember it was very peaceful. Toward the end, as everyone left, Jackson stood. He walked to the water's edge. I watched him, his hands stuffed deep in the pockets of his jeans as he faced the pink-orange sky with a resolute stare. *Like a prophet*, I thought, *a fiery prophet.* And at that moment the certainty of our fated love rang in my mind with such clarity and confidence that I never doubted it to be true. I knew it was God telling me.

Over the summer our shift from friendship to romance happened by slow degrees and with several false starts. One day we were close, and the next uncertain. It was awkward. Or I was. It was my first time, and I fell in love the way Alice fell down the rabbit hole. I was curious, mildly alarmed, and completely thrilled. I wrote that in my diary: "Jackson thrills me." So in the autumn, when the kisses finally started, it was bliss. It was also, due to my complete inexperience, base and muddling and I reacted with some confusion. This may have scared Jackson. I know it scared me.

We never officially became a couple. We never went steady or held hands in public or did any of those things that teenagers do to indicate monogamy or mutual bodily possession. In church or at school, Jackson paid me no special attention. (Or that's how it seemed to me.) So it hurt when he flirted

with other girls—like Nancy who was bouncy or Clara who
had boobs and Susan who would always flirt back. But to him
I never said a word. By then Jackson was a senior. I was only
a sophomore. I was pleasant looking in a childlike sort of way,
and not too shabby at conversation as long it was about horses and
books or questions of moral intention, but I was also skinny and
titless and under such circumstances, at least in high school in
my hometown in the 1970s, there were rules for girls in love.
No whining was one of them. Besides, the devil takes advantage of your fears and I knew that.

   In private, though, we were happy. We hung out, goofed off,
and drove around a lot. We stayed up late, usually at Tommy's,
sitting on the kitchen counter and finishing off leftovers. We
played gin rummy and charades and laughed so hard our sides
hurt. I had fun. I'd never had so much fun. Our time alone was
intimate. Jackson played his guitar and sang for me. I read him
my poetry and he read me his. We rode my horse together in
the woods for hours, often starting out before dawn. On Christmas Eve, Jackson came to my house and handed me a present
all wrapped. I was so excited that as soon as he left I took it to
my room to open.

   I can't say what I expected, maybe jewelry or some traditional
token of affection, but what Jackson gave me, after months of
my unguarded adoration, was a bell jar. Dried flowers under
glass. They were yellow and delicate and I studied them, wondering if they meant something to him, hoping they did. But it
was still a dead plant.

   On New Year's Day, Jackson invited me to a football party
with all his old friends, the soon-to-be graduates and other

jocks. I felt queasy about it. The boys were big and they were loud. They crowed at the television and made lewd remarks at the girls, who were curvy and cute and sat on their laps. There was beer I couldn't drink and jokes I didn't understand. I had a mouth full of braces and my hair was in braids. The host of the party disappeared with his girlfriend into a room with a water bed at the back of the house. We left early. I didn't even have to ask.

That night I tossed and turned. I relived, in detail, every embarrassing thing that had ever happened to me, including, in particular, a time in second grade when I fell off my bike on the way to school, stopping traffic with carloads of kids peering out the windows of their station wagons as I brushed off my skirt and gathered my books that were scattered all over the road. The next day Jackson told Tommy to tell me that we should stop spending so much time together and go back to being just friends.

I had no idea. I don't mean about Jackson breaking up with me, because I could see that coming, or the fact that he sent his message through Tommy, though that did surprise me, but of how it would feel. The heartbreak, I mean. The shattering of trust, the brutal sense of loss and sudden awareness of my heart's true vulnerability, like a tree branch snapping off in an ice storm. I had no idea about *that*.

Hide. That was my initial strategy. For weeks I kept my pain private. I tried to be useful and considerate and keep my bed made, but progress was slow. Hours after dumping me, Jackson started dating Rhonda. Rhonda was pretty and popular and older than I was, so the whole thing was troubling. It's hard to say how troubling, except to say that it undermined my personal sense of the creative and sustaining force of the universe. Plus, it put me in a very bad mood.

It was Tommy who took me to the revival. I didn't want to go. I wanted to join the circus. I wanted to become a missionary in a foreign country—immediately. I had things to do, like clean out my closet and give away all my favorite clothes. There were all kinds of things I wanted to do rather than see Jackson and Rhonda.

"You're moping," Tommy said, standing in the doorway of my bedroom, one eyebrow raised, mouth pursed and twisted in that expression of sympathy and insolence he had been perfecting since nursery school, challenging me to retaliate, which I did, by reading out loud from an extremely nasty section of *The Exorcist*. Still, he would not go away.

"You're moping," he said, "and you suck at it."

I put down my book and we left.

It wasn't a long drive to the Assembly of God. To get anywhere in my hometown took less than ten minutes; if you drove longer than that, you were on a trip. In the concrete parking lot that spilled over into a field, there were lots of cars. There were teenagers and small children and grown men pushing elderly women in wheelchairs across the grass. It was the same crowd as at the state fair, only without the livestock. On the marquee, the speaker, a famous athlete, was billed as a "Quarterback for Jesus," and I tried to imagine the Son of God with a whistle in his mouth.

The sanctuary was huge. It was white—white robes, white pews, white people—and the air-conditioning was turned up high. Tommy and I sat near the back. Jackson and Rhonda were sitting a few of rows ahead of us and slightly to my right. If I cut my eyes real hard, I could watch them without moving my head.

Something was wrong. Jackson kept glancing at Rhonda. She was looking around and he looked uneasy about it. This surprised me. It surprised me because I'd never seen Jackson nervous before. I didn't even know he was capable of that kind of discomfort. Worshippers lifted their hands. There were hallelujahs and amens, moans and shouts. The Spirit was moving. Jackson was fussing over Rhonda. I felt nothing.

When the altar call came, I went. I went twice.

Still nothing.

I stared. In his agitation, Jackson seemed smaller, less Jackson-like. And it was then, but not before, that it hit me: Jackson never wanted to fall in love with me. It had happened. I knew it. He did too, and I knew that. (Years later, he told me as much.) But sitting on that plank pew at the revival, watching him, nothing made sense. Or it made perfect sense. But I didn't know it until then. I began to cry. Considering where I was and all the emotion in that room, no one noticed. And I began to laugh too. I guess I was hysterical, but I wasn't loud. I felt like a child, and suddenly I was tired of childhood. I wanted to grow up. I needed to. It was time. Tommy eased me out of the pew, out of the church, and into his car.

It was only on the way home that I got loud. Tommy said later, he thought I was hallucinating. He drove. I have no idea for how long, but it was for as long it took, until I calmed, which I did, gradually. The night was clear and warm, and as we crossed the old drawbridge over the river, I put my head out the window. He said something, Tommy did, as I pushed myself up and leaned my whole body out, hanging shotgun out of the Chevrolet and into the moist, moving air as far as I could, which was far. Tommy grabbed the seat of my jeans and tugged. He may have yelled too. But after a minute or so, without warning, he just let go. I wobbled. I flailed and screamed because I was out there on my own and it scared me. I slipped back through the window and into the car seat and cursed. Tommy cursed back. We looked at each other. Our faces were red, mine was wet, and we laughed. We laughed hard. Tommy began to hum.

The Book of Love and Transformation

Michael Taeckens

By junior year of college, in the early 1990s, I had been without a boyfriend for over three years. It made for a drab and dreary life. I lived in a "historic" housing complex and worked part time at a used bookstore. My house, set back in a wooded area where dozens of stray cats prowled, was composed of a series of add-ons constructed like afterthoughts. Rooms were stacked on top of rooms, hallways jutted out at weird angles, windows were too low or too high, with lofts made of the flimsiest wood, everything askew. Mold seeped through layer after layer of paint. Yet I found something comforting about the disintegration and decay, the ghetto perversity. Like an old childhood tree house, the place made me want to crawl inside and take a nap. Which is mostly what I did: nap, and smoke, and read and write, show up for some classes, and nap some more.

But when I wasn't sleeping, I wrote poetry as if my life depended on it, stark and bleak poems full of barren and blasted landscapes. It was as though I had grown up in a gulag, albeit a *lyrical* gulag. I used words like *susurration*, stage props like a full moon, crows in a tree, a reflection on a lake. I tried to create pretty little snow globes, then fill them with ashes.

I had been confusing beauty and sadness for a long time, apparently. My belief that they were intertwined was like a double helix in my genetic code. And perhaps the sadness and beauty were mixed up with masochism too. Emily Dickinson was my favorite poet. (Funerals! Flies buzzing!) Ingmar Bergman was my favorite film director. (Death! Schizophrenia!) The Smiths was my favorite band. (You don't even know I exist, but I love you!) Even as early as age fourteen, my predilection for the maudlin made itself known—the theme song I chose for my relationship with my girlfriend was Chicago's "Hard to Say I'm Sorry / Get Away": *Even lovers need a holiday far away from each other.* The song just seemed so romantic.

But despite all this—my melancholy disposition set on autopilot—I still held out hope that I'd meet the man of my dreams, someone who would fill the exact shape of my emptiness and thereby make me happy. I'd already fallen in love with an ideal I had created: a worldly, academic, artistic sort; someone who read and understood poetry and philosophy; someone with dark hair and blue eyes. I had crushes on all of my male professors, even the ugly ones. As a kid I even had a crush on the Professor from *Gilligan's Island*—handsome in his white Oxford and khakis, and the surest bet for a way off the island.

Perhaps that's why Theo's appearance in my life, after years of hoping I would meet someone like him, seemed so miraculous—even mythical. I was rereading one of my favorite books, Ovid's *Metamorphoses*, when he walked into the bookstore where I worked. Maybe it's just easy in hindsight to frame our meeting in classical terms, since he was a classics scholar and I was studying and translating Latin. But it seemed like more than that. There was something of a divine intervention about his sudden appearance, this man from out of town, here at my college for only the fall semester.

He was exactly what I was looking for.

Theo stopped at the front counter and smiled at me. He was bookish, bespectacled, in his early thirties, Mediterranean with Frank Sinatra eyes. Through the fog of my self-loathing, I could sense he was attracted to me.

"I see you're reading one of my favorite books!"

"Wow, really? I mean . . . this is one of your favorite books?"

"Yes, I teach it in my classes all the time. It should be required reading, don't you think? The great book of love and transformation."

He was a professor! He taught *Metamorphoses*!

He asked if I had read Ovid in Latin, and I told him that I was taking Latin but had only translated some Catullus and Virgil. He enthused over the poets I mentioned. He said he taught Greek and Latin and classical literature and had recently published his first book, on Aristotle's *Poetics*. I was in awe. He asked me to dinner that evening. I said yes.

We spent that first night together. And all next day as well. In bed, naturally. It was like the first Catullus poem I translated:

Give me a thousand kisses, then another hundred,
then another thousand, then a second hundred,
then yet another thousand more, then another hundred.

Our mouths were raw and red. We were happy.

Meeting someone who not only spoke five languages but translated Greek and Latin poetry also was like winning the jackpot. Theo was my personal professor, and I his perpetual student, just as in classical times. He was a walking museum of art and history: bring up any topic and he would produce a virtual light box, a diorama outlining its history, pertinent etymology, relation to art or politics, and various interpretations of the subject throughout the ages. We spent as much time together as possible—at cafés, at the library, at his apartment. He read poems aloud to me in Italian, in French, and in German, and even though I couldn't understand a word, I swooned. To impress him I memorized the entirety of Rilke's first Duino elegy and recited it to him in bed.

For the first two weeks we saw each other constantly. He told me how brilliant I was. I tried to demur, pointing out that I hadn't attended an Ivy League college, hadn't even done very well on my SATs. "It's not about that," he said. "Intelligence is something you carry within your soul. It's a way of approaching and viewing the world."

He thought I was beautiful and told me so frequently. I walked through campus with my entire body buzzing, feeling successful, heightened. Was this . . . *happiness?* We talked about me moving in with him when he went back to the West Coast the following semester. We were rushing things, of course, but there seemed no need for thoughtful consideration, despite our rudimentary knowledge of each other. Everything just *felt* perfect. And that was all that mattered, right? This was love, this

"Just make the list and see how you feel. It will empower you."

PROS
Says he loves me
Incredibly well-read and brilliant—a genius
Likes my poetry and encourages me to write more
Beautiful eyes
I would never meet anyone smarter, ever
The only guy who's attracted to me

CONS
Cuts out pictures of hot men from magazines and collects
    them in a scrapbook
Blatantly checks out other guys all the time
Watches himself in the mirror while dancing at club (narcis-
    sist!)
Always wants to have sex the same way, and loses interest
    after he gets off, which is always first (narcissist x 2!)
Arrogant
Uptight
Likes Cyndi Lauper

I read the list over and over, but it did nothing to change my feelings.

Nights went by when I called his number repeatedly, letting the phone ring dozens of times. Was he there? Was he punishing me? Was he alone?

I'd tell myself, *Okay, I will let the phone ring twenty times.*

was how it worked. I had shed my old persona and was ready to forge ahead into my new life of rarefied contentment.

In retrospect, I realize it was almost *too* perfect. The manner in which he appeared in my life, like my personalized dream incarnate, should have made me suspect. Now that I was finally getting the love I always wanted, what was the catch? Because, according to the very book I held in my hands when we met, there was always a catch. Romance was possible, but romance was also doomed. Love could turn you into something else, an exalted being, but you could also end up a tree, a rock, a fountain, an antlered animal chased by hounds.

Gradually, of course, it emerged that there were a few things about me that Theo didn't find so enchanting. He didn't like my apartment or the way I lived—the mismatched kitchenware, the double-stacked mattresses for a bed, the boric acid spread around the perimeter of my studio in a futile attempt to ward off cockroaches. When he picked me up, he wouldn't come inside but waited in his car on the main street, down the wooded hill, a walk of several minutes.

He wasn't thrilled with the way I dressed—my plastic-frame glasses, my jeans with the holes in the knees, my old and scuffed Doc Martens.

He said that Greek culture prized manners above all else; I was rude, tactless, and my humor too sarcastic. My smoking was morally objectionable. In bed I stole all the covers; I snored like an old man; I talked in my sleep. Whenever possible I slept in until 11:00 a.m.; he was an early riser. He complained because I didn't always shower in the morning. I didn't comb my bed head. I didn't say *Please* and *Thank You* and *No, you first, I insist.* I didn't cook for myself or for him. He told me I could do my laundry at his place but then resented it when I did. I turned lights on and off depending on my mood. He pointed out that it was *his* place, I should ask *him* if he wanted the lights on or off.

All these issues seemed so individually tiny, but taken as a whole there was mounting evidence that I'd have to change. The mere thought that I might lose him made my brain stem thrum with panic. The more I fretted, the more I tried to keep things the same, the way they were when we first met, before he figured out what I was really like. Couldn't we just go back to the beginning, when this was about poetry? *You like poetry, I like poetry. You're attracted to me, I'm attracted to you.* What more do we need?

It seemed so easy—*just don't do the things that annoy him*— but it felt like a calculus equation I couldn't wrap my mind around.

Just as he seemed to start inching away from me, what I was beginning to suspect about him made me want to stay by his side at all times, as vigilant as a German shepherd. He no longer always answered the phone when I called to say good night. He was away at odd hours, said he had to study at the library or attend a departmental symposium. Sometimes his car wasn't in the driveway when I drove by his apartment late at night. I felt like a B actor in some crappy late-night TV show, trying to piece together the clues.

But I just couldn't imagine that he would start dating some-

one else without telling me. He would never do that—he said he *loved* me. I tried not to act overly suspicious but failed one evening when I opened his car door and saw that the passenger's seat had been moved forward several inches. That was my seat; it was always set for my body. I felt all the breath leave my lungs. *Oh fuck, he's seeing someone else.*

"Why is your car seat moved up so far?" I asked him.

He stared at me incredulously from the driver's seat, then grimaced and looked out the windshield.

"Why?" I repeated.

"Because I needed space for my library books!" he snapped.

"Your library books? How many did you have, a hundred? You could have just put them in the trunk or on the backseat!

He was hiding something. His defensive behavior proved it

"*Who* was in your car?"

He narrowed his eyes and told me I was a lunatic, that I acting inappropriately and irrationally. I got in the car bu refused to talk to me. It was our first fight.

Later I was wracked with guilt, second-guessing my reaction. Maybe the problem was my intuition—mayb an overactive thyroid that pumped out paranoid hor Whatever it was, I had to figure out a way to reverse age, and fast. A rift was already growing between us. never figured into my romantic fantasies.

Out of sheer desperation I visited the school cou suggested I make a list of pros and cons. I was f much on what *he* thought of *me*, she said.

"You need to ask yourself if you really want to

"Umm, I do want to be with him. I know I do

If he doesn't answer, it means that he truly doesn't love me anymore.

The phone rang twenty times. He didn't pick up. Maybe he didn't hear it. I tried again an hour later. And then a few more times, just to be sure. That became my nightly ritual.

It's over, I realized, after about a week. *Fuck.*

He finally picked up the phone one night and agreed to meet me for coffee. At the café he told me I was too jealous and suspicious, that he just couldn't handle it anymore. He said, "I think you're afraid to be alone, but you don't have to be," and, "Please know that I will always love you," and, "It will be okay, you will find someone else." I didn't say anything. I just wanted to get back to my apartment and into my bed as soon as possible.

The worst part was, I didn't feel angry. I just wanted to figure out a way to get him to want me again. I listened to my old standby, The Smiths: *Well, I'm still fond of you, oh-ho-oh.*

My melancholy came back in full force, as if it had only left for a couple of months to visit some cousins. I lay in my crummy bed and cried, embarrassed that my neighbors could hear me through the cheap, flimsy walls.

If only I hadn't commented on the passenger's seat being moved forward.

If only I hadn't called the Comp Lit Department to confirm there was a symposium on Interdisciplinary Studies.

If only I hadn't kept flicking the light switches on and off.

If only I hadn't done my laundry.

If only I wasn't me.

*   *   *

In the mornings I woke up early and couldn't fall back to sleep.
I would drink a glass of orange juice, sit back on my bed against
the wall with an ashtray on my knee, and smoke four or five cigarettes. One morning I walked to the cemetery a few blocks up
the street. I wanted to sit at the top of the hill, my back against
a tombstone, and wallow. It was raining but I managed to puff
away in the drizzle. I thought about a poem I had recently read,
Hopkins's "The Leaden Echo and the Golden Echo," and repeated the one line over and over in my head: "O there's none;
no no no there's none." The scene was perfect: the graveyard,
the rain, the melancholy poem. I was inhabiting one of my own
ash-filled snow globes. But this wasn't what I wanted at all.

In less than a month Theo would be gone, back to the faraway city from which he'd magically appeared, and unless I did
something quickly, I'd never know whether or not I'd ruined
my one chance at real love and happiness. It took persistent
pleas—many, many phone calls—to get him to agree to meet
me for one last dinner.

We went to the same fancy Chinese restaurant at which
we had our first date back in September. I thought meeting
here might rekindle our affair, as if the maroon leather booths
and tacky Chinese art had bestowed some kind of good fortune
upon us. But everything was wrong from the start. He was wary,
coolly polite, holding back, avoiding eye contact. I could tell
he wanted to get the meal over with. He acted like this was a
business meeting and I was pitching an unlikely proposal, one
he was sure to reject.

An aura of desperation hung over the table. I receded into

myself, separated from the chattering din of the other diners. The scenario had the familiarity of a bad dream: I was onstage in the middle of a play and I'd forgotten not only my lines but my entire role—and I didn't even know I was supposed to be in this play to begin with. But I attempted to push through with a goofy smile, trying to recapture the charm that once captivated him. (Who was the person he fell for? How do I get *that person* back?)

"Is there anything I can do to convince you that I deserve another chance?"

He looked me in the eyes, finally, weighed the question with a lengthy pause. I could sense his hesitancy, but also a dawning possibility of *something*. He suggested we continue the conversation at his place. But it was a quick statement, somehow off, no real warmth behind it. Reading between the lines, I could tell he was communicating something else: *we will sleep together, one last time.* I was desperate, though, in romantic free fall. I grasped at the moment as if it were a cartoon tree limb jutting off the side of a cliff.

At his apartment he tossed aside all pretense and walked straight back to his bedroom, taking off his clothes. We had never done it this way before, but, as always, I followed his lead. I took off my clothes too, got under the covers. I felt completely disconnected from my body. It was as though I was looking down at us from the ceiling—there was my body, going through the motions. And there was his, evidently experiencing some form of pleasure. It was a one-sided experience, over too soon. He quickly turned away and fell asleep.

After our good-byes the next morning, I didn't hear from him again. I called a few times but he never picked up.

A few days later I couldn't stop scratching.

My entire knowledge of crabs came from the *Porky's* movies. I thought you got them from a prostitute in Florida. I didn't even know they *had* crabs in the Midwest, let alone that you could get them from a professor. When I realized what had happened, it was too late to confront him; he had already left town. It was like a joke, told days earlier, that I was only now just understanding—and the punch line was in my underwear.

I fumed, my anger mounting each day. My myth of romantic happiness had not only veered off course, it had crashed into an embankment and died a fiery death. There was nothing exactly poetic or classical about body lice. I had to call student health to find out what to do. I was so mortified, I thought about disguising myself when I went to the drugstore to buy the shampoo and nit comb. I used half the bottle, lathered it all over myself, and then rinsed off in scalding water and did it all over again. I took all of my bedding and clothes to the laundromat and washed them, twice. I even washed my cat.

Shortly before winter break, I related my tale of woe to a new friend, and she asked what the guy's name was, how long we had been dating. When I told her, she asked if he was teaching classics here for the fall. When I said yes, she replied, "Oh honey, I hate to tell you this, but he's been seeing my friend Paul for most of the semester."

I felt like a complete idiot for not trusting my instincts to begin with. *Of course* he was seeing someone else! That entire second month he had been seeing both Paul and me. I couldn't help but wonder if he invited Paul to move back home with him, too. I also felt a betrayal of another sort: how could Theo possibly have been attracted to me if he was attracted to Paul, my exact opposite—a blond, petite, smooth nymph of a boy? Was everything just a lie?

I considered sending him a special Christmas gift: a bottle of Rid Lice Killing Shampoo wrapped in bright and cheery holiday paper. But I chickened out. The truth was, I hated him, but, despite myself, I still loved him too.

I thought about sending him a Christmas card with the Catullus poem "Odi et Amo":

I hate and I love—why I do this I do not know,
but I feel it happening and I am tortured.

But I decided against that as well—it would have been too creepy.

Even in the midst of my winter of wrath, I was trying to think of ways to win him back. The intellectual me still yearned for him. I couldn't imagine I would meet someone else who would come even remotely close to my romantic ideal. Everything had been so perfect—except that he hated so much about me and cheated on me and left town without saying good-bye and gave me crabs.

In May I sent him a long letter, honed to precision over several revisions. It contained not only an apology for my jealous behavior and annoying habits but infusions of the over-the-top campy humor I knew he loved; effusive reviews of books I had recently read; details about my classes and what I was learning from them; and a couple of new poems I'd written. I didn't bring up Paul or the crabs.

He responded with an even longer letter, and it echoed mine point for point—an acceptance of my apology and a sort of apology of his own; an equal dose of campy humor; some clippings from the *Weekly World News*; thoughts on books he was reading and reports on his classes and research; and hearty praise and analysis of my poems.

We volleyed letters back and forth throughout the spring and summer. I always spent hours elaborating on everything I could think of, intent on dazzling him with my wit and intellect. In one of his letters he suggested that perhaps we should try a rematch at some point in the future, maybe in ten years. *Ten years?* But instead of questioning him about it, I took it as a test. *Okay* . . . I decided I could wait it out. I could improve myself in the meantime and really impress him when I turned thirty-one.

In one letter he let me know he was returning to my college in the fall for a weekend symposium. I took this as a hint. I was still living in the same city and told him I had moved to a new place, a clean and sunny house with two roommates who would be out of town that weekend, and I invited him to stay with me. In his next letter he said, "I'd love nothing more than to spend time with you again."

I planned out everything beforehand: *Don't get jealous. Don't be sarcastic. Don't be yourself.*

I was over the moon, envisioning the two of us back together, just like in the very beginning, before it all went haywire. I did stomach crunches every day, tried to cut back on my smoking, got a new haircut, bought a new shirt. I secretly hoped he'd invite me to move back home with him. But when he showed up at my door, I felt strangely disappointed. His smile was big and looked just like his smile from the year before, but it was contrived, an impostor's smile. His skin was oily, and he looked tired, a little worn around the edges. Older, but striving to appear younger. He wore a baseball cap turned backward, baggy jeans, colorful Converse shoes, and sported a newly pierced left ear.

We hugged and gave each other an affectionate kiss on the lips, but it felt clammy and hollow. The fantasy I had nursed for so long was deflating before my very eyes. A new panic arose: *I've just made the biggest mistake of my life.* I felt, instantaneously, all of my romantic feelings vacate my body. They had been purged. It was as if his act of physically showing up was all I needed, a permission slip to let go of the past. I thought of a line from the Rilke poem I once recited to him: *Strange to no longer desire one's desires.*

I even felt pity for him. How sad that he accepted my invitation, thinking we could rekindle something. How sad that he expected me to sweep his cheating, crab-giving ways under the rug. How sad that he thought I would give him another chance.

How sad that I'd never realized all this before.

I smiled at him, minded my manners, picked up his suitcase, and showed him to the queen-size bed where we would be sleeping. Only, I realized, *we* wouldn't be sleeping there.

After he left for his Friday evening meeting, I decided I just couldn't spend the night with him. He could stay in my bedroom, but I'd be gone.

I went to a bar, where I ran into some casual friends. I spilled the beans about everything—how badly he'd broken my heart, how he cheated and gave me crabs, how he was now on his own, not only for the night but, I decided at that moment, the entire weekend.

I had no idea where I would stay but I didn't care. I felt free and oddly exhilarated. My friends and I drank pitcher after pitcher of beer, and I laughed as they congratulated me and offered a variety of toasts:

To Itchy and Scratchy!

To the Crabby Professor!

To Michael's Rent-a-Room Service!

And as I laughed, I imagined Theo lying in the bed I had made for him, resting his head on the fluffed-up pillows, waiting for me to show up. It was a mean and small act of revenge, something I never could have committed, let alone conceived of, just a few months earlier.

I thought of the opening line of *Metamorphoses*: "Now I shall tell of things that change, new being/Out of old." I was the new me now—at least for tonight. And for the present, that was enough.

Texas

Gary Shteyngart

My strange gentle giant. She was a head taller than me, a great big straw-covered head taller. I could spot her from a kilometer away—this long Texan gal dressed in a tight pink miniskirt and sweaty embroidered T-shirt, stepping off the train in Rome's central station, all around her little Italian men bobbing their heads upward, craning for a look at this impossible blonde in their midst, muttering "Madonna!" and whatnot. And there I was at the other end of the platform, her lover—a short, hairy, overly civilized hamster waiting for his monumental girl-friend to bend down and embrace him and smack him on the lips. After which she would start to cry.

She cried right after I met her, cried when I left her, cried when she stepped in dog shit, cried over the morning's cappuc-cino, cried over the evening's last espresso, cried, cried, cried. I never knew that a stunning twenty-four-year-old American expatriate, who also happened to be the daughter of a former Miss Texas (or so she said), superbly educated and with several languages under her belt along with Daddy's credit card, could find the world so cruel and distressing a place. But she taught me that suffering came in at least two sizes, hers and mine. She taught me there was pain even a selective serotonin reuptake inhibitor couldn't cure. A Texas-size pain, if you will.

We were introduced by mutual friends at a steak-and-bean place high in the hills over Florence. She was studying art history in Florence, and I was in Rome, trying to knock another novel into submission. We had ten drinks the first night we met at a terrible bar near the Piazza Signoria, and she kissed me as a twenty-four-year-old American girl kisses, that is to say slowly and without preconceptions. A short while later she was in Rome, perched over my windowsill, her miniskirt on the dusty marble floor, the Alban Hills shimmering in the distance.

I loved her. It wasn't just that she looked like the cool, long blonde on the cover of my first novel, as someone pointed out. There was a sweetness to her, an ordinariness, a sense of place. "How's it running, Dad?" she'd say over the phone, referring to one of the cars in her Texan father's stable. She told me Gypsy women pinch each other's nipples in greeting. She knew where to find the "best fucking doughnut" in Florence. She quoted hours in military and "demilitarized" time. When we were apart, there were references to masturbating slowly with her cardigan unbuttoned. When we were together, there were the soft blue eyes looking down at me as she draped her elongated frame across my lesser one. I thought I had finally stepped into something good.

The frantic, tear-soaked phone calls started almost immediately. She would take the train down to Rome or I would take it up to Florence, and suddenly there would be this fierce, angelic head floating above me, sometimes smiling, often bawling, always hungry for what little affection I could muster under the circumstances. I began snapping photos of her after the waterworks. In one particular shot she looks as sad and innocent as a toddler who has misplaced her rattle; the mouth is twisted, but the eyes are hopeful, needy, desperate for acceptance. She had a little attic apartment in Florence, so centrally located that the Duomo loomed through the dormer windows, fat Italian pigeons cooing and crapping all over the place. I would work on my book there, and she'd spend hours chatting away with her folks in San Antonio about dropping out of her prestigious art history program and becoming a doctor or a stockbroker. But mostly she just wanted to be my wife. *Sposata subita,* my Italian friends called her. A ready-made bride. *Be very, very careful,* they told me.

It took two cities for us to break up. I began the process during a visit to Naples, we took our plight onto the Eurostar train to Rome, and it ended there. Only it didn't. She left Florence and suddenly appeared in the Italian capital, where she left distressing voice messages about wanting, *needing,* to "hold my hand" in a way I'm sure the Beatles never intended. Once she invited me to dinner, where she undercooked a particularly bony fish and then catapulted her sturdy frame onto my lap. "You need to communicate better," she told me with a half smile. I nervously glanced at the door.

It wasn't all bad, of course. It never is. She knew more than most people about Pope Adrian IV and the status of women in fourteenth-century marriages. She had Princess Superstar on the stereo and wore an unironic SOMEONE IN AUSTIN FUCKING

HATES ME T-shirt. When my parents came to visit she listened very politely to my father's sonorous speeches about Pushkin, the mistreatment of Soviet Jews, and the importance of filial piety. But in the end I couldn't make the tears stop. I couldn't pinpoint their source. I was like some hapless pith-helmeted explorer paddling the wrong way down a gushing South American river. The falls appeared quite suddenly, and then came the precipitous drop. Even the breakups are bigger in Texas.

Love and War Stories

Michelle Green

By the time I turned thirty, my life in New York had taken on a desperate edge that made me easy pickings for sorry specimens. Maybe it was because I was grabbing at the tail end of the disco-ball era—doing poppers and getting rowdy in dance clubs, sharing coke in the loo at the Odeon—and maybe it was because I was an anxious Southerner trying to pass myself off as a smart-ass city chick. The men who went for me did it for all the wrong reasons, and I was happy to take them for a ride.

It didn't help that I was suffering from phantom-limb pain, alone after a decade with a writer who knew my every tic and kink and loved me anyway. Sean was a literary climber, but he looked like Robert Redford without the facial warts and he thought I was a genius. I'd clung to him while we cycled, like army brats, through reporting gigs at newspapers across the South. Though we both were incapable of monogamy and had even cheated on one another with the same chick, when I left him in LA to write for a celebrity glossy I felt like I was ripping my heart out. Without Sean (who'd gone on to marry a Hollywood heiress with cartoon boobs), I was lost in the big-city jungle, hacking my way through the underbrush—and making a mess of it.

Which could be why, when I first beheld the sloppy Jude— five years younger and infinitely ballsier than me—all I could think about was sex. At that point I was craving Jewish guys because they were the obverse of Sean and seemed . . . challenging. A swaggering, hyperambitious brat whose office was next to mine, Jude had broad shoulders and disarming dimples. He'd worked his way through Harvard before taking off to explore the backroads in Asia. Improbably, he was as perverse and profane as I was, and he could make me explode with laughter.

But then . . . he wiped his plate with his finger when we went to lunch at an Indonesian place, and he let me pay with my corporate Amex. He never bothered to wear anything more grown-up than running shoes and droopy jeans, and he was a shark when it came to snatching high-profile assignments and turning expense reports into lucrative works of fiction.

And I wasn't the only female in our company who found him against-the-odds irresistible. I knew he'd broken the heart of a credulous poet who toiled in the library and that he'd schtupped an icy corporate type. While men seemed to perceive him as brash, brilliant and unprincipled, women saw Jude as a puppy: a few sharp words and a smack on the nose with a rolled-up newspaper, and he'd be eating out of your hand.

I no longer recall how we found our way into bed, but it was a drug-addled blast. We stayed up all night riffing and shrieking with laughter; Jude's brain was even more compelling than his body and when he left my apartment the next morning, I was still high.

Work, however, was a bit awkward. Back at the magazine, I could hear every word that Jude said on the phone, and none of them were about me. (I did catch the names of our college intern and the poet he allegedly had dropped.) In the hallways Jude went blank when I happened to pass, but in private it was different. He began sidling into my office and flirting for what seemed like hours, even when we were on deadline.

Our dating life was a bit of a wash, because Jude acted like a thug when we were in public. On a steaming wet Saturday not long after we hooked up, I persuaded him to meet me at a bar and then head to a friend's party in Tribeca. Jude peeled away the minute we walked into Nina's place, which was crammed with head-tossing assistants from the network where she was a producer.

At some point, I realized that my bad boy had disappeared. Nina helped me check the bathrooms, the bedrooms, even the stairway outside, and I felt queasy when he didn't turn up. "God, I'm so sorry," I said. "He had a headache earlier and he probably just split."

I walked alone into one of those rainstorms where streets were flooding and rivers of trash were sweeping by the curbs. My flimsy sandals were sodden by the time I made it to the subway; they were still damp the next afternoon when I called Jude. His explanation: he'd met an old classmate at the party and walked her home to Eighty-sixth Street. They'd said good-bye at her door.

Wouldn't that have been a good place to end it? To just kick his ass out and bask in the sunshine of self-righteousness? But I would have missed out on the character-building angst and frustration that I thought I was learning to handle. What I wanted were street skills: some sort of power that would allow me to engage in sexual drama without getting burned. So I allowed myself to savor the adrenaline highs, surf the pheromones and imagine that I was earning my cojones when Jude did something shameless like describing his interlude with a prostitute during an assignment in Thailand or taking me to a birthday party for the woman with whom he'd "walked home."

The smart people in my life, of course, began to lobby for me to boot the lout. "Honey, you'd be just fine with your typewriter and your kitty for a while," said my gay friend Ron, who'd grown up near me in Georgia and who rubbed my feet while we watched TV. But the women who understood the impulse to countenance bad behavior trumped my Jude stories with tales about their own no-account lovers. I felt I'd been initiated into a sisterhood of the damned.

Since defending Jude was impossible, I attempted to recast him as a boy toy. "This is what I do for sex," I said in a tone that I hoped sounded ironic. In truth, Jude did enjoy making love—particularly in places where we were apt to be discovered—but my libido trumped his. The more I wanted it, the more elusive he became.

We'd meet in Central Park at night to run and, though we'd inevitably get stoned afterward, Jude began to balk when I suggested that we head to my apartment on Ninety-sixth Street. Eventually, I tried to block him out: I reconnected with a video producer I'd once seduced, did time in gay bars with Ron and even tracked down a rock guitarist with whom I'd had a moment. None of it helped; before long, I was sobbing every night I spent home alone.

I have a photo from that time that captures my battle fatigue; it was taken on a working visit back to LA. In my suite at the Chateau Marmont are friends who've been helping me dive into rivers of Stoli and heaps of cocaine. Lying on a chaise, I'm wearing sunglasses in the deep of the evening; my face is both puffy and drawn, and beside me is a plastic flamingo. Neither of us looks particularly festive.

Of course I scored a souvenir for Jude while I was away—winkling magic mushrooms out of my loyal friend Jane, though I'd felt like a loser when I explained that I was branching into psychedelics because of a man she loathed. (When she'd come to New York with her new husband, I'd rolled out my playmate for dinner at Indochine; his shirttail had hung halfway out of his jeans. Later, I'd learned that they'd had to pick up the entire tab because Jude had stiffed them.) "You gotta lose the Jew boy," she'd mock scolded as she'd handed me the foil-wrapped plunder.

"I know, I know, I know," I'd told her. "But every other man I've met is a bore. I can't do mainstream. And every now and then he comes out with something really perceptive about me. The other day he said, 'You have a kind of energy that affects everyone around you.' Isn't that—"

"Talk to me when you're straight," Jane said.

On a sultry Saturday back on Ninety-sixth Street, I was setting the scene for a night of psilocybin and sex when Jude arrived, slimy and sweating from a run. Twenty minutes after we'd popped the freeze-dried mushrooms, chasing them with Heinekens, I was lying on the sofa with my freshly pedicured feet in his lap, wearing an expensively insubstantial black dress that I'd found at Charivari. Jude hadn't bothered to shower, but no matter; he was there. We were giggling over one of our jokey themes and the agenda was becoming muddled. Plus, the Santa Fe peachy coral of my walls was pulsing a little, going fluorescent around the edges and taking on a certain . . .

"I've gotta make a phone call," said Jude, pushing my feet to the floor. He walked into the bedroom and sauntered back after two minutes, still on the phone, speaking in a low, intimate voice and chortling before he hung up.

I believe I said, "So?"

"I've got to meet somebody," Jude announced. "I have to leave in ten minutes."

I did tell him, "No, you fucking don't." But yes, he did; in my three-week absence he'd acquired another chicklet. And somehow, even with both of us tripping extravagantly, he went out into the night.

My stoner posse picked up the pieces: Robin, an artist I'd known for years, and her college roommate Mitzi, a Chinese translator who'd been a lesbian until she met Harry, the round Brit who was her boyfriend. They arrived within thirty minutes and whisked me to Robin's place on the Lower East Side, where we sprawled on the bed and listened to Bruce Springsteen until morning.

Ironically, Jude and I kept going. In the following year, he even grew up a little: He apparently ditched the other women and, after one of his friends developed a crush on me, moved into my new place in the Village. He took me to visit his father and stepmother in Brooklyn and went with me to the south of France. "It's not the Philippines," he said archly, "but you have to walk before you can run." When we returned, Jude even allowed me to throw a small party for his mom, who was turning fifty. (As I gave a toast, his champagne glass fell to the floor and exploded into shards.)

No surprise, though, that my anal-expulsive honey still needed a very long leash. Soon after we merged households, we stopped having sex altogether. I began to feel like a toad.

In the end, the sexual boycott became irrelevant, because Jude had a plan. He was going to ditch the weekly where we were still putting in sixteen-hour days and find work as a freelancer. Before long, he was able to cobble together enough assignments to spend several months in Africa, which meant that the man who wouldn't sleep with me was disappearing altogether.

At this point I'd been through two and a half years of semistarvation, and I was ready to make the break, or so I thought: I'd started to weigh the pros and cons, and not much was coming up in Jude's favor. Before I had time to hoist a single celebratory cocktail, however, my juvenile offender called his own bluff. Six days into his trip, he left a message on the answering machine: "I can't do this. I want to come back. I want to be with you."

How impulsive! How romantic! Of course I'd take him back! The first thing Jude said when he walked in the door was, "After I called, the trip got a whole lot better. I had an amazing time on the beach in Tanzania and I almost changed my mind."

Then he began to plan a summer expedition for both of us—five weeks in India, most of it trekking in the Himalayas.

Those who knew me best were alarmed by the notion of my trying to negotiate terrain where room service could be inconsistent. Ron warned that I'd be dependent on a man who'd sell me into slavery on a whim, and Jane pointed out that Jude was capable of disappearing with a local and leaving me to find my way back alone. Only Henry, whose father was born on a tea plantation in the Punjab, liked the idea. "Look at it this way," he said. "You'll learn how to handle yourself in a part of the world that's a symphony of human suffering."

Me, I was revved. I'd always wanted to be at home in alien terrain that stank of diesel fuel and black tobacco. Jude was the guy to show me the moves; the cutthroat impulses and bravado that made him such a shoddy boyfriend could only help in less-developed zones. Hadn't he told me he could no longer do it alone? At the very least, he needed an audience. But could I trust him?

That spring, we began mapping out the trip: In Sonamarg, a town barely visible in the atlas, we'd pick up a couple of ponies and guides to help us get to 12,500 feet, where we would be motes amid glacial lakes and lethal-looking peaks. Jude reminded me—gleefully, I thought—that once we hit the Himalayas we'd be chugging water perfumed with iodine and taking toilet breaks behind boulders *en plein air*. I bought serious hiking boots and an expensive sleeping bag that would zip on to his to form a double-wide.

I don't think I've ever laughed as much as Jude and I did when we reached Delhi. Stunned by the heat, rendered goofy by sleep loss and a sense that we'd somehow escaped from the grown-ups, we created our own Monty Python take on India's glorious absurdities. Riding down a polluted roadway in a slap-dash vehicle that involved a motorbike, Jude broke us up by belting, "There's a bright, shining sun on the Janpath . . ." We could make each other do spit-takes by saying the word "hell-hole" or by pointing out tin cups chained to water fountains or noting other chilling manifestations of Third World hygiene.

When the giddiness evaporated, what remained was reality. The truth about the world into which we had ventured set in with a ten-hour trip on a fetid train and then on a classically harrowing Indian bus ride that took us through miles of switch-backs to the dusty town of Srinagar in Jammu and Kashmir. When a rat scampered across our room in a "three-star" hotel there, I cried and begged Jude to turn back. "We can go to Italy!" I sobbed.

Jude talked me into staying for one more day, which turned into three, and we kept going. On lily-padded Dal Lake, we rented a charming wooden houseboat where we could retrench and stock up for our trek. The place came with two servants, a hookah for smoking hashish, and a bedroom suffused with light and birdsong.

It was during our idyll on the houseboat that I realized why I was so weepy, and why I'd thrown up so much on the bus to Kashmir: It wasn't the crowding or the cigarette smoke or the earsplitting videos of tinny Hindi love songs that melded into the chatter all around us. My period was two weeks late. I had to be pregnant—Jude and I had had drunken sex just once in New York—and I was far, far away from home, with the perp right beside me.

Still, without a little blue line to confirm my diagnosis, I could retreat for a time into denial. Jude and I went to Srinagar to mine the dim market stalls for tinned milk and tuna fish. Riding rusty bikes, we competed for road space with clattering sheep and indolent cows. Jude took photos of me in a Mogul rose garden and in a boat that we rowed over the vast lake; with us was the cheerful mongrel to whom I'd been slipping the bone-laced ground lamb that appeared on our dinner table every night.

Not until we'd launched our trek, however, did I reveal my theory to Jude. On day three, I was dizzy after scrambling over scree all day and had to crawl into my sleeping bag as soon as we made camp. When Jude joined me after dinner, I said, "You won't believe this, but I think I might be pregnant."

"Oh, man," he said. "Look at where we are. What do you want me to do?"

On our fourth day out, squatting behind a car-sized boulder, I saw that I'd begun to spot. If things went badly, I knew that the chances of my getting timely help—or of Jude even speeding up our little procession so I could make it to a doctor—were pitiful.

As we reached remote meadows where flakes of toilet paper left by other hikers were the only signs of human activity, I began dreaming about avocados and orange juice; I awoke to chai and biscuits and raw apples. I was tired and sick to my stomach all day, but our guides jollied me into getting back onto my feet after breaks. "Oh, memsahib!" cried one, playfully rubbing my calves. "We will kill a chicken for you. We will find some eggs."

By the time Jude and I finished that seven-day expedition, I'd lost twelve pounds. I know because I weighed myself at the airport on the way to Ladakh, an even more-remote corner of India where we'd planned to attack yet another part of the Himalayas. That would be the airport where I was followed into a bathroom stall by a hunched woman seeking rupees, and where Jude informed me that he planned to tackle the next leg of the trek on his own even if I couldn't manage it.

Lucky for me, then, that I spiked a dramatic fever when we reached the steep, otherworldly town of Leh, and that the hotel where we landed could summon a physician. Otherwise, my take-no-prisoners partner might not have believed that I'd been slammed by a bloody awful crud, and that he would have to abort our second hike and return with me to Delhi so I could catch a flight home. "But I'm not leaving India," he had announced. "I have that assignment in Calcutta and I'm not gonna blow it off."

On our only evening in that ancient outpost where Buddhist monks walked the streets in saffron robes, Jude left me in our tiny room to drink beer with other trekkers. High on my own body heat, I lay in bed and stared at endless stars stabbing through the thin blue air.

Italian, Japanese, Swedish—the bar outside was filling with languages I couldn't understand when it came to me: True, Jude was never going to change, but it didn't matter. Even with the pregnancy scare (my period would start again in New York), I'd felt like I'd been on LSD every second I'd been in this carnival of a country; the experience had had its nightmarish elements, but it was also like coming home. Without another ravenous traveler to frog-march me along, I'd never have watched jewel-like prayer flags undulating against a navy sky or sipped tea with salty yak butter or learned to say "fuck off" in Hindi. I'd never have learned how to hire guides or shed touts or cope with unwashed strangers slavering over the sight of my legs beneath a flowing skirt.

Floating above the beery laughter, I realized that Jude would never be Sean's replacement. And that he wasn't the guy I wanted to marry. My friends might have described my two-plus years with him as a bad investment and my relationship with him as a failure. But he'd served his purpose. The man who'd often behaved like my worst boyfriend had been, in many ways, my best. Now, I needed love more than I needed war stories, and I could let him go.

The next day, I jammed my feet into my boots and threw my muddy backpack onto a flatbed truck headed for the airport in Ladakh. A bearded, sunburned Jude tossed his gear in beside it and hoisted himself in ahead of me. He didn't offer a hand to help me up, but then again I didn't need it; my fever had broken that morning.

Leave Me Something When You Leave Me

Brock Clarke

She didn't leave me with a broken heart, but she did leave me bleeding from both wrists and lying faceup in a puddle of someone else's vomit, wearing someone else's shirt.

This was in college, during a time when I tended to steal people's clothes and wear them while pursuing women who only had moderate-to-little interest in me while spurning the advances of the few women who were deranged or misguided enough to actually be interested in me. A year before I was left bleeding from both wrists and lying in a puddle of someone else's vomit, wearing someone else's shirt, I was in the top bunk bed in my dorm room with a woman—not the woman who left me bleeding from both wrists, etc., but someone else, someone who I barely knew but had seemed like someone I might like to know better. We were just lying there, for the time being. She was pretty; I remember thinking she was pretty and also wondering what my problem was. Why, if she was so pretty, did I feel the desire to get out of the bunk bed *right now*? It made no sense, but nevertheless I did have the desire and started to act on it. I climbed over this pretty woman and she grabbed me—who knows why: she couldn't have actually *wanted* to stay on that bed with its sheets that hadn't been washed in too long and when they had been washed had been washed by this guy-she-barely-knew's mother. In any case, she grabbed me, but I had both legs over the side of the bunk bed by this point; there was no stopping me, nor was there any stopping her, and we fell, together, twisting in midair so that she landed, back first, onto a typewriter, which was on the floor and not on the desk (why, I don't know: I have no memory of typing on it on either surface), and then me on top of her. *Ding!* the typewriter went as the pretty woman landed on it and I on her. Years later, she became a successful journalist, but I doubt our falling on the typewriter had anything to do with her success. In any case, she groaned, pushed me off her, and got the hell out of there, fleeing the scene of our lover's leap—except that we hadn't been lovers and we hadn't leapt romantically and tragically from some precipice into the depth below but instead had fallen from six feet onto a Smith Corona. This is the kind of story that will cement your reputation as a guy to stay away from—if the story gets out, that is. And it did. Soon I noticed that fewer and fewer women seemed deranged or misguided enough to risk an encounter with me and my top bunk and my sheets and my typewriter.

Two things seem worth mentioning here. One, the story about me and the pretty woman and my typewriter got out not because the pretty woman told it but because I did, over and over again—to my friends, to people I wanted to be my friends, to anyone who would listen. And why would I do that? Why

would I tell this story that made me look so bad? Do we fall in
love or in like or have sex or try to so that, when it goes bad, we
can tell a story about it? Is it that when the relationship goes
bad, which it almost always does, we at least have the story to
keep us warm? Or, would we rather have the story we know
is good than the relationship that might turn out bad? In any
case, I told the story—*ding!*—and I often told it while wearing
stolen clothes.

This is the second thing: when I fell off the top bunk with
the pretty woman and onto my typewriter, I was wearing someone else's shirt. It was a red T-shirt with the name of a prep
school on the chest in white block lettering. I'd stolen it from
someone who lived on my hall and who went to the prep school
advertised on the shirt. I tended to steal articles of clothing
that advertised, or suggested, prep schools, probably because
I hadn't attended one: I'd stolen varsity crew raincoats, barn
jackets, a type of shoe called bluchers. I even stole a pair of
lime green shorts three sizes too big for me and still wear the
shorts too, much to the dismay of anyone who sees me still
wear them.

There is a special place in hell reserved for writers—for
people, for that matter—who look back at their former selves
and try to force some larger meaning, to attach some redeeming
lesson, to all the random, idiotic, hurtful, wrongheaded things
they did. But I'm going to risk that place in hell by saying that
I stole people's clothing for the same reason I kept telling the
story about falling with the pretty woman onto my typewriter:
because there was something terribly dull about me. But I
thought that maybe if I wore someone else's clothes, maybe if I

did something spectacularly bad and then kept telling the story about it, thus making the bad thing I did even worse, maybe I'd be something better, or other, than dull. Maybe that's why I kept telling the story of the pretty woman and me falling on the typewriter—*ding!*—telling it, that is, until the night when the woman, not the pretty woman who fell on the typewriter, left me bleeding from both wrists and lying in a puddle of someone else's vomit, wearing someone else's shirt.

The shirt I had stolen and was wearing that night was white: a lived-in but not worn-out white oxford shirt I'd stolen from my roommate, who was more or less my size, which is possibly why I'd chosen him for my roommate. The shirt was beautiful: very white, very soft, and in this way had a lot in common with the woman who left me lying in it, who was also very white and very soft. I met her a year after the typewriter incident. She had long, whitish blonde hair that she wore in a braid hanging down to her waist and a softness to her that suggested, not obesity, but rather generosity, comfort. There was something cherubic about her—her cheerful smile, her apple red cheeks—something that screamed volunteer work, which makes sense, since I think she ended up in the Peace Corps after graduation. She was as beautiful as the white soft shirt I had stolen, which is saying something. And I liked her; I didn't love her, but I did like her. But more than that, I was *crazy* about her, and here's why: she didn't feel the same way about me, and it drove me crazy. Oh, she liked me well enough to spend time with me, a good bit of time. We took walks; we went to parties together; during a given week we had more lunches together than not. That kind of thing. We could have been seen as inseparable, except that I knew that she would, at any minute, separate from me. There was something absolutely missing between us, and she knew and I knew it, but she would be the one who'd get rid of me because of it; she would be the one who would rightly suggest that we be friends and nothing more, which was all we more or less were anyway. I knew this, and this knowledge, this anticipation of the day to come, pained me. It made me *crazy*. Why don't you like me quite as much as I like you? Why can't I make you? Why am I sticking around until you get rid of me? What will I be left with once you leave me? Why are you *doing* this to me?

Of course, there is nothing special about these feelings, these questions. They are part of an old, tired story. Which was probably the thing that drove me the most crazy. I wanted to ask this woman, Don't you know this is an old, tired story? Don't you know that the story of me liking you more than you like me is so tired, so old? Don't you know how dull this story is? Don't you know how dull you're making me? Don't you know that this is why I steal shirts? Don't you know why I became the kind of guy who sandwiches women between him and his typewriter and then tell stories about it? For that matter, don't you know how tired I am of being that guy with that story? Because I was getting tired of it: tired of that *ding!* tired of being the bad guy in the story, of being the worse guy telling it.

Luckily for me, the beauty of having a story is that another one, a better one, is always ready to take its place. This happened on a Friday night. I was in someone's dorm room, sitting next to the woman who was as beautiful as the white shirt I was wearing. I was drunk and she wasn't; the drunks were laughing at the story, but she wasn't. She'd heard the story before, and while she never said so, I knew she didn't much care for it. If I had stopped to think about it—the way I told it in public in front of her, the violence of me falling on top of the woman on top of the typewriter—maybe I would have stopped telling the story. And if she had stopped to think about it—that I was a fuckup, but if I told a story about being a fuckup and it was a good story, then maybe I might be less of one—maybe the story wouldn't have upset her so much. But she was destined to end things, and I was destined to help her. *Ding!* I said, and she got up and walked out the door. I followed her. I was holding two bottles of beer: the one I was almost done with and the one I was just starting. I was wearing that white shirt and was barefooted, for reasons that now escape me. The room we'd been in was on the fifth floor. By the time I caught up with her she was on the stairs. I said I was sorry, and she said nothing; I said that I was really sorry and, still, she said nothing. "What are you thinking?" I asked her. But I knew: she was probably thinking of how she was going to say good-bye to me, and I started thinking of how I was going to take it. We were alone on the stairs until we hit the second-floor landing, where there was a crowd of people surrounding an enormous puddle of vomit. It couldn't have possibly come from one person—indeed, several of the men in the crowd had queasy but proud looks on their faces—but there was a decent-sized strip of clean concrete on the other side of it, and before I bothered to ask myself why, I leapt, from the fourth step up, feeling like Errol Flynn, until I landed on the very edge of the puddle, on my bare heels, slipped, and fell backward, in my borrowed white shirt, into

the puddle of vomit, cracking the back of my head in the process. Both beer bottles shattered and sliced open my wrists, and
I began bleeding like crazy. No one in the crowd said anything;
they were looking at me like they'd been looking at the vomit just
a moment earlier. No one moved to help me; no one moved at all
until the woman, the woman who was now much, much more
beautiful than the no-longer beautiful, no-longer white shirt I'd
stolen, leaned over me, her lovely white blonde braid swinging
over her shoulder, and said, "Brock, I don't think this is going to
work." Then she tiptoed around me and the mess I'd fallen into,
the mess I'd made, and continued down the stairs.

Sometime later—it could have been a week, it could have been
several months—I'd heard she was back in my dorm. This was
yet another Friday night, and I was in someone else's room,
drinking too much beer, again. But once I heard she was in the
building, I stopped what I was doing and went to find her. It
turns out she was in the room next to mine, hanging out with
these two guys, brothers, fraternal twins who were known as the
Dirt Twins (nicknamed so because they actually were twins and
because they were generally unshaven, unkempt—although I
never saw either of them fall backdown into a puddle of vomit
and then lie there, bleeding from the wrists; they were never
as dirty as that). She might have been dating one of them at
the time. I didn't care. I walked right into the room, over to
where she was sitting, leaned over, kissed her on top of her
head, said, "Thank you," and then walked out of the room. As
I did, I could hear one of the Dirt Twins ask, "What the fuck
was *that* about?"

"I don't know," she said, and maybe she really didn't. She knew that she had to leave me. But maybe she didn't know how much better I would feel if she left me with a good story to tell about her leaving me. Maybe she didn't know how relieved I was that she got rid of me when she did, how she did, and not at a more conventional time, in a more conventional manner. Maybe she didn't know how crazy and sad I'd been, waiting for her to leave me, and how sane and happy I felt, lying there in a puddle of my blood and someone's vomit, her beautiful good-bye words still in my ears. Maybe she didn't know that those words—"I don't think this is going to work"—have endured the way "I love you" never could have. Maybe she didn't know how grateful I was then, and still am, which is why I kissed her on the head and said, "Thank you," and why I've been saying it every time I've told the story since, and why I'm saying it now too.

The Story You Will Tell

Jami Attenberg

You meet your new boyfriend at a holiday party for a Web site you write for, one that doesn't pay you except in parties. You do not know you are meeting the person you are going to spend the next year of your life with right away, because you are there with another man, a friend who you like, but who you just figured out doesn't like you, not like that anyway. Well. Tonight could suck.

You bum a cigarette off your new boyfriend because he is cute and has nerdy glasses and because you want a cigarette. You start to talk. He has a lot of energy and makes dumb jokes with great enthusiasm so they sort of turn out funny in the end. Somehow the conversation swings to politics. He likes to talk about politics a lot. And it's not even an election year. He tells you he writes a column for a small midwestern monthly political magazine, one that doesn't pay him except in credibility. *He's just like me, only boring,* you think. But also: he knows about things you don't.

You sit with him, and then your friend joins you, and suddenly they are arguing about politics and you write a little story in your head in which they are in fact fighting over you, and then you notice your new boyfriend keeps watching you whenever he makes a Very Important Point and that's when you realize he's your new boyfriend.

Two days later he goes out of town for the holidays and you e-mail every day. You send each other ten personal questions at a time, and you have to pick three of them to answer in response.

> Who was your best friend growing up?
> Have you ever been in a fistfight?
> Who did you lose your virginity to, and what song was playing on the stereo?
> Yes, that counts as one question.

When he gets back from the holidays you meet in the East Village for a drink, at 7B. It is unseasonably warm and you ride your bike into the city. Before he gets there you make a deal with yourself not to get drunk and sleep with him. So there is nothing, no flirting, no touching, no knee bumping, the whole night. You just talk. You are kicking ass at this date! You talk about drugs and music, and you realize he is not as boring as you thought. He talks about his ex-girlfriend and you wish he would shut up. You drink whiskey and you smoke cigarettes and you take pictures of yourselves with your digital camera, and it is a great date because you know you are not going to get drunk and sleep with him.

    At the end of the night he calls you a cab. He won't hear of you riding your bike across the bridge at this time of night. He wedges your bike neatly into the trunk of the cab. He opens the door, and then he kisses you, three times, before he leaves.

You swoon in the backseat. And you are not a swooner.

The first time you have sex he makes a joke about how he is glad he doesn't have the Irish Curse. You ask him what the Irish Curse is. He mumbles something about penis size. You think to yourself: he doesn't have the Irish Curse, and he doesn't *not* have the Irish Curse. But you don't believe in curses anyway.

The second time you have sex he pushes you up against the wall of your apartment and grabs you all over. There are no jokes about curses ever again.

In the first three months you break up with him a few times for no particular reason. This is what you do, what you have always done. You are aware this is a problem you have. You find yourself staring at him and thinking: *What next?* And wishing he would know that you are thinking that and that he would have some sort of answer and that he would just say it without you even having to ask, because if you have to ask, is his answer going to be really real?

And then you think about the way you have nothing in common, except for the struggling writing thing, and the love of indie rock, and the past with drugs, and while that is enough to last for a while, a date or two, can it really get you through a life together?

And also he is hiding something, you can just tell.

This is why you are always alone.

He still wants to be with you though. He always comes back

for more. Maybe he knows something you don't know. You take him back.

You pretend to care about politics. One morning, you wake up and join the ACLU.

He loves open-bar media parties more than any person you have ever met. You think open bars are stupid. They only last an hour or two, all those people pressed up against a bar to get their one free drink. You would rather pay for your drink, get the kind of drink you want, and drink whenever you like.

"But it's free," he says and looks at you like he does not recognize you, and you remember that he is a dirt-poor writer with no backup plan, and then you feel like an asshole.

You survive things together. Like:

- Meeting each other's friends
- The ex-girlfriend who keeps picking up things she's left behind at his house
- How you will always love your work more than any man
- His shitty apartment and his subtle seething toward his roommate
- The fact that he is almost always broke.
- That poli-sci grad student girl who hangs out at his local bar and always talks to him while you're in the bathroom
- Quitting smoking

You go away for the summer, to a small cottage in northern California, to write. You write every morning. In the afternoons you take large mountain dogs on hikes and then do yoga for two hours. In the evenings you drink a lot of wine and masturbate and cry about everything horrible that has ever happened to you. It is a good thing you are by yourself most of the time, or you would be insufferable.

After a month he scrapes up some money and flies out to visit you. You tell him that you love him. He is shocked. "I didn't think you were like that," he said. Neither did you.

When you get back to town he tells you that he loves you too. It just took him a while to figure it out. He tells you all the things he thinks are great about you and says, "If that's not love, then I don't know what is."

Later that night he tells you your toes are cute and you say, "You've got it bad, man," and it doesn't bother him at all. You are in love. He really did know something you didn't.

Bliss lasts about a month. Right until the freelance market dries up and he has to start borrowing money from his room-mate for rent.

You realize that he only has one sex trick, the sex against the wall. Like he saw it in a movie once and decided if he could just do that he would be the best lover ever and then he never decided to learn any other trick again. A one-trick pony. You picture him whinnying and waving a long, dirty mane in the air. Pawing the ground sadly.

Love. There is nowhere to go but down. Will you marry this man, the one who can't pay his rent? Will you even move in with him?

The sex gets boring for both of you. No one is even standing up anywhere at all anymore. You lost weight and he didn't even notice. Or maybe he did notice, but he liked you when you were bigger, who knows? The freelance market doesn't improve, and then it's the holidays and no one ever has any work during the holidays. He gets depressed. Then you stop having sex entirely. You never go out anymore because you are sick of paying all the time. So what's left behind?

This is something you can't survive.

You break up on New Year's Day at 6:00 a.m. You tell him it's because you're too different. You have bigger dreams than him. You wish you could travel more. You feel you are on the verge of something big and he is still writing the same book reviews for fifty dollars a pop that he was writing when you met him. *Can't you see what I'm saying?* When you leave in the morning you hug good-bye.

It is the easiest breakup ever. You don't even cry.

Three weeks later you miss him on a Sunday morning when you are alone. He would have been making you an egg and cheese sandwich on cheap Krasdale white bread and a cup of Café Bustelo, which you would have eaten on the green couch with the sunken pillows in the living room. The couch that smelled like smoke and cat, even though he didn't have a cat. His life was shitty and he was struggling, but at least he made you breakfast.

You have made a terrible mistake, it's clear. He loved you and you threw him away. No one ever loves you. You are going to be alone forever. Writing. Alone.

This is when the power shifts.

You spend the next nine months talking about getting back together but never really doing it. You go out for drinks and hold hands over the table. He swears he's not dating anyone else, you're the only one he thinks about. There is a long hug at the subway entrance. The next day you send him an e-mail talking about how you feel, that you want to move forward, and he never replies, or if he does it's noncommittal. Or you call him and he never picks up.

This happens, like, eight times.

You would not tolerate this behavior if you had just started dating someone, but because you have a past together, you think it is just part of your bigger story. It does not occur to you that he is kind of treating you like shit or, at the very least, leading you on. And you don't do that to someone you love.

You come home early from a trip out West because he thinks he has made some kind of breakthrough in his life, and you are thinking maybe you are that breakthrough.

It is August in New York. It is the kind of hot you can't escape even with air-conditioning. You are wearing a tank top and a short skirt, and it does not matter how close to naked you are, you are going to sweat. Everything is stained and damp. The subways smell. The streets smell. All around you people are drugged with heat. It is maddening.

You both drink beer to cool down, too quickly and too many. He talks about how he knows what he finally wants to write about. He knows what makes him feel important. He is inspired. You keep waiting for the rest of it, but he just keeps talking about his writing.

You are excited for him. But.

Later you make out under a streetlamp, the bugs swarming the bright light above your head. There is a distinct buzzing. You can hear it.

He doesn't call. Three days later you finally call him at work. You force him to admit that it's over, it's really over. Why did he do this to me? Secretly you wonder if he's right, though. Finally you cry.

You are never talking to him again. Start writing a story about a guy in a coma. Put *him* in a coma.

He is *so* going to die at the end.

Six months later you both decide enough time has passed. Go out with him for a drink. You know you want to. You've got a lot of awesome things going on in your life. Your work is solid and inspiring. You just lost even more weight and started coloring your hair. And sure, you're single and haven't been really dating at all and you work all the time, but you don't necessarily count that as a negative if one were keeping score, because you aren't. Keeping score, that is.

At the bar he's late as usual. He's still cute, you notice, and funny in his way. Those glasses always helped. But then he talks for a half hour about something really dull that happened to him that he clearly thinks is fascinating. You are having a hard time paying attention. You realize he is telling you his stories, that this is the best he has to offer from the last six months, and you are really glad you weren't with him for the last six months. Or for the next six months or ever again because these would be the stories you would have to listen to. You relax. This is going to be okay.

He has gotten an actual job, one that pays all right, with a political Web site. He tells you he has a new apartment, finally, after all this time of wanting a new apartment, and wanting to live alone. He and his old roommate are even friends again. You are proud of him for accomplishing this goal. He says it's amazing, that he loves not having to talk to anyone. You understand completely. This was one of the reasons why you liked him. Because he understood why not having to talk to anyone was a good thing.

You were the same, but different.

He takes you out to dinner after the drinks. It feels comfortable and easy and you are having fun. It is not quite like you are friends, and it is not like the way it used to be when you were together. It is something in between, but maybe it is always going to be in between with the two of you. Maybe that's the way it works sometimes.

You go to another bar and have more drinks. Now you are both getting drunk. He brings up things that happened in the past. The time you had sex in the woods (standing up), the time you yelled at him because he showed up late for your party. These are things you hadn't thought about in a while. You wonder why he thinks about them so much. The reminiscing makes you feel close to him. You touch his hair. He touches yours. You have another drink, and then suddenly, it is time to go.

You stand in the entryway of the bar together and smoke a cigarette. It is a long entryway and it is quiet and empty. He notices your heels, the red ones, your favorites that you wear so often you have forgotten that they even exist.

"You wore those the last time I saw you," he says. "With that skirt."

And then you kiss him because when a man remembers what you were wearing six months ago, he should be kissed. That's what warrants a kiss in your book. And all of a sudden the both of you are kissing and it is strange and sort of good but mostly strange. It is not like when you first met and it was dangerous and new and hot, and it was not like when you were together and you loved each other and it was so sweet because it felt like it was going to go on and on forever and ever. It is just simply familiar.

Then he pushes you up against a wall and pushes his hands up underneath your coat and grabs your ass. You kiss each other's necks and lips hard. It is a serious make-out session outside a bar in Brooklyn on a Wednesday night, and it is real and it is happening and all you feel is numb. That's what it is. He led you on for so long, how could you feel anything but nothing at all? The only other option would be to hate him, and you can't do that anymore.

Eventually you stop. The people walking by the bar are loud and it throws off whatever little connection you were feeling. He walks you to your bike. He tells you he wants to see you again. He is lying, you think. You agree to see him again. You are both standing in Brooklyn on a Wednesday night, lying to each other.

The next day you tell your friends that you made out with your ex-boyfriend and that you felt nothing, and most of them are pretty uninterested because they have seen him bounce you around for a year now and they are starting to find him boring. In fact, you feel a little dumb that you did it.

*   *   *

He doesn't call or e-mail. But it's okay. You are already turning it into a story in your head, that time I made out with my ex-boyfriend. Because this is what you do, you turn things into stories, and then it's okay. You don't need to be in a relationship. You are already in a relationship with yourself. You are going to love yourself forever. It is a little bit sick, but it is a little bit healthy too. And you will never not call.

A week later you're out with another friend who knows your ex-boyfriend. You mention you saw him, and then, just because you're in the mood for it, you tell her you made out with him.

And your friend says, "Oh dear, he just moved in with that girlfriend of his a month ago. Didn't you know?"

And you think to yourself: *What girlfriend?*

You are flushed with shock and humiliation. You literally cannot close your lips together for a half hour because your jaw is so firmly dropped. You burn with anger for the rest of the night. *He really knew something I didn't,* you think. If you could see him at that moment you would punch him.

You bring yourself to ask your friend: *What's the girlfriend like?*

And she says: "Oh, you know. *Boring.*"

You barely hear her because you are already turning it into a story in your head: that time I made out with my ex-boyfriend and he turned out to be a total fucking prick.

And then you think, that's the most interesting thing he's ever done in his entire life. Then you think after that, actually *I* was the most interesting he ever did in his life.

And that is the story you will tell.

Marking Territory

George Singleton

The cat didn't get hurt physically. I don't know how to measure a cat's psychological damage due to insult and embarrassment, but if there's any chance that a mean old house cat can comprehend outright embarrassment, then this particular Darlington cat suffered enough to make a pet psychologist wealthy, I'm sure. I'm not saddened. I *do* stay awake still—these twenty years later—in fear that this old tom will show up outside my door, but that might have to do with other paranoid tendencies on my part.

I will change the names—I can't even remember the stupid cat's name, so I'll call it Zorro—and I will come out of this, I'm sure, as an idiot. An idiot and a heel. So I'm going to plead my case from near the beginning of the end.

I'll call her Ms. Pearson, because David Pearson was a great stock-car legend, and this particular ex-girlfriend shared the name of another stock-car legend. Not Petty or Waltrip or Earnhardt. Not Fireball Roberts. Another one. This all took place in Darlington, South Carolina, home to a racetrack known to be "too tough to tame." I was twenty-nine, then thirty, and she was about twenty-five. Ms. Pearson looked a lot like that Cybill Shepherd actress. Not that I'm a bastion of responsibility or rational behavior, but sometimes she acted like the woman in *Sybil*, the movie.

It all came down to Ms. Pearson's frequent AA meetings— she didn't drink, and from what I remember she never had partaken of the drink, but she believed in that genetic theory of alcoholism—and my disdain for AA meetings. Maybe I was wrong, looking back on it.

Also, I need to throw another important cog into this dysfunctional relationship. I'll call him the Remora. I worked with the Remora—a remora's better known as a suckerfish to anyone who is not an ichthyologist—and his girlfriend had left him. I can't use her name either, but I swear to God it wasn't that far from being Fifi or any other poodlelike name. Fifi left the Remora, and then he kept calling me up to say, "Hey, I'm really lonely, man. If you and Ms. Pearson go out this weekend, keep me in mind," et cetera.

So I'd call. I didn't want a suicide on my conscience. That has to count for something. I couldn't stand thinking about a poor guy sitting alone in his house, pining for Fifi, a gigantic bottle of Bufferin on his lap, which he'd use as a call for help.

I should mention at this point that Ms. Pearson and I lived in the same house—owned by her grandmother—but I had to park a few blocks away each night so her grandmother wouldn't drive by in the morning and see my truck. She was a matriarch straight off a bad soap opera. Anyway, Ms. Pearson and I lived in the same house, split the rent money that she paid her grandmother, and there was also that mean cat Zorro in the house that Ms. Pearson loved. This cat—on my very first date with Ms. Pearson—came out of another room and attacked my ankle. He shredded my sock and scratched me so deeply that I bled. He never blinked over the entire six months or year or however long the relationship lasted. Ms. Pearson kept a Dixie cup on top of the litter box, so that when the cat used it she would immediately scoop out his business and flush it down the toilet. The cat waited for me around corners daily, and the girlfriend sat around within eyeshot of the litter box's front door at all times.

The litter box comes back into play in this story.

The Remora would go out with us, usually to a bar on the Darlington square. He'd be all hangdog faced. He kept a pocketful of quarters and paid for draft beer thusly, as if the bar was only a side trip on his way to the laundromat. When Ms. Pearson would excuse herself to go pee out six gallons of Coke and water and iced tea, the Remora would always say, "Man, I don't know how you can take it. She sure does bitch a lot about your drinking. That's got to be rough. How can you take it? She sure does bitch a lot about your drinking," on and on.

Then, from what I learned later, when I went to rid myself of, say, a dozen beers and a dozen shots of bourbon, the Remora would say to Ms. Pearson, "Man, I don't know how you can take it. George sure does drink a lot. That's got to be rough. How can you take it? He sure does drink a lot."

Classic Remora MO I later learned from either the Learning Channel, the Discovery Channel, or a Wikipedia entry I may or may not have written myself later on in life.

*   *   *

For some reason I moved out of the house, but she and I kept dating. Maybe her grandmother discovered the arrangement, I don't know. Maybe the cat sent me some kind of subtle, subliminal messages while I slept. More than likely—looking back—Ms. Pearson tired of my coming home late and passing out, and she rightly figured that I'd never amount to much more than an idiot itinerant English instructor working semester by semester on an adjunct basis, trying to teach future plumbers and welders the importance of complete sentences. Or maybe my eye strayed toward women without a love for sock-shredding felines. In my defense, I didn't know I suffered from "stray eye." I didn't even know it was an official syndrome until I saw it on *Oprah*. Or read about it on Wikipedia.

Anyway, I moved into a four-room house about three hundred yards away. Ms. Pearson moved some of her belongings, or at least a highboy, into my little brick place. I kept a desk and typewriter at hers, for some reason. More often than not, I kept my truck parked at my house and scurried over to hers after dark. The one time that I drove over there and parked, she woke up the next morning, got in her own car, and rammed it into my passenger-side door. Ms. Pearson always promised that she didn't mean to do it. She did so with a slight smile on her face, kind of like when Cybill Shepherd smirked at Bruce Willis in that old *Moonlighting* show.

We split up, we made up. The Remora continued his long, arduous, timed plan of attack until, finally, Ms. Pearson said that she and I could no longer see each other. I guess that she finally realized that I wasn't going to change anytime soon, that it was hopeless to wait around to see if I'd ever get published, quit drinking, and be kinder to the ones closest to me as opposed to complete strangers. I do not think she made a bad decision there.

Maybe a week passed before Ms. Pearson came over to my house to get that stupid highboy thing back. I'm not even sure why it ever seemed necessary to have this giant piece of furniture taking up so much of my so-called den. It's not like I owned an array of raincoats and slickers and ponchos to hang on the thing. I didn't have extra blankets to put in the bottom part of it. She came over to get it, and she said, "I have a date on Friday night."

Perhaps I said, "Good for you," but I doubt it. I said, "You know, this highboy thing is probably going to topple over on the way to your house. You're going to have to sit on it to weigh the thing down."

Like I said, it was only a few blocks away, but involved a sharp descent and two or three hairpin turns. Ms. Pearson said, "Don't do anything stupid," and climbed into the bed of my pickup.

I said, "I'll be careful."

Then I took a left-hand turn instead of going straight across Mechanicsville Road. Ms. Pearson sat on the highboy, looking, I imagined, like the queen of England. Or maybe the queen of whatever country had a good-looking empress.

I drove straight onto the Darlington square, and—I'm not sure how I got all the lights to work in my favor—drove laps, my right hand on the horn, my left hand holding the wheel as hard as any stock-car driver trying to maneuver a track too tough to tame. People looked at Ms. Pearson riding in back. In my mind I saw her staring straight ahead—or behind—not waving the classic queen salute, but clenching her strong jaw in a way that only correct women can clench.

So on that Friday—I hate to admit it, but I'd gotten kind of depressed over this woman understanding that I would not change my self-destructive ways—I left my job teaching college English and I drove straight over to the Remora's house. I thought, I was there for him during all those crybaby sessions, so he owes me. The Remora lived near a blue-collar bar I liked called Rosie's. One time I was in Rosie's and this man with a jet-black, hard pompadour said, "My name's spelled D-A-U-G-H-N. I'm one of only about four people in the world who has the name Don spelled that way." I was with a good Irish ex-all-American distance runner named Jim, who said to Daughn, "I know about three thousand men named Daughn back home, spelled that way."

Daughn pulled out a pistol and aimed it at Jim. I said something like, "Whoa, whoa, whoa," and tried to push the barrel back toward the bar. Daughn said to Jim, "I think you're some kind of spy. Who're you working for?" and so on. Daughn, from what I understood later, got sent to prison soon thereafter for other reasons.

Anyway, I drove my banged-in truck to the Remora's house to find, of course, Ms. Pearson's car parked in his driveway. Only later—the next morning—would I find out that she was going out on a date *with him*, that he would drive her all the way down to Murrells Inlet, and that he would say that she was the prettiest woman in the seafood restaurant. If the Remora ordered shark off the menu, would that make him even more of a traitor? Answer: yes.

So I went to Rosie's alone and drank a few beers. Then I drove to the next bar on my way home and drank a few beers. There are a lot of roadhouse bars in the swampy Pee Dee region of South Carolina, by the way. I went to the next place, then the next, finally ending up at the bar on the square that I frequented more often than not.

I told my tale of woe to the bartender, who was also named George, and to anyone else who'd listen. I made people make vows to curse the Remora whenever they ran into him again. And then I realized that it was absolutely necessary that I drive my truck over to Ms. Pearson's house, hop over the back fence, jimmy open the unlocked back window, and retrieve my desk and an arm lamp and the extra typewriter I had over there.

I did so. Then I got to thinking about how, maybe, the Remora and Ms. Pearson might end up at the house later, so I found a photo album, pulled out all the photographs she had of me, and taped them on the den wall.

I could've unlocked the front door, packed up my truck, returned inside to make sure the back window was shoved down, and so on. I could've made it out of there.

But I looked at the cat. He sat hunched near his litter box, staring at me. He waited for me to look away, or busy myself with something else, so he could pounce.

I said, "You stupid son of a bitch," and walked toward him. He scrammed into the bedroom.

The litter box was a fancy one with a hood that attached

with four side clamps. I unclamped the things and lifted the lid. All those beers, understand, had built up.

I might've peed two gallons into the litter box. I'm talking the cat litter floated up. I secured the lid, told the cat to have a nice life with the Remora, and left.

Understand, I didn't bang into any of her possessions. I didn't torch the place or go over to the Remora's and crash into whichever car was left in the driveway there. I didn't shoot out any lights, harm an animal, short out the electrical circuit. I just peed in her litter box. Then I drove home and thanked God for the Darlington cop's absence in my life on this particular evening.

I awoke to someone knocking repeatedly on my door at six in the morning. I heard Ms. Pearson yelling out my name. I got off the bed and thought, uh-oh—she's going to be pissed off about all those pictures I taped to her wall. What if the Scotch tape takes off some paint, and then her grandmother asks what happened?

I opened the door to find Ms. Pearson standing there, crying. Her car was parked beside mine, in the yard. She left it running. She blubbered. I said, "Hey. What? What's the matter with you?"

I couldn't make this up, and it's exactly how I've told the story for the past two decades. Ms. Pearson blurted out, "I need you to help me get the cat to a veterinarian. I think his bladder burst!"

At that moment, to be honest, I'd forgotten all about pee-ing in the litter box. I remembered breaking in the house and getting my stuff, and about the photos, but not invading the cat's personal space. I said, "Hey, I saw your car over at ——'s house"—this was before I called him the Remora—"yesterday. What're you doing going out with him, anyway? Is that the kind of weasel you're looking for?" I went on and on.

She said, "He went into his litter box, and then he came out shaking his front and back paws like crazy. I looked in there and it's filled up." She spoke about the cat, not the Remora.

Then I recalled everything from eight or nine hours earlier. I started laughing and said, "His bladder didn't burst, fool. I peed in his cat box last night."

She quit crying. I'm talking she turned off the tears just a little too fast. I think Ms. Pearson knew all along. Composed, she evidently decided that this would be the perfect time to let me in on all that stuff about going out on a date to Murrells Inlet, being called the prettiest girl in the restaurant, and so on.

But I could tell she wasn't ecstatic about the Remora. I don't want to brag or claim soothsaying capabilities or anything, but I think that, deep down, she *wanted* a man in her life who did things like pee in the cat box. I think she *wanted* a little danger and excitement and unpredictability in her life, though she wouldn't admit it on a Saturday morning, her cat in one of those pet traveler things that don't look a whole lot different from fancy lidded litter boxes.

She called me an asshole and left. Her relationship with the Remora lasted about another two dates, from what I understand. He stayed away from me, then went off to finish his Ph.D. and write a dissertation called something like "Passive-Aggressive Tendencies in the Works of F. Scott Fitzgerald" or "T. S. Eliot Really Needed Ezra Pound" or "Truman Capote's

Workout Regimen" or "I Rode on Peter Benchley's Underbelly While He Wrote *Jaws.*"

My next real relationship was with a woman who owned a pit bull.

Ms. Pearson ended up marrying a man who played drums for a band that played cover songs in hotel lounges. They moved to Kentucky. The cat, I'm sure, acclimated well there. I turned out okay and even have a cat along with all these ex-stray dogs. I don't play tricks on my cat. The dogs do.

The Rules of Repulsion

D. E. Rasso

The moment I opened the Camden College catalog and saw a photo of a girl with pink hair, I knew I'd finally found someplace where I wouldn't feel like an outcast. Simpatico! At Camden you could create your own major and live with a roommate of the opposite sex and call your professors by their first names (both in and out of the bedroom). I applied, and for whatever reason, they liked me so much that they offered me a four-year scholarship.

I had grown up in a rural upstate New York town, and I'd been itching to get out forever. *Eighteen years of tribulation in this backwater, and finally some recognition,* I thought.

After our first "house" meeting (Camden was too progressive for dormitories), the "house chair" (Camden was also too progressive for RAs) invited me back to his room to drink beer and meet upperclassmen. That evening I met bored, arty types who chatted me up long enough to bum cigarettes. I sat and quietly listened to stories about summer breaks spent on Tortola or interning with Mark Kostabi, wondering at what point it would be appropriate to chime in with anecdotes of my own summer drinking lukewarm keg beer in the state forest and smoking weed in the cornfields. I sort of wanted to ask the kid who'd spent the summer in Tortola why he wasn't tan.

That's when Booth walked in.

Carrying a thermos emblazoned with the Black Flag logo and wearing Doc Martens, slim trousers, and a vintage button-down shirt, Booth sported the definitive early nineties proto-hipster style that I'd only ever seen in music magazines. My hometown had one stoplight, and my high school boyfriends favored dirty jeans, motorcycle rally T-shirts, and engineer boots. In my limited worldview, Booth was the Platonic ideal of cool.

People hugged him mightily and announced how happy they were that he was back. When he sat down next to me and said, "Hi, I'm Booth," I felt the most inchoate sense of longing an eighteen-year-old has ever felt. I knew that if I could make him love me, I would be the happiest girl in the world.

It seemed he wasn't quite as entranced but was keen to chat. He told me about his summer, which, as I recall, included some sort of cross-country road trip involving ironic tourist destinations. And he'd been to San Francisco to get a tattoo. He lifted up his shirt to show me his scrawny, pale back. He had a line of tattoos down his spine and described the provenance of each. I recognized each one as a totem of absolute fucking cool.

Booth possessed an encyclopedic knowledge of music. We had very similar tastes, save for one genre: jazz. In fact, Booth was a jazz music major. He played the contrabass, which seemed to suit his personality—the largest and most formidable instrument on any given stage.

I was awestruck. I forced myself to say good night, however, knowing that I faced a long day of orientation symposiums on date rape and the importance of gender-neutral pronouns. I told Booth that I hoped I'd see him again.

"Good night, Dana," Booth said. "It was nice to meet you."

That night, in my unfamiliar and lumpy institutional bed, I replayed that final exchange ad infinitum. He had remembered my name.

The next day, my roommate and I decided that we knew enough about how "NO MEANS NO," so we skipped orientation and sat on the lawn outside of the classroom building, under an old apple tree. Our housemates—none of whom had attended the symposiums either—joined us, and while everyone else chatted amiably about their hometowns, I thought about Booth and absently tossed half-rotten apples down the hill.

A little while later, a Ford Bronco rolled down the school drive and stopped ten yards away. Booth stuck his head out the window. "Hey there!" he called to me. "What are you up to?"

"Nothing," I said, and abandoned my housemates.

He drove me to his off-campus apartment in North Camden, and while he was making coffee, I scanned his pedigreed library. "I see you like Henry Rollins," I commented, noting that Booth seemed to own every record and book the turgid, parochial moron had ever produced.

"Yes! He's my hero!" Booth bounded over to the shelf and pulled out a Black Flag tour diary. "Lemme read you something. It's so great."

It was a passage in which Rollins recounted jerking off into a sleeping girl's hair because she had kicked him out of bed. I stood there patiently for five minutes as Booth read and wondered if maybe I should've attended that date-rape seminar after all.

He finished and looked at me expectantly.

"That guy's an insufferable douche bag," I said.

"You're wrong," Booth countered, unrankled. This would turn out to be one of Booth's greatest and most irritating qualities—I couldn't get him riled up about anything. "You're wrong" was the only thing he'd ever say when we argued.

We sat on his couch, drinking black coffee, smoking, and listening to a Japanese Ornette Coleman bootleg. I tried to make conversation, but he shushed me every time. "You have to listen to this part," he said, pointing reverently at the stereo speaker.

I began to wonder if maybe he wasn't all that interested in me. And how was I supposed to *make* him interested if I couldn't stun him with my erudite, witty observations?

After thirty-five torturous minutes, side two ended, the tone arm returned to its cradle, and Booth emerged from his reverie. "So," he said. "Wanna fuck?"

For the next few weeks, this is how it went. I would go to class and stare into space. Then I would come back to my room hoping to find an answering machine message from Booth. If there wasn't one, I'd sit on my bed and listen to mopey college rock. If there was, I'd forgo dinner, neglect my homework, and blow off my friends just so that I could spend my evening sitting quietly on a couch and listening to rare recordings of duets for tuba and vibraphone. And then have sex.

We didn't *always* listen to music; sometimes we talked. Or

he talked. He'd seen every cool band in the world, before they got big. He'd gone to boarding school. He knew all of Alec Baldwin's monologues from *Glengarry Glen Ross* and could imitate any celebrity. He was from an old-money Southern family who attended the same church as the Clintons. He'd read Céline's entire oeuvre, twice. He lost his virginity in South Africa. He'd recently been to Amsterdam and gone to the red light district to see a sex worker but couldn't get it up, so they talked instead. He probably did his Alec Baldwin imitation.

I couldn't decide if these stories were more for my benefit or his. He clearly liked to hear himself talk. Listening to him was like didactic foreplay, and I felt rather boring in comparison. We'd have sex and then he'd kick me out so that he could practice. I'd walk back to campus happily, because I was ass-over-teakettle in love with him. In this irrational state, I justified his behavior by constantly revising my definition of the Platonic ideal of cool.

I wish I could say that the sex was mind-blowing, but it wasn't. (What does an eighteen-year-old know about mind-blowing sex anyway?) It was not unlike his monologues—educational. Booth introduced me to a number of sex acts I'd only ever read about, and he did so with flaming-baton-routine vigor. (I would frequently return to campus bruised, scratched, and—one time—bleeding.) The way he performed in bed, you'd have thought there was a camera crew in the room.

He bragged about banging his high school girlfriend so hard that her gynecologist thought she'd been raped. And as disturbing as *that* sounds, it paled in comparison to other things. He told me about a mason jar he'd once kept under his sink, its contents a dead squirrel and God knows what else suspended in urine and phlegm. His favorite Bukowski story involved a man raping a little girl in a garage. But things like this don't matter when you're singularly, obsessively in love. When I think about it now, I can understand the *Dateline NBC* stories about those women married to serial killers—the wives who blithely freshen the makeup on the decapitated heads in the fridge while their husbands are disarticulating the limbs in the basement.

About a month into the semester, as I lay in bed watching him perform some new arrangement, I offhandedly asked Booth if we were serious . . . as in, "going out."

He stood there, naked behind the contrabass, and said, "No. Of course we aren't."

I couldn't make words.

"Listen," he said, putting the bass down and sitting next to me on the bed. "I'm at a point in my life where monogamy just isn't my style."

I think I lapsed into a fugue state or had a stroke, because I don't remember anything that happened until the following day. That was when the heartbreak formally commenced, and I wandered around campus like a shadow trapped in hell.

Without Booth around, I had plenty of time to focus on my precarious academic standing. I had known for weeks already that I'd tragically misjudged both Camden and myself. Apparently, a "self-made major" required aspirations and intellectual curiosity. It hadn't occurred to me that college would involve more than just sitting around, listening to the Clash, and talking about the Shining Path and vegan shoes. I was really floundering.

My daily routine began at 9:00 a.m., when I would sit in French class and puzzle over love poems by medieval nuns. At noon I was too frightened by the cool kids to sit in the pantheon of the dining hall—the smoking dining room—and I would sit in the adjacent room with my back to the door, too self-conscious to get up to refill my drink. During my afternoon painting class, I would nervously pick at the pimples on my forehead while the professor would chain-smoke Marlboro Reds and say things like, "Look, if you want to learn about color theory, go to RISD."

At 4:00 p.m., exhausted from all this self-flagellation, I would arrive at Literature and Colonialism, the toughest class on my schedule. I came to Camden having read none of the Great Books. In fact, I'd only read three books during my entire senior year: *Tess of the d'Urbervilles*, *King Lear*, and *Invisible Man*. Ellison had been my choice for the final paper. My English teacher had suggested I pick something less "transgressive," but I'm glad I stuck to my guns because, of the three, *Invisible Man* was the only thing remotely related to our syllabus. So whenever I was called on, I'd compare whatever we were discussing at the time to *Invisible Man*.

There was only one student floundering more than I was, and she related everything to Plato's "Apology." *At least Ralph Ellison was black,* I reminded myself.

Who was it that said, "Art is suffering"? It's probably on a coffee mug somewhere. As I adjusted to life without Booth, I began to channel my angst into my schoolwork. Had Goya been a heartbroken eighteen-year-old girl, he would have created something like what I was churning out in painting class, artistic depictions of suffering that could have filled the Louvre floor to ceiling. In French class, I breathed new, maudlin life into Baudelaire's "Spleen." And in Literature and Colonialism, I suggested that *Wretched of the Earth* was really a metaphor for failed relationships.

This is not to say I was doing well in school, but at least I was trying harder than I had before.

Socially, I was trying even harder. But even at a school full of maladroit, narcissistic, and completely unhinged personalities, I wasn't fitting in very well. I had a few friends, but for some reason I was more concerned with the majority of the student body who were, at best, uninterested me. Why weren't they interested? I'd watched Fassbinder! I'd read Iceberg Slim! Yet at parties, I would haunt the corners of the room, or get too friendly with upperclassmen who didn't tell me they had girlfriends (or boyfriends, for that matter). I made a drunken nuisance of myself, comforted only by the knowledge that by attending these gatherings I wouldn't run into Booth. He too was a bit of an outcast at Camden. Unlike me, however, he seemed happy about that.

By December the ground was covered with snow, and I had begun wearing the same clothes every day and sleeping in my snow boots. The agony of heartache was being supplanted by the very legitimate fear of flunking out. If it weren't for the lenient grading policy and the administration's desperate need for tuition dollars, I might not have squeaked by.

The winter break at Camden was especially long, to allow us to spend two months doing an internship related to our interests. I lacked the ambition to find something fruitful or re-

warding to do. So while others spent their winter in Phuket or
Seville, I went home, interned at a local graphic design firm,
and spent a lot of time thinking angry Booth-related thoughts.

A few of my friends had stayed behind at Camden, though,
so on a lark I drove up to see them on Super Bowl Sunday.
You can't imagine a group of people less interested in watching
football, but there we were, muting the TV and discussing John
Dewey. I was surprised when Booth showed up. He seemed
lonely, and I felt sorry for him. That night, before I left, we
stood in the North Camden town square and I let him kiss me
good night. "It was good to see you," he said. I heard, *You are
the only girl I could ever love.*

I made him a card for Valentine's Day. I wrote, *Have you
started liking me again?* His reply was a single-spaced letter
with quarter-inch margins typed in **HELVETICA CONDENSED BLACK OBLIQUE
SMALL CAPS**—the official Henry Rollins font. It began, "Thanks
for the card. I never stopped liking you in the first place." This
was followed by a four-thousand-sentence quasi-philosophical
rant. I memorized the entire letter.

During the break, I read in the *National Enquirer* about a
scientific study that analyzed babies who become addicted to
electrical shocks. They crawl over to an electrical socket, stick
their fingers in it, and get sent flying across the room. Then they
crawl back over and do it again and again. I don't remember if
the scientists concluded that this is because of the adrenaline
rush, or because some people are just born masochists. Either
way, it resonated with me.

Predictably, Booth and I were back to our routine by the
third week of spring semester. Then one afternoon, as we slid

into bed, I noticed a long, dark hair on the sheets. It wasn't the first time he'd slept with someone else. On one occasion, it had been with a preppy senior and he'd told me about it the next day, clearly excited by how exotic it seemed. Another time was with a sculpture major, I think, but it's difficult to recall, given how often it happened. I'd forgiven these infelicities because I understood that he'd never promised he would be faithful. But the thought that he couldn't even be bothered to change his sheets—that was the last straw.

I held the hair up. "*Whose* is this? Whose *is* this?"

He shrugged. "It was just something that happened," and added, apropos of nothing, "It wasn't that great. She had a really small clit."

"That's comforting, thank you." I put my clothes on and stormed out.

I had reached what I thought was the nadir of humiliation: the only man I wanted was indiscriminately fucking every girl within arm's reach. My classes might as well have been taught in Esperanto. I didn't want to go to parties because I'd earned the enmity of too many jealous girlfriends. But like teens exploring the abandoned mine shaft in a slasher flick, I went even deeper and discovered there were much lower levels of humiliation to be found. The semester was coming to an end, and I knew that I wouldn't be seeing Booth for a while, so I invited him on a picnic, because the weather was so lovely. I put together sandwiches and lemonade.

He never showed.

I didn't even have enough energy left over to be sad. But I craved some sort of reckoning. I entertained letting the air out of his tires, destroying his Rollins collection and *Lustmord*. In the end I decided to fuck his closest friend instead.

This involved a lot of self-sacrifice. It wasn't challenging to cajole him, a music major ten years my senior, into the act. It just wasn't particularly rewarding. For one, he had a ponytail. Another thing: he couldn't keep it up. (At the time, I chalked this up to his advanced age, but it's probably because he sensed that I was using him as a grudge fuck. I don't recall there being a lot of seduction on my part. It was more like, "Pants off, Ponytail; let's do this.") Worst of all, there was a really good chance Booth, ever blasé, would be unmoved.

The next day, Booth came up to me in the dining hall and snarled, "So, you fucked him. Good for you." Victory!

That summer, while ruminating on how much I hated Booth for breaking my heart, I realized that I hated Camden for the exact same reason. Fuck those people and their self-made majors and exotic vacations and ambiguous sexuality, I decided. It went beyond just not fitting in; there were plenty of people just like me, the ones who didn't go to parties and didn't come from absurdly wealthy backgrounds. I felt as though I wasn't emotionally prepared for the experience, like I wasn't intellectually braced for the endeavor. I arrived at Camden with an absurd, distorted sense of confidence, and by the end of spring semester it had completely dissolved. I was just another shiftless asshole, a failure who didn't even have a summer internship at a Taos glass-blowing studio to look forward to.

So I dropped out.

I gave my friends explicit, blood-oath-enforced instructions:

they were not to tell Booth where I was, or what I was doing, ever, I added, optimistically, *no matter how many times he asks*.

I thought about him from time to time. Two years after I left Camden, I flew up to see my best friend Jen graduate. "Booth will probably be there, just so you know," she warned.

I arrived itching for a fight, and the afternoon before the ceremony I saw him coming right at me from across the commons lawn. He was wearing a fez and a sly grin.

He looked me up and down and said, approvingly, "Damn, you've been doing your homework."

"Go shit in your stupid fucking hat," I replied.

He had the nerve to tell me that I'd hurt *his* feelings by disappearing.

I countered that my hurt eclipsed—nay, *engulfed*—any hurt he could possibly feel, and that he had knowingly toyed with me for his own enjoyment. And that if I ever got around to therapy, it would take years for me to recover. Beads of sweat formed on my forehead. I shouted and hopped up and down like Rumpelstiltskin.

He was quiet for a moment. *At last*, I thought. *He grasps my suffering. He's overcome with guilt and regret.*

"So are we gonna fuck or what?" he asked.

I won't say what happened.

I still hadn't exactly gotten around to therapy when I visited Jen in San Francisco—where all Camden grads moved—a year later. It would be the last time I saw Booth. He and I spent twenty-four hours together. He showed me the city on the back of his Vespa and took me to a concert at the Fillmore, where

we got in for free because he "knew" the girl at the ticket counter. That night, we went back to his place and, of course, we
fucked.

The next morning, I woke him up and asked if he could take
me back to Jen's. He was living in the Haight, and Jen lived in
the Mission District, and I didn't know the city very well, having been in San Francisco all of forty-eight hours.

"I can't. I have a lot of things to do today," he told me, and
rolled over.

And so I walked home, scratched and bruised, again. This
time, it didn't ruin my mood, even when I stopped to ask someone for directions and she told me, "Oh no, you can't possibly
walk that far." *Lady,* I wanted to say, *you have no idea how far I
can walk.*

Head Lice *Lynda Barry*

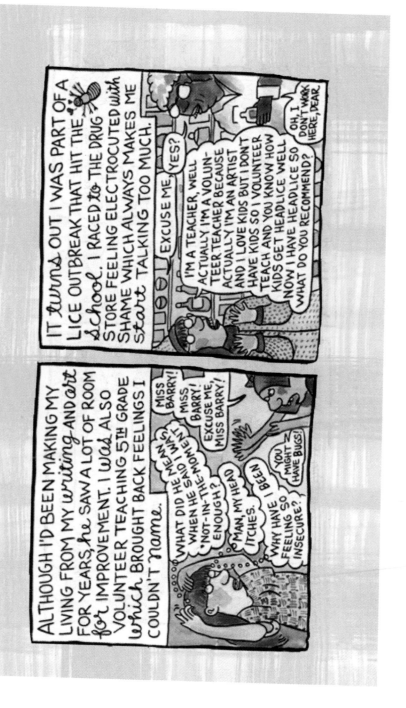

Why Won't You Just Love me?

Emily Flake

WHEN I WAS 20 I FELL IN LOVE WITH A DUDE. LET'S CALL HIM "K" THROUGH HIS COMIC STRIP.

HOLY CRAP THIS GUY'S A GENIUS—

I GOTTA MARRY HIM LIKE RIGHT NOW

USED-NEW

LUCKY FOR ME I WAS A MEMBER OF A STUDENT-RUN ART GALLERY AND IT WAS MY TURN TO PICK A SHOW.

I KNOW! I'LL GIVE HIM A SOLO SHOW!

THEN I WON'T SEEM LIKE A CREEPY STALKER FAN, I'LL SEEM LIKE...LIKE A SEXY BENEFACTOR!

ETHICS, CURLING UP AND DYING ON THE FLOOR

I SCREWED UP MY COURAGE AND CALLED THE PAPER TO GET HIS CONTACT INFO (I'M SORTA OLD SO THIS WAS BEFORE YOU COULD JUST GOOGLE THAT STUFF).

NO, NO, I'M NOT A CREEPY STALKER— I WISH TO OFFER HIM A GALLERY SHOW.

SO WE MET, I SET UP THE SHOW, EVERY-THING WAS FINE AND I WAS KEEPING IT MORE OR LESS PROFESSIONAL—

AT THE OPENING...

SO, UM... YOU WANNA COME TO MY BIRTHDAY PARTY?

WELL SURE—

TOTALLY INAPPROPRIATE SLUTTY DRESS

(WHILE BECOMING CONVINCED THAT THIS GUY WAS INDUBITABLY THE ONE)

BUT OF COURSE AFTER THE SHOW "PROFESSIONAL" WENT RIGHT OUT THE WINDOW.

THE REST OF THAT CONVERSATION DID NOT GO AS I'D PLANNED

I FOUND HIS LOGIC FAULTY.

AFTER A WHOLE LOT MORE BOOZE I WEASLED MYSELF AN INVITATION TO HIS APARTMENT, LIKELY BY CLAIMING TO BE TOO DRUNK TO DRIVE (CERTAINLY TRUE BY THEN)—

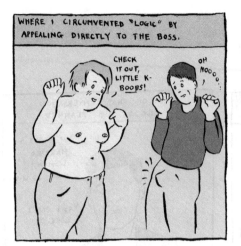

Dear Ugly, Dear Fatso

Patty Van Norman

Dear ugly,

I will Never love you

Never

I am going to california

to my ugly

Dear Fatso

You are Fat and ugly and DumB

You do not Love me at all

Just Like the Movies

Pasha Malla

Over his career as a film actor, the American novelist Ethan Hawke has appeared in two Richard Linklater pictures set in France. In the first of these, his character, a writer, meets a beautiful young Frenchwoman (played by Julie Delpy) on a train. They spend the day together and maybe fall in love a little bit, and then Ethan Hawke goes off wherever he has to go on another train, away. Then there is a sequel: ten years later the writer is back in France, promoting a novel he has written about his last visit, and Julie Delpy's character appears at his book launch. Then they fall in love for real. I assume. I've never seen either of these movies.

In the spring of 2006 I broke up with my girlfriend, Lisa. My stepmom was fighting lung cancer, I was being tested for multiple sclerosis, and the grant that paid my job ran out. I dealt with these things first with beer, and then in June I ran away to France.

Two years prior to that summer, like Ethan Hawke, I had met

a beautiful young Frenchwoman on a train. Originally from Paris, she was staying for a few months in Montreal, where the train was heading and I also was living. Her name was Lolita.

But this Lolita was not a thirteen-year-old nymphet: she was a children's author with a book coming out from a Quebec press. And while she didn't seem averse to chatting with me, I had recently gotten together with Lisa, who lived in Toronto, so when the train arrived in Montreal and Lolita gave me her number and suggested we go out for drinks before she moved back to France, I didn't call her.

At some point Lolita returned to Paris, and my long-distance relationship with Lisa picked up enough speed that the following autumn I moved to Toronto so we could be together. Then Lisa started talking about moving in together, planning for the future, buying a house. When we'd been living in different cities, things had been fun: we'd hook up every few weekends, drink our faces off, and nurse our hangovers with sex. But now I was facing a real relationship and, suddenly, fantasies of that mysterious girl from the train began to rear up again—fantasies that were exciting and international and often appropriated scenes from arty French movies.

Right around Valentine's Day, Lisa and I broke up. Soon after, my stepmom's health began to decline sharply, and I started developing symptoms that seemed like a checklist for any number of horrible ailments: constant buzzing in my hands and feet, shakiness, fatigue, blurry vision, you name it. An array of doctors ran blood tests and brain scans and, for some reason, made multiple jabs at my prostate. At the same time, my job started looking as though it might be running out of funding.

As springtimes go, this was no joyous leap toward the sunny days of summer.

By March it seemed likely that my stepmom would need a transplant to fix her decimated lungs, and I went to Montreal to visit her and my dad. Wandering the city one afternoon, I stopped in at a bookstore, where greeting me at the front door was a children's book, newly released and prominently displayed, written by a certain Lolita. I raced home to e-mail the publisher to pass my congratulations along to the author, whom I was pretty sure I'd met once but likely didn't remember me.

A few days later, back in Toronto, I got a reply from Lolita: why had I never called her? She was living in Montreal again. We decided to get together on the Thursday evening before Easter weekend, when I would be back in town to see my family. Lolita would be returning to Paris a week later, this time for good. But first, we would have our drink.

For years I've entertained the following fantasy: I'm living in a bohemian sort of apartment with a girlfriend whose looks fall somewhere between French movie star Anna Karina and Audrey Hepburn. One day I emerge from the shower and make my way to our bedroom, with a towel wrapped around my waist. There my girlfriend is sitting on a mattress on the floor, smoking a cigarette. She glances at me standing in the doorway—dripping in my towel, unspeaking—and the look on her face is one of seething, absolute disdain. She blows a cloud of smoke at the ceiling and looks away. My soul withers. I realize that I have nothing. I realize that I am nothing. The fantasy is in black and white. It is totally pretentious and totally awesome.

This fantasy was on my mind for much of the Easter Thursday train trip from Toronto to Montreal. But what awaited me that evening was real life, and real life I tend to fuck up, so I invited some friends for a few predrink drinks to steady the ship. Except I predrunk a bit too much, and when Lolita appeared at the door of the bar—looking breathtaking, *smelling* breathtaking—and I rose to do that double-kiss thing, I stumbled and headbutted her off her feet into a chair.

Sensing potential disaster, my pals stuck around to finish their drinks. They were funny and chatty and compensated for my hopelessness as only good friends can. But then, on their way out of the bar, one of them leaned over to me and whispered, "You know she's got a boyfriend, right?" Apparently I had somehow missed this piece of information. Or ignored it.

But then my pals were gone. Left alone, Lolita and I ordered more drinks, and then more drinks. We talked about her writing: she was working on a sequel to the children's book, a novel about a woman who kills chickens, and a short story collection about her family—particularly her dad, who was some make of musician. I figured this meant that he played bass in the house cover band at some shitty roadside tavern with slot machines in the back—a "musician," sure.

Near the end of the night, after several more pints, finding out about this alleged "boyfriend" finally seemed possible. It turned out that, yes, there was a boyfriend—living with Lolita in Montreal, no less. But things were "not so good." Not so good! Not so good could be good.

Then the bar closed, so I walked Lolita home. Standing on her doorstep, I chose to read our awkward, protracted good-bye as pregnant with possibility—certainly not just me blocking the way, hoping for a good-night kiss. But the moment, if there had been one, passed. "Maybe I'll see you in Paris sometime," said Lolita, and slipped past me into her apartment, where her boyfriend was no doubt waiting.

That I ended up in France for the summer I'd like to say was coincidence. A cousin of mine had offered to let me stay in the nineteenth-century Limousin farmhouse she and her husband were converting into a ten-bedroom home. My health was tenuous, as was my stepmom's, and my work situation still looked bleak. But a neurologist I'd visited a couple of times seemed to think the trip was a good idea. "Part of how you're feeling has to be stress related. Get away, relax. The countryside will be good for you." Sure—but first, of course, I'd be flying into Paris and spending a few days with Lolita.

After our meeting, we had e-mailed. She would write and I would respond within hours, and then I would wait a week or two for her to get back to me. In her messages were often encouraging but confusing statements like, "We don't know one another at all. But sometimes you feel something that you can't explain . . . like those crazy cats staring at something in the air."

By this point, an oxygen compressor was all that was keeping my stepmom alive, but she had made the transplant list at Toronto General and, after making a temporary move there with my dad, was waiting for new lungs that would hopefully save her life. Meanwhile I'd received a small grant, and my symptoms, although still bizarre, didn't seem to be getting any worse. I rationalized the trip to France as an opportunity to work on my writing, suppressing any feelings that I might be abandoning my folks.

Then, a week before leaving, I lost my shit. One afternoon while checking my e-mail, I saw that Lisa was online. We hadn't talked since the breakup nearly four months before, but suddenly I was compelled to make contact. I told her about my stepmom, my health, my job, everything—except, of course, who I'd be visiting in France when I left seven days later. Naturally, Lisa was concerned, so I invited her over. Within minutes of her being in my apartment, I broke down. I wept long and hard, not even really sure exactly what I was crying about, while Lisa held me on the couch. I felt like a tool, but it was hard to deny the security of being with someone familiar and comfortable.

For the following week, Lisa and I saw each other every day. I tried to convince her that the moment in my apartment was a clear indication that we should get back together, but she was skeptical: with so much going on, how could I possibly think straight? I did my best to convince her that planning for the future was a good idea. But first I needed go to France—to clear my head, I assured her. And when the week was over, I left.

I arrived in Paris on the eve of the World Cup final between France and Germany, which Lolita and I had arranged to watch in Montmartre with some of her pals. I waited on a bench outside the Abbesses Métro, my hands shaking—either from nervousness or whatever weird shit was going on in my brain, I couldn't be sure. Fifteen minutes after the match started, Lolita pulled up on a scooter, unleashing her hair from her helmet like something out of a shampoo commercial, and then we made our way to her friends' place.

The apartment was crowded with cheering, drunk France supporters. Lolita and I huddled together in a corner, sharing beers, her hand occasionally brushing mine as we passed the can back and forth. But then Zinedine Zidane headbutted away the country's chances at victory, and everyone decided a visit to the bar was in order. Jet-lagged, I opted out and asked Lolita if we could hook up again the next day. "Where are you staying?" she asked. When I told her the name of my hotel, she shook her head. "That's a bad place," she said. "Tomorrow I will get you somewhere new."

Back in this "bad place," water stains on the ceiling and more suspicious stains on the sheets, I couldn't sleep—partly from nerves, but mostly because of French lovemaking (not my own). In the room next door a woman brayed "Oui! Oui!" while her partner rumbled "T'aimes ça? *T'aimes ça?!*" and their headboard rattled against our shared wall all night long.

The next day Lolita called me with instructions to meet her in Montparnasse at her mom's place, where she was staying. The apartment was like something out of the nouvelle vague: three floors stretching around a winding central staircase that culminated in a rooftop veranda overlooking the neighborhood. "Want to see my room?" she asked, and led me down a hallway to an open door, where the only object was Lolita's bed: a mattress on the floor.

We picked up the keys and walked over to Lolita's own apartment—directly across the cemetery—that she had been renting as a TV-commercial set to make some extra money. A luxury loft with twenty-foot ceilings, two walls of books, and a third of DVDs, it was unaccounted for until the next production company claimed the space. The bathroom was furnished in dark wood, with an ornate claw-foot tub of gleaming marble and brass. Through the kitchen window stood the Eiffel Tower, silhouetted against the horizon halfway across the city.

"My father bought this apartment for me," Lolita admitted. The musician? "Yes," she said, and then produced a DVD from her library. It was a live concert recording of someone named Renaud. Renaud is a grizzled-looking, hugely popular singer of socially charged rock anthems and gravelly voiced love ballads. (Think Bob Dylan fueled by Leonard Cohen's sex drive.) Remembering our conversation back in Montreal, I felt more than a little stupid that I'd passed off Lolita's "musician" father as some crappy nobody playing classic rock to drunks.

Over the next few days, Lolita met me whenever possible: for walks around Paris, for lunch, for supper, for drinks. When we weren't together I relentlessly checked my phone to see if she'd called. Usually she hadn't, and I avoided thinking about what she might be doing—and who she might be doing it with.

Despite my best efforts, I was still finding myself exhausted, muddleheaded and shaky, so in the evenings I would forgo hitting the town in favor of Internet cafés. I e-mailed my dad for updates about my stepmom's condition, kept tabs on the situation at work, and checked in regularly with Lisa. I wrote her effusively about our potential life together when I got back to Toronto but never made any mention of Lolita. What was to tell? We were just hanging out. Nothing had happened.

Four days after I'd moved in, Lolita called to say that a film crew would be shooting at the apartment on the weekend, so I'd have to split. Fine: my cousin was expecting me in Limousin anyway, and ostensibly I had some writing to do. For my last night in Paris, I took Lolita out for dinner and then drinks. Having brought only flip-flops to France, that afternoon I bought a pair of complicated, angular shoes in Les Halles. During dinner I found myself tucking my feet under my chair, attempting to hide one shoe underneath the other, feeling absurd.

At midnight we started heading back to Montparnasse. I invited Lolita back to my place—or her place, whatever—for tea. We talked about writing, and she asked to read something of mine. I gave her a story (about, among other things, a couple breaking up), which she put in her bag and promised to get to later.

"So," I asked casually, "what's going on with your boyfriend?"

"We're on a break," she said.

This seemed like a window.

"And what about us?"

"Us?"

"Me and you."

"You and me?"

"Us."

"Us," she said, eyes narrowed, taking a sip of her tea. "Pasha, you're my friend from the train. We're friends."

Friends. "But," I said.

"Did you think we were going to get together?" I tried not to read her smile as mocking.

"I thought . . ."

"It's a nice story," Lolita explained, standing, ready to leave. "But it's not real life."

When I arrived at my cousin's place in Limousin, I was greeted with mayhem. While the surrounding countryside was serene, consisting mainly of farms with cows clustered chewing in their pastures, the house was in shambles. Piles of lumber were strewn around the yard, men in hard hats milled about constantly, and I woke up every morning to hammering, always hammering. I did my best to block out the noise by sequestering myself with my laptop in the shuttered dining room. Meanwhile Lolita was at a beach house in Saint-Tropez, working on her book—without e-mail, impossible to contact.

I thought about how she'd left me, as a friend, and wrote embarrassing notes to myself to figure things out. Eventually, I came around: she was right. We were friends from the train—strangers, really—and anything else was fiction, the stuff of movies and books, with no connection to real life. Real life was waiting for me in Toronto. Real life was Lisa.

Via e-mail, I started trying to convince Lisa to come over to France. We'd travel around, it'd be fun! Another cousin needed a house sitter in Basel, Switzerland, while she and her family were on vacation; I figured Lisa and I could stay there and try to get things back to where they'd once been. Lisa remained skeptical, admitting the offer was attractive but doubting it was the right thing to do. "But you can argue with me," she wrote. So I did. I employed my best techniques of persuasion—or manipulation, whatever. One day she called me, and I assumed I'd helped her reach a decision.

"I think this is a bad idea," she said.

"The trip?"

"No. Everything."

Lisa went on to say that we'd obviously broken up for a reason, and it was better to leave things alone. But this time she didn't mention that my situation—with my stepmom, my health, my work—might have influenced my thinking. I listened, agreeing, realizing for the first time in weeks how exhausted I felt. Then there was nothing more to be said. Lisa hung up, leaving me with the sound of a chainsaw chewing through the beams of the barn next door.

A few days later I headed to Switzerland. Basel is a funny town with not a lot going on—a perfect chance to get to the work that I hadn't really done while in France. But, with my cousin and her family away, it was boring being alone in a place where I knew no one, and my writing still wasn't really happening. So, instead, I watched a lot of TV. One night I found *Doctor Zhivago* as the first half of a classic-movie double bill. I watched until the end, when the character named Pasha goes insane and ends up driving a train around the Russian countryside. Then the second movie started. It was *Lolita*.

I turned the TV off and sat there in the living room in the dark. It was August 1, Swiss National Day; in town fireworks were going off, people were cheering, music was playing. Need-

ing to get out of the house, I headed down to the Rhine, where
a boat laden with pyrotechnics was tracking back and forth,
getting ready to detonate its cargo. Crowds lined the banks of
the river, waving Swiss flags and sparklers, waiting for the show
to start.

Beside me was a young woman who was intermittently
checking her cell phone. From behind she could have been
Lolita: same dark, shoulder-length hair; same svelte physique. I
overheard this girl leaving a message for someone in American-
accented English, so when she was done I tried to strike up a
conversation.

"When do the fireworks go off?" I asked.

"Ten," she said, barely looking at me. Then she turned,
beaming, as a lanky blond guy with sparklers in either hand
came bounding toward her and into her arms.

The next morning I got an e-mail from my dad: lungs had arrived
and my stepmom had successfully received her transplant, but
it would be good if I could come back to Canada immediately.
Alone in Switzerland, the relief I felt about this summons ex-
tended far beyond my stepmom's well-being.

My emergency trip back to Toronto consisted of a flight from
Basel to Paris, a train to Limoges, and then a car ride out to my
cousin's house in the country to pick up my stuff; the following
day there would be another drive to Bordeaux, a flight to South-
ampton, a train trip to London, and then a final flight home. I
would be back on Canadian soil within thirty-six hours.

I was scheduled to arrive in Paris at seven in the morning,
and the train trip south would leave that afternoon. On the off

chance that she was back home, I e-mailed Lolita to let her know that I would be in town for a few hours, and that if she wanted to have lunch—as friends, friends from the train!—before I headed out, she could call me.

At the airport in Paris it was raining. I headed into town, hoping to wander around a bit—not waiting for Lolita to call, of course, just playing the tourist. By one thirty I'd heard nothing from her and assumed it was time to go on my way, so I took the Métro to Austerlitz and lined up to buy a train ticket to Limoges. As I got to the counter—*as I was handing my credit card over to pay*—my phone rang. It was Lolita, who had been trying to get hold of me all morning. She might be able to get away from work for an hour; could we have lunch?

I booked myself on the last train of the day, leaving at eight that evening, and walked over to the Jardin des Plantes, where we grabbed some sandwiches and sat near a bridge with a river underneath and a canopy of trees overhead.

Lolita took a few bites of her sandwich and started crying.

"I read your story," she told me, "about the breakup."

I held my breath.

"It was so sad, so real." Was it really? Then: "I'm going to break up with my boyfriend."

She went on to explain the reason for her split, but I wasn't listening. My thoughts derailed to renegotiating having to leave the country now that Lolita was single. I couldn't stay—but maybe she would just have to come to Canada, the obvious next step in our own story.

We strolled the gardens together until it was time for Lolita to go back to work. I failed to ask about her coming to Canada or what the breakup might mean for us, so when we went to say good-bye, there seemed something unfinished. Apparently Lolita felt it too: She wanted to see me again before I left.

"Can we meet at seven for a beer at the train station?"

Yes, we could. Yes.

I decided to kill two hours at the nearby Institut du Monde Arabe, a gigantic, modern place with cabinet after cabinet of relics from around the Muslim world. An hour before closing on a weekday, I was pretty much the only person in the museum and trailed absently from room to room, checking the time every five minutes.

While I was hovering over some parchment verses of the Koran, one of the security guards, clearly as bored as I was antsy, came up to me. Upon discovering that I was from Canada, he grew animated, wanting to know why I was in Paris. I told him about Lolita.

"The daughter of Renaud!" he exclaimed. "My friend, you have to make this work."

"Yeah, I know, but I have to go back to Canada."

"No, you can't go to Canada—not yet. You can stay at my house. My wife will understand."

I explained that I really couldn't, that family duties required me home.

Dejected, the security guard took me by the shoulders. "My friend," he said, "you have to go for it, sometimes, in life."

With this stranger's words ringing in my ears, I made my way over to the pub by Austerlitz station where Lolita and I would be having our drink. I was ready to go for it. I never do, and the one time I had, it had backfired. But this time I would succeed. The security guard told me so.

Lolita showed up on her scooter and we ordered beers. For some reason, my hands weren't shaking at all; the constant buzz in my feet was little more than a dull hum.

Our beers came and we drank, meeting eyes over our glasses. Lolita put her pint down.

"You know," she said, "I've been thinking I'd like to come to Canada to see you."

"Oh, yeah? When?"

"Now. Today. I want to come with you now."

"Right now? Like on the train with me, then fly back to Canada?"

"Yes."

"You can't," I said.

"What?"

"You can't. I have family stuff. So not now. But later, yes. Definitely later."

My train was about to leave, so we raced across the street to the station. On the platform, Lolita and I stood for a moment, eyes locked.

"Well, good-bye," I said, and went in for the hug.

Lolita hugged me back, and it was fine, and then I went to get on the train—except I'd forgotten to punch my ticket. The conductor pointed to the end of the platform. "Hurry," he said, "the train's leaving in one minute."

So I ran, I ran down the platform waving my ticket in my hand, and Lolita turned to see me running, and I ran into her arms, right by the ticket validating machine. You probably think you know what happened next—but you've seen too many movies with the kiss and the steam engine puffing clouds all around and a blast from the train whistle and the conductor hollering "All aboard!"

What actually happened was that I reached over Lolita's shoulder, slid my ticket into the machine, and explained, "I forgot to punch my ticket." That was it. I pulled away, waved, and got on the train.

Sitting on the train as it eased out of Austerlitz station, I realized my mistake and sent a frantic text message: *I should have kissed you, shouldn't I.*

A few seconds later, Lolita's reply came back: *Ideally.*

At home in Toronto, my stepmom was doing okay—out of the ICU and into a regular bed in the hospital, very close to breathing on her own. But, shamefully, I still felt empty. Not only had I failed to make my fantasy come true, I'd also let the real relationship I had back home slip away.

I made one last-ditch effort. In the movies sometimes this happens: all seems to be lost and then the hero does something cute and endearing and the girl comes around, and then there is an airport reunion with tears and soon enough they are doing it to violins on a rooftop and there's a sunset and everything's amazing.

Lolita's birthday happened to be a few days after I arrived in Canada, so I sent her a quirky package: a Mad Libs, fill-in-the-blanks sort of letter, the requisite mix CD, and a letter of my own, which included an offer to pay for her flight—right away!—to Canada. And then, yes, I included the DVD box set of *Before Sunrise* and *Before Sunset*, the Ethan Hawke movies of serendipity and French love that I've still never seen.

For weeks I heard nothing. I followed up the package with multiple e-mails. No response. Finally, weeks later, a reply arrived.

Feeling "unloved and unable to love," Lolita had gone back to Saint-Tropez; she hadn't received my package until well after her birthday. She said it was nice to return to so many e-mails and a parcel of presents, but then added that "it was a bit too much."

The e-mail went on to say that I was and had always been far more "into it" than she was, and that "scared" her. There was no mention of my invitation to come to Canada. Beyond a curt thank-you, neither did she rave about how charming she'd found my package of gifts. The e-mail ended with the words "Good luck with everything."

Nearly two years have passed since my botched French love affair. Typing these words has been a trying process. Not emotionally, of course, as by now there's more than enough distance to see how goofy and misguided the whole business was. No, the tough part has been remembering what actually happened, beyond fantasies and plots from movies I've never seen.

When I first got back to Canada, I told this story so many times that I began to wonder if I was just creating a series of embellishments upon embellishments, each version of the story distorting the last. But then the story faded away: my health got better, my stepmom was doing okay, a publisher decided to publish my first book. I started dating someone who, while maybe a bit reminiscent of a young Geneviève Bujold, is very, very real. And if our relationship has ever made her "scared," I'd hope it would only be because I was growling weird stuff in my devil voice while we were watching *The Texas Chainsaw Massacre*.

So all this—the meeting on the train, the trip to France, the shameful return to Toronto—I look back on now as little more than a script for a film that never got made. (No big deal: projects get killed all the time!) The spring of 2006 was a period in my life when I was a little lost, a little overwhelmed, and it was nice to sink myself into fantasy. That things didn't work out proved to be the best way, for me at least, that the story could have gone. And besides, if I ever want a story with a happy ending, I can always rent those Ethan Hawke movies—he and the Frenchwoman *do* get together in the end, don't they?

Scout's Honor

Amanda Stern

At the turn of the twentieth century, a group was created to promote the social welfare and moral character of young men by plying them with knives and matches and setting them free in the wild. They call themselves the Boy Scouts of America and their motto is "Be Prepared." A proud and overzealous bunch, the scouts defend against nonscout infiltration through a series of exclusive codes. There is a Scout Law, a Scout Slogan, a Scout Sign, a Scout Handshake, a Scout Salute, a Scout Promise, a Scout Oath and a Scout Motto. It was only after camping with a fully grown Boy Scout that I wondered whether memorizing all those signals prevented the boys from absorbing other important information, such as the bit about moral character and being prepared.

After two months of dating, Billy asked me to go camping in Washington State. "What could be more fun?" he asked. Being stuck in an elevator on a holiday weekend, diagramming sentences in braille, leading the Janjaweed through a series of trust exercises . . . all that, I thought, could be more fun. It was

August, and uncertain about my off-season commitment, Billy was simply where I was "summering." At that moment we were sitting on my bed, and I watched as he nervously tugged out puffs of batting from a vintage quilt I stole from my mother's house. As I stubbed out a half-smoked cigarette, I explained that joining him was impossible. I was sorry, but I couldn't go.

"Why not?"

"Uh—because I don't want to?"

"You have to go camping at least once in your life."

"I already have!"

"When? Where'd you go?"

"I made bed forts when I was little."

"That doesn't count."

I propped a pillow behind my head. "I'm not going."

"Don't you like nature? Don't you want to sleep outdoors?"

I relit the cigarette, took a movie star drag.

"No, that's why I rent an apartment." I let smoke french its way into my nostrils.

"You'll be amazed at how beautiful it is. Don't you want to have this experience with me?"

I sat up, propelled by a realization. "*Winged Migration* is playing at the IMAX. We'll get blankets and bug spray! My treat!"

"What are you worried about?"

I stubbed out the cigarette. I was trying to quit and allowed myself twenty puffs per day. Seven left.

"Here's a hint. It rhymes with death."

Fear of my own death insulted him. He stood, thrown upright, because defending one's honor cannot be accomplished sitting down.

"I was a Boy Scout!"

His raised voice steadied into the cinematic bravado reserved for hostage-negotiation movies starring Robert Duvall.

"I'm an expert camper. How could you be afraid? You'll be with me. I can tie and untie any knot. I know what I'm doing."

"Will you be securing me to a tree with rope?"

He sat back down and watched as I stuffed the batting back into the quilt.

"You know what? Never mind. I'll go by myself."

"You'd camp by yourself? Is that safe?"

"Well, if *you* don't come I guess that's my only alternative."

Did this mean I was responsible for *his* death?

The next night, he flexed the flaccid tarpaulin in the living room of his Brooklyn apartment.

"Excuse me, sir, but I think your tent has an erection."

He moved toward the tent and crawled inside. His head popped out of the opening.

"If you make friends with it now, you won't be afraid of it then." It wasn't the tent I was afraid of, but his gesture was so thoughtful I crawled in next to him.

That night we slept in sleeping bags. He set his noise machine just outside the plastic dome, filling the living room with the soothing patter of light rain. I slept deeply, comforted to be dry while the simulated rain fell around me as a sound effect. I found myself reconsidering my iffy commitment to him, and to camping. Based on one night sleeping in a tent on the living room floor of a rent-stabilized one-bedroom apartment in Clinton Hill, Brooklyn, I realized that camping might not be as hard as I thought. Perhaps it *was* recreational. His consideration won me over. I am a sucker for gesture, which, it turns out, is different from action. Setting up the tent made me say yes.

He forwarded me links to trails. I didn't know what a switchback was and couldn't visualize elevations in terms of floors much less thousands of feet, so I investigated trail routes in the Cascade mountains based on camping taxonomy I could understand. All trail links I sent Billy were preceded by the words *very easy*. While I wanted to be laid-back about the situation, I also wanted to make certain that I had conveyed my message clearly. I wrote him an e-mail so we'd have something in writing.

Dear Billy,
This is to confirm Amanda Stern's fear of:

Camping
Mountains
Darkness while on a mountain
Darkness while camping on a mountain
Darkness
Killers
Rapists
Camping in the vicinity of killers and rapists
Bugs that are larger than my fingernail
Bugs
Fingernails
Animals that are not dogs

Dogs
Exercise
Climbing
Shortness of breath
Trail mix
Sleeping when it's too quiet
Sleeping when it's too noisy
Sleeping when it's too dark
Sleeping

His response was affirming and, in my mind, legally binding.

Dear Amanda,
Don't worry. You are in good hands.

I believed him.

I looked through the worn parts of clouds as the plane glided over the mountains I would soon be camping in. I was blindsided by my own sense of wonderment, overcome with nostalgia for something I hadn't known to miss: Mother Nature. Could it be that leaves and dirt really *were* restorative?

Our first order of business in Seattle entailed driving to REI, the camping store. In the car he began calling me Slugger the Sly Little Fox. At the store, after grabbing a canteen and some trail mix, my nickname was reduced to just Fox. He never called me by my real name again. Sometimes I wonder if he had just forgotten it. Billy led the way to the Pinnacle, the tallest freestanding indoor climbing structure in the world. With over a thousand climbing holds, its surface resembled a tree in need of Accutane.

"I meant to add this to the list of fears," I said.

"Fox, it's super fun. I promise."

Well, I did like how toned the arms of the female mountaineers were, but I wasn't certain what the point was.

"Is this really necessary?" I asked, picking at the nicotine patch on my arm.

"Stop being so afraid." There was irritation in his voice. A square-shaped woman with an underbleached upper lip put a harness on me and clipped on a rope. I laughed when she introduced herself as my belayer. When she didn't join me in merriment, I understood she wasn't making sex jokes. She was not a cutup.

"Please, do not let go," I said to my belayer. I implored in a tone of grave consequence, but it sounded thin and stringy, like tinsel.

She smiled and said, "I won't," and then she did something that was very out of character for a person whose character I did not know. She handed the rope to Billy.

"Don't worry," she said. "I'm sure you're in good hands."

"Um, how do you do this?" I asked Billy, expecting a short tutorial, a lesson, some rah-rah for Team Fox, but he just stood back holding the rope, looking irritated.

"You just climb, Fox. It's not math."

Somewhere along the way, from the airport to the Pinnacle, Billy abridged not only my name but his patience. I grabbed on to a peg and began to climb. I was actually having a bit of fun, once I discovered that I was innately very climby. But then I made a novice mistake and looked down.

I could feel the quick breeze as I fell through the air, the crush of ground against my face as I landed on it. The unnatural way my arm would bend as it broke. I struggled for continuous breath.

"I need to come down."

A couple of people stared, but Billy just smiled, looked up, and yelled, "Go higher!"

"No, no. Really, I'm ready to come down now. Please let me down."

"You have too many fears, Fox. You need to face your obstacles!" I did not want to introduce Billy to panic attacks by actually having one.

"Billy, I'm not kidding. I need to come down immediately." But Billy was not making a move to lower me.

"You're not even up high. I can reach the top in seconds. Challenge yourself. Show me you can go a little higher, then I'll let you down." The idea that Billy might teach me something was becoming questionable.

Even my heart wanted down because it spasmed—a cockroach trapped under Tupperware. Sweat dripped off my face and fell fifty feet below me. My arms ached, weakening from white-knuckling the climbing pegs. My legs shook from terror and shame. No one explained what would happen if I let go. Was he expecting me to overcome my fears *right now*?

"Do you promise?"

"Yes, I promise. Just go a little higher. You're stronger than you realize. You just have to believe. Keep the faith." He was beginning to sound like a tough-love counselor at a Christian-themed fat camp. I turned and faced the climbing wall. I was

so close to it we were practically frenching. My throat ached
at the Adam's apple from gripping my tears. I grabbed the rung
above me and pulled myself up so that my straightened arm
bent a mere forty-five degrees. I quickly lowered to my original
position.

"There! I went higher. Let me down now, please!"

"That didn't count!"

"Billy, let me down. Now!" I shouted.

He took his time to consider. I felt like a visitor in my body,
my skin a material I could feel without touching.

"Okay, but next time you have to go even higher, okay?"

"Okay."

"Promise me," he called up.

"I promise!" I screamed, too overwhelmed to process the
words "next time."

The rope finally lowered and I floated down. On the mat, my
legs felt too weak to hold me, so I sat, head between my knees.
It took hours until I felt normal again, until I couldn't feel every
single one of my heartbeats. And all the rests in between.

"That was really scary," I said.

"We have to toughen you up," he said. "That was pathetic."
Some coach he was. Ten bucks Bela Karolyi didn't speak to
Dominique Moceanu this way. I felt homesick for the first time
in years.

We were supposed to wake early the next morning and head
out. That night in bed, something in me didn't feel right. I
couldn't put my finger on it, but it felt like . . . distrust. I was
confused. Was there a difference between the things he said
and the things he did, or was it just me? Was human communi-

cation one more thing for the tally of all I couldn't understand? I tried to push my doubts away. *He's so good! He wants you to overcome your fears! What other person wants that for you?* But I didn't want to follow through with the trip and I woke him, crying.

"I can't go, Billy. I can't do it."

"Yes you can, Fox. You can do anything."

"I couldn't climb the wall."

"We're not climbing a wall tomorrow, we're just going on a little hike. It's not a big deal."

"Will you stop if I need to?"

"Of course."

"And you will go at my pace?"

"There's no other pace I'd want to go." He soothed me with niceties and vowed we could always turn back. The fist of doubt released. He did understand me; he was good. REI was a fluke. He was jet-lagged, hungry. He said all the right things and I was persuaded. Especially by the part about turning around.

The next morning rain pitched down in inconsistent gushes. The sudden and exaggerated downpours reminded me of a low-budget movie set. I imagined a prop master tipping an awning of water over all of Seattle. I considered being embarrassed by my late-night tearful confession but I was too elated for humiliation. Camping was canceled! When I emerged from the bathroom, I was surprised to find Billy dressed and carrying our backpacks toward the front door.

"What are you doing?"

"Packing up the car."

"It's pouring," I said.

"By the time we get to the base of the mountain it'll have stopped." I was dumbfounded. But when we got to the base of the mountain the rain had not stopped. I turned to him, faking disappointment.

"Another time, I guess." I stayed buckled in and stared straight ahead trying to convince him we were still moving, but instead of going in reverse Billy opened the car door. A minute later the trunk hood popped. He knocked on my window, motioned me out.

"BUT IT'S RAINING!" I called from inside the car, refusing to roll down the window.

"WE'RE STILL GOING. IT'LL STOP ANY MINUTE NOW."

Reluctantly, I exited the car. Billy put a backpack on me and I tipped back, nearly falling over. At the time I weighed 101 pounds and so, it seemed, did my backpack.

"It's not *that* heavy."

So the backpack was lying?

He started out in front of me and I followed. We must have parked on the wrong side of the mountain because there was no entrance. The only way to get on the mountain was to literally climb it, which, to my horror, was what Billy had begun to do.

"Billy?"

He raced up the side of the mountain, moving as easily as he did on flat ground. When he stood on the first semiflat landing, he towered a good ten feet above me. I looked up at him.

"This doesn't look like the trail I chose."

"It's not," he said. "That trail was too easy."

Too easy was the point. I looked back at the car and cursed

myself for not knowing how to drive. I looked back at the mountain, trying to find the holds, but they weren't apparent like on the Pinnacle. Then I stretched my arms up, so he could pull me, but nothing took hold. He was gone. I grabbed the burl on a knotty branch and pulled myself up in the pouring rain, wearing a backpack that was as long and heavy as a ten-year-old boy. I grunted; I heaved. I used every last reserve of strength and energy I had. Ten minutes later, when I had finally scaled the very first steps of what would be a four-hour trek, I was so out of breath I had to sit down. But the knapsack was too heavy for sitting, so I leaned against a tree. Those ten minutes felt, at that moment, like the most physically accomplished I'd ever been. I was ridiculously, ludicrously proud of myself. So naturally, it was time to go home.

Billy was already scampering up the first of the very steep switchbacks. The first of twenty-five. For the three of you who are as unfamiliar with switchbacks as I was, let me draw you a verbal picture. A switchback is a sharp reversal of direction in a trail, a 180-degree zigzag turn that ascends a steep incline. With consistent torrents of water pouring down on me, turning an already heavy bag heavier, man-made switchbacks, to me, suddenly felt personal, racist even. Billy brought me to an anti-Semitic mountain! After the first switchback, I was completely without breath, so without breath that when I stopped to catch it, I feared my last real breath was gone for good. I was a twenty-puff-a-day smoker who did not exercise. This trip was a very bad idea. Billy continued on.

"I'm . . . out . . . of . . . breath. Can . . . you . . . just . . . wait a minute?" I called. He stopped and turned, annoyed.

"You're already out of breath? We've been climbing for five minutes." Fifteen actually, but I measured time sequentially as related to the dimension within which I traveled, whereas Billy seem to regard time as an illusion. So, I was hiking with a Sophist.

"I need some water."

"Already?"

"Yes, already."

He looked at the canteen and then at me as if he were making Sophie's choice.

"Just a sip. We don't have a lot."

I tipped it back and when the first drops hit my tongue he pulled it away.

"Don't drink it all!"

"I barely got any."

"We need to save it for later."

I was in his hands now and I did not like what they were doing. I turned around but couldn't see the car anymore. There were too many ways to leave—I'd get lost trying to navigate my way out. I had little choice but to follow Billy's lead. His endurance seemed superhuman and his expectation that mine match, supercilious.

We scaled another switchback and then another, and when I was nearly in tears, I stopped again.

"I thought this trail was easy."

"It *is* easy," Billy said. "*I'm* not out of breath."

"I need to rest."

He rolled his eyes. "You just rested."

"I need to rest again."

His impatience with me was becoming frightening. What happened to last night's aphorisms, to the overtures of understanding? What happened to *turning back*? Here I was, completely at the mercy of a person who, let's face it, I didn't know very well, but who was my sole source of survival. I feared the one person I was relying upon. And that realization made me come down with a slight case of Stockholm syndrome. It wasn't identification that I felt, it was concession. We were too far into the mountain for me to take any independent action. My free will had been usurped. I felt abducted. On we went. At points he was so far ahead of me, I couldn't see him and I'd dovetail into minor panic. I was relieved when he came into view; he was annoyed to have been kept waiting.

"Can you go a little slower?"

"Can you go a little faster? What's up with your endurance? Let's get to camp already. I want to set the tent up and get dry."

Our boots sank into the marshy grass, making sucking sounds each time we lifted our feet. We walked through a rock creek that was so slippery I had to crawl through it to reach the other side. There wasn't an elementary particle of me that was dry or warm. Changing into the clothes we carried on our backs became my sole reason for survival. As we scaled a slick terrain of mountain face, I could no longer feel my body. Billy pointed out small alien rock piles. *Blair Witch*, I thought.

"Cairns," he said.

"What are they?"

"To show people where you've been."

I stared at the piles of rocks and then up at the sky. *Com-*

munication! Perhaps a plane overhead would read these tonsil-sized stone clusters as distress signals, toss a rope ladder down, and reel me up. We passed hundreds of cairn piles as we crossed the slippery rock face, and I wondered how so many people enjoyed the treachery of this experience enough to stop and stone-pile about it.

During the next hour of flat trail hiking, it turned dark on us. I had starvation shakes, and when I asked Billy for some trail mix he hesitated before rationing out a small handful of nuts. There were almonds and raisins, cashews and macadamia nuts in there, even chocolate, but Billy managed to root out and offer me the worst kind of nut, the wet blanket of nuts. Walnuts.

We walked in quiet for the next couple hours, and when it was too dark to see, he pulled out his flashlight. We walked through a spotlight of rain until the light illuminated a seemingly endless surface of grass cratered with black marshy lakes. The topography of the land, the existential infinity of wet grass, the surreal atmospheric silence of high altitude, made me spacey. The land struck me as prehistoric, something we studied in sixth-grade Earth Science. Billy stopped walking.

"We made it."

"This?" I asked. I thought campsites, were, well, sights. I was under the impression that there would be other campers and picnic tables, not just dungy lakes and swamp grass. Worse, we were the only ones there.

He started hammering in stakes for the tent, and I took off my pack. The rain had become punishing and the darkness brought a biting cold. Once the tent was up, I went in and immediately opened my knapsack for dry clothes. I grabbed the jeans on top, but they were wet. The shirt under that, the sweater under that, my socks, underwear, bra, every single thing in my backpack was as sopping as the clothes I was currently wearing. I opened the pack with the sleeping bags: drenched.

"Everything's wet," I called.

He entered the tent. "Are you kidding?"

"Feel."

"Jesus Christ." He investigated his knapsack and then said, "I guess I didn't wrap them for the rain."

I was too run-down for tears. "What are we going to do?"

"Just put something on anyway, it's freezing. You'll get sick."

I swapped out my soaking wet pants for a new pair of soaking wet pants. Billy handed me the flask of whiskey.

"This will warm you up."

I did not drink it to warm up; I drank it to get drunk.

Once I was drunk I didn't mind that the tent was filling up with water. Or that I'd be sleeping in a wading pool. And after the flask was nearly emptied, it didn't bother me that there were things about Billy that seemed highly questionable. It didn't bother me, not just because I was drunk, but because I had Ambien. And I was not sharing. I washed an Ambien down with the whiskey, while Billy hovered in the rain, cooking our shared dinner—one cup of miso soup. I drank more whiskey; he drank what was left. It seemed the only thing dry on this trip was the bourbon. We unpeeled the wet sleeping bags and molded them back into their intended shape. We had drunken mountain sex and then I passed out.

I awoke in the middle of the night to cracks of life-threatening thunder, neon shards of lightning, and the fainting of a tree or three. I quickly returned to the battered dreams of Ambien sleep, and when I woke in the morning, it was still pouring. There was no sign it would abate.

"We have to get out of here," Billy said.

"Thank God."

I shoveled all the wet clothes into the knapsack. I didn't bother to fold or roll anything. I pushed everything into the knapsack like kale through a juicer. I wanted out—fast. Outside the tent, he placed the backpack on me.

"I'll catch up with you," he said.

"What? What do you mean?"

"Start down, I'll pack up and meet you on the trail."

"What? No way. I'm waiting for you."

"Fox, listen to me. I know what I'm doing here. I was a Boy Scout. Just start down and I'll catch up with you."

"I don't know how to do that, Billy."

"You just follow the path."

"What path? I don't know how to follow a path!"

Rain dripped down our faces. There was no way I could follow a path. Upon exiting the subway, I've played tourist while asking which way was north. Sometimes I add an accent.

Billy was aggravated and stomped toward the lip of the trail. I followed behind.

"How hard is it to follow a path? It's a path! A path is a path is a path!"

Learn about paths.

"Billy, I really don't think this is a good idea."

He scoured the ground.

"Hmmm, it must have washed away."

"What?" I was terrified. Not only did I not know where the path was, the path was now invisible.

"Maybe it wasn't here. Maybe it was over there?" He started walking in the opposite direction and I followed him. We walked fairly far and into a grassy cavity surrounded by high rolling hills. The visible landscape of the entire world from where I stood included only hilly drenches of green enclosed by the gray dampened dome of a showering sky. I felt like Brooke Smith trapped in that pit in *Silence of the Lambs*. Only, my pit was prettier.

"Wait here," Billy said, and before I could answer, he ran off.

I stood there, in the middle of an alien plain, alone, in the battering rain, silent, weighed down by a backpack and fear. I felt miniaturized, suctioned through a vent in Billy's tropical rain machine. He must have been gone twenty minutes when I realized that he was not coming back. My sense of reality began to slip and the familiar sense of dread calcified in my arteries. When he was gone about a half hour, I felt a strange type of re- solve about dying alone on the mountain. What a calm place to die. Probably very pretty when it wasn't pouring. But I worried my family wouldn't find my body and they'd go on pretending I was alive somewhere although I was already compost. When I saw his figure descend a nearby grassy hill, I cried with relief. He waved me over; he found the path. We walked in a direction that felt counterintuitive.

I stared at it, stared at it like a person new to planet dirt.

"I don't see it. I don't see how that's a path."

"It's a path. It's a goddamn path. Just follow it. Come on! Just go. Go!"

And then he gave me a push. I stumbled and fell into a tree. When I turned to glare at him, he was gone. I stared at nothing else but that path as I began my descent down the mountain. When it split into two segments, it took me minutes to choose one. When I found myself walking through an unfamiliar forest whose floor was covered in ingrown branches, I knew I chose wrong. I considered turning around, but when I looked behind me I could no longer see a trail. Everything was being washed away. I tripped over some twigs, scraping my knees but, even with the heavy pack, managed to stand back up.

I was lost.

The inhabitants of the world, it felt, had disappeared as well. Even in my deepest, most fearsome depressions, I have never felt as literally alone. I felt nothing else: not scared, panicked, hungry—just alone. That's when I began to sing. I was so outside myself I think I needed to hear myself to know I existed. Singing is not an area I am gifted in, but the mountain acoustics made me sound like Dusty Springfield. When I exited the unfamiliar forest, I spotted the cairns at the rock face and I finally felt something.

The rocks were slick with rain, and I made the lateral passage on all fours. I stopped partway through to catch my breath and then built my own cairn to show people I was here but would never ever return. There was no sign of Billy. I called for him but heard nothing. I thought about the *Brady Bunch* episode where Bobby and Cindy get lost in the Grand Canyon and come across Jimmy Pakaya, the Native American boy. All the Bradys go looking for them, yelling in drawn out calls:

"*Bobbbbby?*"

"*Ciiiiinnndddy!!!*"

In two days, that was the only time I smiled. When things began to look unfamiliar again, I reentered a state of complete dissociation, comforting since at least *that* was familiar.

The thunder picked up and I felt my pack grow heavier with water. I semicrawled across a creek, wading in to settle my hands on a rock, but I was pulled suddenly by the weight of my knapsack and fell in up to my waist. A sharp pain rose in my wrist. I ignored it, using both hands to push myself out of the creek, and that's when I felt the ominous tear. Somehow I managed to get myself out of the water, but I was still on the wrong side of the creek. And now that my wrist was injured, I couldn't crawl. I had no choice but to leap from wet rock to wet rock in order to get to the other side. I spent minutes concentrating before each jump, and after about thirty minutes, I made it to the other side. Still no sign of Billy.

By the time I got to the first switchback, I watched my legs as they walked. Who was moving them? I slipped and banged my tailbone on a switchback, so I stayed seated. I held my hurt wrist in one hand and used my feet to scoot myself down and around each steep zigzag. I had been hiking, crawling, hopping, and soaking for four hours and counting. When I slid down more than halfway, I saw something white in the distance. *Something!* I didn't know what it was, but it wasn't natural and I was assured by the promise of inanimate objects. The next time I looked up at the white thing, I realized it was the car. I had made it to the bottom of the mountain. I had done it. I pulled off the straps of my pack and kicked it over the side. It landed with a thud next to the car. I continued on my butt and slid off the deep incline.

Billy had given me the keys to the car in case I got there before he did. I let myself in and turned on the heat. I felt relieved and starving and shaken, and my wrist throbbed. It took four hours to walk down the mountain. Three hours later Billy arrived. When he got in the car I said something that to this day surprises me.

"Take me to a hotel right now and get me sushi."

"What?"

"You heard me. Take me to a hotel."

"Okay."

"Okay."

I stayed in the hotel bath for an hour, my bad wrist (fractured, I'd learn later) hung limp over the side. He ordered sushi and we watched bad television, and I was so overjoyed to be among processed and man-made materials I think I even looked at him. My body was weak and broken, but a tourist of newfound strength came to visit. I smoked, didn't exercise, but had climbed down a mountain for four hours alone. It would be months before I recognized I'd been alone when I scaled it.

When we arrived back in New York, I stopped speaking to Billy—briefly. When I told people about the trip, they were appalled, pointing out what I overlooked: he had put my life in danger. For some odd reason, the angrier people got, the stronger I felt, until soon I was awash in gratitude. I mistook that gratitude and misdirected it toward Billy. He was right about my fears. I had too many and he was helping me face them. Maybe he deserved another chance. Why couldn't my friends see what Billy saw? I needed to be deflawed. Didn't they also want me to overcome my fears?

Is that why I put up with it? Blindly followed him while feeling unsafe, because I wanted to believe he had my best interests at heart? Did I slog, trip, and fracture myself across country and up that mountain because I wanted the worst to occur and force him to prove his worth to me? Or worse, prove mine? Had I believed so much in the Boy Scouts myself—the codes and laws, oaths and ethics—that I didn't stop to consider that Billy learned those rules when he was eleven? Applied to the forest, Boy Scout skills may get you home, but applied to life and relationships they'll get you lost. On that mountain I saw the extreme limitations of Billy's camping skills, but it took me longer to see his limitations in the world. I followed him because I wanted him to turn around and take care of me, make me a better, stronger person, but he never did. I didn't yet realize that job was mine. So there I was in my early thirties, chasing a boy through the mountains, trying to get him to see me. Maybe in our own ways we were both eleven.

I believed in the words he said, and he believed that by virtue of having been a Boy Scout he was an authority, not just on the woods, but on me. But I also believed in my desire to find my mate—to find that one person who truly saw me, who wanted to push me forward to reach my goals. I wanted so badly to think I'd found that person that I overrode what I knew to be true. My instincts were right, but I ignored them. The climbing wall was boot camp. A push prehike so I'd keep up with him; wouldn't slow the pace. I don't think it was malice that drove him but self-interest. Still, on that mountain I learned something invaluable: there are two types of people. The first kind pretend to know things they don't, the second kind choose to ignore things they do. I'm the second kind.

Billy mistook his wish that I were different to mean that he knew how to change me. And while I didn't want to be changed, I turned my back on the metaphorical NASCAR flags waving to alert me. I gave him the chance to know better. Yet for all the Scout Oaths, Scout Slogans, Scout Handshakes, and Scout Vows he claimed to have mastered, for all his talk of overcoming my fears and pushing me to rise above them, Billy seemed truly capable of only two types of transport: flying me to Seattle and pushing me down a mountain.

This Guy Who Was My Boyfriend for Like Three Weeks

Dave White

"My boyfriend likes to _____."

The words that would complete the preceding blank spaces refer to a sexual act—one irrelevant to this story, one that would only shock and dismay any family members who happen to read it, even though the sexual act in question is pretty mundane. But it's what this guy said to me when we woke up the morning after the night we met. And by "my boyfriend" this guy meant me. And when I say "this guy" instead of the name of the man who said, "My boyfriend likes to _____," it's not because I care about his privacy. It's because I never knew his stupid, crazy, stalker-ass name. And if I ever did know it, then I forgot it moments after he told me what it was. That is because I was a little drunk at the time. Buzzed enough to do it with a stranger and then forget his name. It happens. And because every subsequent conversation I had with this guy involved him announcing, "Hey, it's me," or leaving a phone message in which he referred to himself as Boyfriend instead

of his actual name, I never actually learned what he called himself. So he's This Guy.

The sentence, "My boyfriend likes to _____," which
was This Guy's version of a good morning, is relevant for two
reasons. The first reason is that the sexual act he referred to,
the one I've self-censored, is, as I've mentioned, a really boring
one. But his voice decorated it with a sort of porny Christmas-
tree flocking and an icky sensuality that transformed him, in
that moment, into a man wearing a Dacron, thigh-length bath-
robe, holding a bottle of massage oil in one hand and a box
of strawberry-daiquiri-flavored condoms in another. He might
as well have just repeated the word *juicy* over and over. The
other relevant fact is that This Guy called me his boyfriend
after knowing me approximately eight hours. Not being very
hungover at all, I picked up on this, noting it as something of a
howling siren of insanity. But then I did nothing to drown out
the noise. I didn't say, "Hey, shut up, This Guy," which would
have been appropriate. I didn't shove him out my front door. I
just chuckled lightly and let it ride. And I paid for that. Juicily.

We met at 1:05 a.m. on a Saturday night in June of 1993,
in Fort Worth, Texas, at a gay bar called 651. It was called 651
because that was the street address. At 651 they played country
music exclusively, except for when there'd be a sudden break
in the George Strait and Reba McEntire and "Baby Got Back"
would boom from the sound system and everyone would line
dance. At 651 I drank Budweiser because it was weak. And I
didn't dance because the mysteries of the two-step eluded me,
even after living in Texas for a long time and spending count-
less hours at the mercy of women who tried to teach me to

lead. At this bar the men had to know how to lead *and* follow. So I just did a lot of not-dancing and a lot of Bud drinking and a lot of chatting to guys I wanted to bang. Fucking was pretty much the sole item on my 651 to-do list. And I assumed This Guy sensed it, because after staring at me a lot—I stared back a lot too, since he looked something like what would happen if Garth Brooks, in the fatter platinum-album years, could spontaneously generate little almost-clones of himself; it's a look I respond to with an almost certain immediacy—he walked over, looked me up and down, and said, "So. How big is it?"

It was like suddenly there was a Bold Gesture Contest happening. And he won. Not only was he good to look at, he had a nerve. And this particular bold gesture made me feel oddly safe. It let me know that we would not be romancing each other that night, something I didn't want anyway. Ever. Gay boyfriends were ridiculous to me. They were matching sweaters and ownership of little dogs with grand names. So This Guy was just the right thing at just the right moment. As a response, I volleyed back something equally bold that set up a very specific scenario that I hoped the two of us would enjoy. And then we drove back to my apartment and enjoyed that very specific scenario. And eight hours later he used the word "boyfriend" on me. Then he wanted to go to brunch. At first I blamed myself. It was my own fault for letting him fall asleep in my bed and stay the rest of the night. Had I kicked him out after finishing the previously agreed upon business at hand, the next three weeks would have been peaceful.

"Your boyfriend?" I said. And I laughed nervously. I laughed nervously like it was a sitcom where people with something to

hide laugh nervously. "That's great," I said. "You should bring
him over sometime."

"I mean *you*, Silly. We have a connection, you and me. I
can tell," he whispered. And he did it in that meaningful whisper way that people do when it's time to be all serious about
true love. That he referred to me playfully by the instant nickname Silly should have been deal breaker enough. That he did
so right after calling me his boyfriend should have been deal
breaker enough. But I just didn't care. I wasn't beer hungover. I
was fuck hungover. I'd gotten what I wanted and it was Sunday
and I was mostly thinking about how good some biscuits and
gravy would be right then. A flicker of a thought passed through
my brain about how he was dead-last wrong about our connection, but I was lucid enough to know that he was still in my
apartment and I wanted his exit to be a smooth one. Eventually,
he did that. And I left to go get the biscuits and gravy. Then I
spent the rest of my Sunday shopping for new records.

The following day I got home from work to find two messages on my answering machine from This Guy! He had gone
through the phone book and called all fourteen Dave Whites
in Fort Worth until he got the machine with the right voice on
it. He wanted more sex. And because I am male and have a
pulse and a penis I said yes. I chose to pretend that the Rupert
Pupkinishness of his behavior was not, in fact, strange at all.
I chose this course of nonaction because he had a nice chest,
the kind people refer to as strapping. And speaking now, from a
position of relative maturity more than a decade later, I realize
that body parts are no reason to consent to sex. I wish I could
explain that male psychosis. But I can't. We are dumb animals

and willing to ignore lots of shit from a potentially crazy person if we think the crazy person will suck our dick.

Afterward, he asked if I wanted to go to dinner. "I'll take you to the best restaurant in the city," he said. "On me."

This was difficult to turn down. I love food. I especially love free food. And I especially love free food after sex, especially-especially free food at fancy restaurants after sex. But my hungry gut said, "You've enjoyed two orgasms on a Monday before 8:00 p.m. Don't lead him into thinking you want more than physical attention." I declined the invitation, claiming I had work to deal with. In reality I had a date with a box of pasta and a jar of Ragu. I ate it while watching *The Slumber Party Massacre*.

Three answering machine messages were waiting for me when I got home from work on Tuesday:

1. Hi . . . It's me . . . Boyfriend . . . Just wanted to say I'm having a great time with you . . .
2. Hey-aaaayyyyy . . . just thinkin' about you, Cutie . . .
3. Oh my *God* my family is driving me crazy. One of my dad's ranches is in chaos right now and I'm the only one in my family who'll lift a finger to help out. I'm going to inherit my family's land and holdings someday but until then it's strangling my life. Help!

In moments of confusion, I turn to the clarity of cake. I'd baked a cake with the remainder of my record-shopping Sunday, for the comforting purpose of making sure that I had something chocolatey on a plate and a glass of milk waiting for me at home after work each day. I sat at my kitchen table and ate a piece while looking at a J. Crew catalog. Pink-cheeked college-jock models with no access to my phone number happily wore rugby shirts and tossed a football around on a beach. If they were actually here having cake too, they'd call me "buddy" or say "hey, man" or something that didn't have a teddy bear holding a Mylar balloon linguistically attached to it. None of them knew how to call another man Cutie.

The phone rang.

I was raised to pick up the phone when it's ringing. I come from the time just before answering machines and voice mail, and when a phone rang you picked it up. If it was someone you didn't want to talk to, you lied to that person to get her or him off the phone. And also having come from the time just before it was cool to be gay, I was very good at lying.

"Hey, Boyfriend, it's me."

"Hey . . . you."

"Did you get my messages? Sorry to fill up your answering machine but this day has just been, like, you can't even believe. I'm like, *gaaaah*, you know?"

"Oh yeah, absolutely . . . so . . . what's up?"

"Oh nothing. I'm just home from work now. Bored. Wanna hang out?"

"I really can't today. I'm meeting my mother for dinner."

"Oh cool, where? I can just show up and pretend it's a co-incidence!"

"Over in Dallas, actually. And my mother doesn't know I'm gay yet so that really can't happen."

"Oh, she'd never know I was gay."

I imagined This Guy greeting me at the imaginary restaurant, calling me Cutie while giving me the big gay kiss hello, then turning to my mother and saying, "Hey gurl!" while my mother, who knew that her son was gay and was, in fact, more excited about it than he was, going so far as to march with PFLAG in the annual homo parade, greeted him with open arms. Later, in This Guy's absence, she would confide in me that she thought he'd make a great "partner." They'd exchange phone numbers and start palling around, shopping for shoes and going to T.G.I. Friday's for happy hour. After getting sloppy on a pitcher of margaritas, he'd say, "You know, my boyfriend likes to _____."

The call ended with my promise to call him back later that night, a promise I had no intention of keeping.

Each day my answering machine would sour my return from work with at least one message in which This Guy reminded me that he existed and that he had thought of me several times that afternoon. A second message would accompany it, usually long and rambling, and would include his exasperation with his family for not understanding that *he only has two hands, gaaaah!* But then he'd remind himself and me of the gold-paved streets we'd walk someday as gay boyfriends, providing an accountant's-eye view of his family's immense fortune. I learned that there were three ranches, lots of cows, a sultan's wealth in horses, and some working oil-pumping thingies all the way out in the middle of nowhere in West Texas near Marfa. As for him, he had three cars, one Mercedes-Benz and two "Beamers," that he seemed to be forever taking in to be detailed. Soon he'd be making a trip down to Rio de Janeiro, just for the weekend, perhaps. I should come with him. He'd love to take me on many trips to lots of places. *His* spots. He was "dying" to show them to me for the first time. Travel was his "passion."

I picked up the ringing phone three more times that week, the travel to exotic locales theme alternating positions with the one about how rich his family was. Then he switched it up to how much he was falling for me. That this was taking place inside his brain struck me as the most mysterious of all, since I barely spoke during our time together. He didn't know a single detail of my life beyond that my just-out-of-college apartment was a too-small four hundred square feet and that I had too many records and books and not enough furniture. And he told me those facts about myself in his two visits to my place. Other than that, our face-to-face time was spent, as he said, "making love." He told me that calling it "fucking" was too impersonal. I wondered with what, beyond his making love and my fucking, he was falling in love. The phone calls always lasted at least thirty minutes. They would begin with me saying hello and then adding an uh-huh during the moments when he took a breath, until it was time to beg off and hang up. It wasn't a lot of work, really, and I became fascinated by how little of me he needed to sustain the conversation.

After the calls, while showering or doing dishes, I'd wonder about what would become of me if he wasn't lying. What if he really was rich and wanted to take me places? What if he wanted to buy me a couch? And pay off my student loans? And hook me up with cable and movie channels? What if? How many records could I buy with a weekly allowance in a job-free life as his sexual plaything? Could I become quietly convenient arm candy like Jane Russell and Marilyn Monroe in *Gentlemen Prefer Blondes*? Would he hire me as his assistant to be discreet about my sudden ubiquity? And could I see the property and bank account statements first, just to confirm that it was all true? Because if I was going to turn my life ass-inside-out and pretend to love someone for the cash and go live on the set of *Giant*, then I'd like it to be real and not just the fantasy of a compulsively lying barfly out to impress his latest fuck buddy.

On Saturday afternoon he showed up at my door. I don't know how long he waited for me, but when I came back from the supermarket he was there, hanging out in front of my apartment building. It was "our one-week anniversary" and he wanted to celebrate by "making love" on my living room floor. And again, the quality of being male is, at least with me, also the quality of being stupidly horny, so I let him in. After the brief anniversary sex, he helped me unbag my groceries.

"Someone likes Pop-Tarts," he said.

"They're my after-work snack when there's no cake."

"Keep snacking like that and this belly of yours is only going to grow," he said, patting it for emphasis, in case I didn't know where I'd left it last.

"Like yours?" I asked.

"I'm not fat!" he huffed.

"I'd say we're both a little chunky."

"I'm just stocky," he said. "My family is German."

"Really. Do you speak German?"

"Only to my dogs."

"Are they German shepherds?"

"Yes, in fact, they are. And I train them in German."

"How many are there?"

"I have five."

"Uh-huh. So if my belly gets bigger we're through?"

"No, but I can only have a boyfriend who takes care of himself. You have to respect yourself and your body. Don't you agree?"

"I sure do."

"Anyway, do you go to the gym? You should join mine and we could work out together."

I stopped answering the phone.

The messages on my answering machine became weirder and more frequent. And the later they occurred at night, the more slurred and drunken the monologues. He wanted me. I was intriguing. He wanted to show me Cher's Sanctuary catalog because it was "amazing," and I'm such a rock-and-roll guy that I was sure to love the stuff she had in there, seriously kind of goth, which is what I'm into, right? He was having second thoughts about me. I ate too much unclean, processed food. He didn't mean to call me fat even though I should really take better care of my body. Wouldn't it be a blast to work out together and then shower together at the gym? I was the best sex he'd ever had. He wanted more sex. I was ignoring him. I was probably busy with work. I should call him and let him know that I'm all right because he was getting worried about me. His parents were still driving him crazy, especially his father, with whom he had a horrible relationship because of the old rancher's religious objections to faggots, but he's the only son they can count on and he has to take care of them and they were going to leave it all to him and it could be just him and me on the rolling Texas hills, gaying it up ranch-style under the stars and then jetting off to Paris whenever we felt like it. Why didn't I call him back? What had he done wrong? When would we "make love" again? Why was I not returning his calls? Did I think I was too good for him? Why was I such an asshole flake? Why can't gay men ever let someone into their hearts? Why are we all the same?

By the end of the third week, the phone messages stopped. The last one was left on a Saturday afternoon. It was full of anger and hurt. I was, apparently, just like every other imma-ture faggot out there. I was throwing away a man of honor and integrity, one who could take care of me. I thought I was too cool for a "true country gentleman." I was instructed to have a nice life because what goes around comes around.

In the week following his final message, my relief was only occasionally stabbed by guilt. I could have handled him differently. I could have broken it quickly, with a promise of friendship that I'd never fulfill. I could have been honest and explained that I had no heart for loving another man because I was fresh out of the closet and selfish and not interested in being pushed into a career as a kept boy. I could have indulged his stories of superwealth and tried to trip him up in a jumble of contradictory lies. Or I could have gone to Rio with him.

The next weekend I went to see some bands over in Dallas with my friend Stephanie. We saw Jawbox and Yo La Tengo and had a really good time. After that I went to this bar in Dallas called the Brick and picked up this other guy who looked like a defensive end. We started dating. Once, This Other Guy even held my head while I vomited. It was his fault I vomited. This

Other Guy had begged me to go on a spinning ride at the State Fair of Texas, a ride I had no business getting on. The relationship progressed slowly and smoothly. Boyfriend status was a quiet given, implied but never spoken. In November I told This Other Guy I loved him. Two weeks later, the day after Thanksgiving, he broke up with me.

I Love You in Twelve Languages

Wendy Brenner

Oh hey, Wendy, it's Jim, and you know, I just wanted to say good-bye, and tell you that you're about the most untalented writer that I have ever run across. I mean these are like, just bullshit stories, I mean they're like little stories and they're bullshit. You know?

So, I hope you can get a leg up and get it together. You have some talent, you're moderately attractive, and, well, I hope you can put a sentence, a phrase, a paragraph together.

God bless you, you got an award. God damn you. Fuck you.

It was my ex-fiancé on the answering machine. We hadn't seen each other in more than a decade. He was calling from his home in Arizona; I stood in my kitchen in North Carolina, listening to his slow, sarcastic singsong voice. He spoke as if he were performing a little piece of theater.

The book of stories he was talking about—my first published book—was several years old. It wasn't like he was just now reading it for the first time. The book was *dedicated* to him.

I thought he must be joking. Then I realized he wasn't.

I knew why he was mad. I had been avoiding him, artlessly and obviously, for months. If I forgot to screen calls and accidentally picked up, I pretended to be in a rush and promised to call back. I *meant* to call him back. It was just hard to talk to him, for reasons I didn't want to think about. Things weren't going well for him; things were going very well for me.

Listening to his message, I felt a weird kind of relief: *Now I had a reason not to call him back.* He had provided us both with the reason—a gift.

I replayed the message for friends, evoking their outrage on my behalf, but I couldn't act like the injured party without feeling ridiculous and guilty. I even found the message perversely flattering—*some talent, moderately attractive.* Nicest thing anyone's said about me in ages, I joked. Put it on my tombstone.

I mean, really, who did he think I thought I was?

After his death a few years later, his sister told me he carried my book with him everywhere, whenever he traveled. *He was so proud,* she said.

When I was twenty, I wrote about Jim: *He literally doesn't sweat over things. His body barely has a scent of its own, beyond soap. He seems exempt from the rush of city living, but really his spirit gets by, undiluted, sneaking around in his slow body. He lets his spine hang in a lazy posture of truth, for anyone who cares to notice.*

When I was thirty, I wrote about Jim: *He was dark and aloof and moved precisely and slowly—very, very slowly. He seemed to exist in some other dimension, a slower, more hypothetical dimen-*

sion, perhaps a dream. Yet at the same time, he showed up more darkly than other people, as if his slight figure had been drawn in a richer, heavier medium. I'd never seen anyone so beautiful, or beautiful in such a way.

Maybe I am guilty of selective memory. But what other kind of memory is there?

When we met I was a senior in high school. Jim was twelve years older, owner of an independent theater and comedy club housed in an old Chicago church, a showcase for the edgy and experimental—Emo Philips, Judy Tenuta, Margaret Smith. Some boyfriend took me there on a date, and I went back on my own, became a regular, driving into the city to escape my parents' suburban house, the daily screaming fights with my mother. Jim's club did not have a liquor license, so I could always get in—they didn't card.

I don't remember the first moment I saw Jim. He was not flashy or loud, never broadcast that he owned the club, but preferred to lurk around the edges, mopping the floor, repairing spotlights, hanging taxidermy on the lobby walls. He dressed elegantly, moved gracefully, had impeccable manners and a beautiful, sarcastic voice. He himself did not perform comedy, though he was funnier than most of the comedians he employed. The audience would never get him, he said—he was too strange.

He was an artist, a writer, a fashion designer, an alcoholic, a bisexual, a former mental patient. I don't remember how or in which order I learned each of these things. His father, a top-level executive for a national bus company, had Jim committed to a mental institution when he was fifteen, because he was on drugs, because he wanted to be an artist, because he was gay—Jim cited all these reasons at various times. In the institution, he received electroshock therapy. When he was eighteen, he signed himself out and enrolled in design school. He had been engaged twice, never married.

Someone once observed about the author Jane Bowles that "the way she said things had the implication that we were all just like real people, but we weren't actually." Real people, the rest of us, seemed to live in one dimension, while Jim casually inhabited them all. When he looked at me, I felt he saw everything, things I didn't yet know were there. In his presence, my brain and life widened and deepened and broke open, broke free.

He hired me on as a girl Friday. That summer, and whenever I was home from Ohio on college break, I sold tickets, cleaned the public bathrooms, anything so I could keep hanging around him. Sometimes he bought me flowers, sometimes he suggested I stay over at his apartment, if he thought it was too late for me to safely drive home—little chivalrous gestures. I worshipped him, found him madly attractive, but could hardly imagine us as boyfriend and girlfriend. He was too different, too important. Plus I was busy sleeping with a million other guys—the main point of college, as I understood it.

When I brought boyfriends to the club to meet him, though, it never went well. He made them look idiotic just by standing next to them. He made faces behind their backs. Then I would immediately have to break up with them—sometimes on the sidewalk right outside the club door. He ruined later boyfriends, men he never even met, just by existing. I would imagine them meeting Jim, then have to break up with them. He once wrote to me while I was away at school that an ex of mine had invited him to go skydiving: *Somehow I just don't trust him in an open plane ten thousand feet up. If he wants to see whose dick is bigger why doesn't he just ask?*

When he asked me to marry him, it didn't seem odd that we weren't sleeping together. That he was gay, or bisexual, depending what time of day you asked (*I'm gay for you*, he once told me) seemed beside the point. We'd be like Jane and Paul Bowles, I thought. He loved to compare us to Calvin and Kelly Klein, or Richard Burton and Elizabeth Taylor. *The excerpts from Richard Burton's diary in* Life *magazine remind me so much of you and I,* he wrote in a letter, *except we never bought any funky diamonds or let the dogs shit on the carpet, or made any films. Or did we?* He was like Jackson Pollock, he said, and I was like Cher. For a while he worked on a plan for us both to marry David Geffen. We did have sex, eventually, but sex was never our central currency—a fact that made our romance more honest, I thought. Sex you could get anywhere. Reality was for losers.

Not long after we got engaged, in the winter of my last year at Oberlin, he called to tell me he was leaving Chicago, moving to Phoenix, where his parents and brothers lived. He'd lost his lease on the club again—relocated twice already since its inception in the old church—and he was sick of theater business, the bullshit and self-seeking, everybody trying to get something from him. He wanted to quit drinking, maybe even cigarettes, start life anew—especially if we were going to get married. The plan was for me to join him as soon as I graduated.

He sent dozens of letters in the meantime, addressed to *Miss Wendy Brenner Queen of the May, Wendy you with the stars in your eyes Brenner, Miss Wendy Brenner & Cheese Hold the Mayo, Miss U Wendy Brenner,* the envelopes overflowing with ephemera both personal and mundane, as if he were trying to send me his life. His school photo from eighth grade. A stenciled satin label for MAJOR MAJOR, a line of T-shirts he planned to design. A garden-store ad for Corry's Slug & Snail Death. His twenty-four-hour chip from Alcoholics Anonymous. A tabloid headline: HEARTBREAKING STORY OF THE SMARTEST BOY WHO EVER LIVED.

March 1987:

I've only been here a month and already my room is a pile of books, newspapers, clippings, and junk—just like always. Collecting ideas.

June 1987:

I told you I wanted to kill my brother at dinner the other night . . . even though he's got a "cute" personality there's only so much I can take. He and my dad look like matching bookends, only their heads are contrasting sizes. Let's get married July 4.

June 1987:

Bad things about me? Well, I'm TOO funny—that's one. And I'm too considerate, that's another . . . I'm losing my hair, and my teeth are a mess (could my ears be far behind).

July 1987:

A car jumped the curb while I was having coffee and almost ran over me—it was reeeeaaaaaal close—I figured it was you thinking of me.

Sometimes he sent cassettes that he recorded, unscripted, on his portable tape recorder, while driving to work, doing laundry, watching TV, cleaning his apartment. *This is great, now I can turn off the light, lay down in bed, I don't have to write anything longhand, I'm not keeping anybody up with my typing . . . and think of how great it'll be for you when you get this, you know? You won't have to go through the bother of holding a piece of paper in your hand and making your eyes go back and forth.*

His slow, precise voice had always made me swoon, and his timing made everything he said seem absurd and hilarious, even the most ordinary observations. The very ordinariness, the dailiness, of his monologues thrilled me. *I have some pink socks that I never wear. You may have them.* On one tape he reenacted for me the song-and-dance number he and a friend performed in the AA talent show. On another he just sang for half an hour, making up lyrics as he went, a long improvised medley that included "Up, Up and Away," "Do You Know the Way to San José?" the national anthem, and a six-minute rendition of "You Light Up My Life."

I played the tapes for everyone, all my friends, strangers who happened to walk by my dorm room, anyone who would listen. I showed them off the way normal girls show off diamond engagement rings. *Doesn't he sound like Jack Nicholson? Isn't he a genius?*

And yet, when the time came, I didn't move to Arizona.

Even now, I cannot fully explain why. I never decided not to marry Jim. It wasn't a decision so much as an inability to make one. A postponement, a procrastination.

I didn't plan to stay in Chicago long, just through the summer. But by fall I'd taken a job answering phones at a hair salon, rented an apartment in the city. I had a useless degree in creative writing, no specific ambitions other than to be "creative." I didn't know how to use a word processor or even make a résumé, and my dead-end job barely paid my rent on my basement studio apartment. But I knew people in Chicago, and streets, clubs, subway lines, good places to eat—a loosely stitched together fabric of familiarity that passed for a life. I didn't know anyone in the entire state of Arizona, except Jim, whose opinion mattered so much it terrified me—more than anything I had ever made or done on my own. I had nothing to bring to the table, no resources, inner or outer. I feared he would see this about me, finally, in the harsh desert light of sobriety and daily routine.

We didn't break up or even argue about it. Our letters and phone calls continued through that fall as though nothing had changed—and maybe nothing had. Our love affair had never been predicated on geographical proximity, physical reality. Anyway it was only temporary, I told myself, just until I felt more secure. I did not yet understand how security makes it harder, not easier, to change one's life, how even the smallest move takes more and more effort with each passing year.

Shortly after we decided to get married, Jim wrote: *Do you love me? Is this going to be okay—even fun? Are we in a big hurry? I don't want to burn this thing out. Is it going to end? Please—I have to know.*

Twenty years later, after his death, I reread this letter, appalled that I had failed to register such straightforward vulnerability. I didn't even remember that these words existed; this was not part of the story of us I'd always told. In my version, Jim held all the power. So large and overwhelming were my own insecurities, I simply could not imagine a future in which he might love and need me more than I loved and needed him. I could not envision the future—my adult life—at all.

In another letter from the same period, he wrote: *Think about getting your butt out here—there's a reason to live.*

When I tell friends that Jim is dead, they leap to assure me it wasn't my fault, nothing I could have done. *Nobody can save an alcoholic, he must save himself! Love the person, hate the disease!* These people didn't even know Jim, but they can't get the words out fast enough. I tell them Jim is dead and am immediately and unequivocally cleared of all wrongdoing.

I don't mean to sound—to be—so ungrateful. I can see that by any sane person's standards my decision not to move to Arizona was completely understandable, forgivable, even "healthy."

It was still the wrong decision.

*   *   *

We kept in touch, though it inevitably grew more difficult to do so. I moved to Florida for graduate school, then to New York and North Carolina for teaching jobs. Jim stayed in Phoenix, worked at an art gallery, a Lucite studio, a furniture store, traveled to Los Angeles and San Diego for design conferences. Eventually we both dated other people, though nothing lasted, on either side. Sometimes I cried on the phone to him about asshole boyfriends or evil landlords. He still drank sometimes, still went to AA meetings. We talked about visiting, tried to make plans, but it was never the right moment, we were both so busy. Sometimes I felt alarmed by how many years had passed since we'd seen each other—the same way everyone feels about everyone. His letters continued, as always.

1991:

The job is okay. My life is dull. I like it that way. I'm into sterilizing everything and have plastic over my door and windows. I have a big portrait of Howard Hughes in my bathroom.

1992:

My friends are here from New York. They're twins . . . Gary (twin #1) has an office in the Empire State Building—isn't that great! I asked him if he worked for King Kong.

1995:

I'm sooo incredibly tired I'm about to have a nervous breakdown. I work a bizillion hours a week.

1996:

Next time you call make up something nice about what might be happening with you. Lie if you have to. Life gets a little divey. Edgy. Boring.

Sometimes, on the phone, when Jim was drinking, he would ask me again to marry him. Sometimes when we hadn't spoken for a while I would think he was right—he was the love of my life, nobody else ever lived up. But then we'd talk, and I'd remember how it was, how he was. The funniest person, the most brilliant, but also the scariest. The most dangerous, most exciting, most unknowable. It was too much, too intense. It could never work. Not in the real world.

At some indeterminable point during these years, I began to morph into the grown-up person I could not envision a decade earlier.

At some point, Jim began to lose everything.

The e-mail came on a Sunday night in December 2007. I recognized her name right away even though we hadn't been in touch for twenty years. I didn't know any other Melodies.

I still had the publicity photo she'd autographed for me back when she performed weekly with her improv troupe at Jim's club and snapshots of her and Jim posing together in the lobby under the giant wall-mounted marlin, looking glamorous in matching aviator sunglasses. I remembered feeling jealous of the easy way they laughed together, as if every single word he uttered was not the most important thing in the world. They never dated each other, but they shared an apartment for a while, roommates and best friends. Both fled Chicago around the same time—Jim to Arizona, Melodie to California, where she married a famous music producer.

I remembered Jim mentioning they'd reconnected a few years back, by strange coincidence: he was visiting another Los Angeles friend who happened to live right across the street from her.

In retrospect, divine providence.

I have been trying to call you, Melodie's e-mail said. *You know that there can only be one reason for this message.*

He'd been in and out of ICU all year, she told me. Cirrhosis, hepatitis C, irreversible liver damage. His parents were both now dead, and he was largely estranged from his sister and brothers, only one of whom still lived in Phoenix. He was alone when he died, in his room at a residential hotel, making beef stew and drinking a glass of red wine, clean laundry neatly folded on the bed. His esophagus started to bleed and he called 911.

Melodie had just spoken with him the night before. They talked every night, she said, all night if he wanted. He visited often, spent holidays with her family, slept in the bed with her, even. Her husband didn't mind—he wanted Jim to move to LA so they could take better care of him. Her kids loved him, called him Uncle Jim. When he died, he was wearing a friendship bracelet her nine-year-old daughter had made for him.

He knew he was dying, Melodie told me. Had known for a year. Made a living will, a regular will. She helped him get everything set up as he wanted. No funeral, no memorial. She was, at the moment, keeping his ashes beside her in bed.

I badgered him, begged him to call you, she said, *but he* would not *discuss it. He always carried your book with him, you know, whenever he traveled. But he would not talk about you at all.*

His number had appeared on my caller ID two or three times that year. I was busy, I ignored it. He didn't leave a message.

We had spoken again, thank God, after his voice mail about my book, the *bullshit stories* message. He said he didn't remember leaving it, and I believed him. He was drinking heavily and could not find an antidepressant that worked or a doctor he liked. His mother was dying, would be dead within the year, 2006. As we talked, I could hear him getting drunker. I tried to convince him, as always, to get online, get an e-mail account. As always, he refused, said he had no interest in computers. I told him about my colon cancer surgery, which had occurred since we'd last been in touch. I was in remission now, cancer free, the whole ordeal a mercifully brief memory, but Jim latched on to the topic in a way that made me uncomfortable, like he was happy to locate an area of vulnerability, to find an in. Like he wanted me to be weak, so that he could again, at least for one moment, be strong.

At least that's what I thought I heard in his voice.

He sent a note a few days later, the last I would receive from him.

Wendy—

I adore you.
I'm thinking of you.
I love you.
Jim

Reading this, as I recall, I felt only cynical and a little sad.

Three weeks after I get the news from Melodie, I am scheduled for more abdominal surgery—not the cancer again, I'm still in remission, but it's my fifth surgery in five years. By now, I think I know what to expect, which drugs to ask for, which foods to stock the house with in advance, whom to call upon for errands. In between presurgical scans and blood tests and grocery shopping and phone-list making, I get Jim's cassette tapes transferred onto CD, dig up his letters and put them all together in a safe place, scan photos into my computer and e-mail them to Melodie. I keep up a frantic pace, can't afford to break down before surgery. How in hell will I manufacture the mind-set, the necessary body chemicals, for healing?

Going into the hospital, I give myself an impossible instruction: *Do not think about Jim.*

Oh, if you've been through colon cancer, this will be a breeze, one of the presurgery nurses tells me. It turns out she's wrong.

I come out with a compression bandage stretched hip to hip, holding everything in. If I lie perfectly still, the pain ceases. If I move, cry, or take a deep breath, it feels like I'm being stabbed. Friends drop off groceries. I can't do the most basic tasks for myself—shower, change my sheets, put on socks. My phone never rings; I've told everyone it hurts too much to talk.

If the phone does ring, it won't be Jim.

I wonder if this is how he felt. If this is half the pain he felt.

After a few weeks I start to feel that my body quite literally cannot contain my grief for much longer. If I even think about

Jim, I start to tremble uncontrollably. The compression bandage is gone, but in its place is a searing pain, as if I've been cut in half. I can't tell if the pain is from the surgery or from holding in the pain.

One night I'm crying so hard I'm sure my scar will split open, and then I hear Jim's voice, just like how people always describe hearing the dead, perfectly clear and distinct, like he's right there in the room.

He says: *It's not like you'd be calling me, if I were alive.*

Recovery takes far longer than my surgeon predicted. During the weeks flat on my back, I watch and rewatch every movie I've ever liked, all the films I missed and have been meaning to see. I try to avoid love stories. Horror films are strangely reassuring. I watch *Rosemary's Baby* every day for a month—for some reason it always calms me down.

I watch *The Hunger* because I remember Jim loved it—urban vampires, gauzy curtains fluttering in architectural windows, crazed monkeys in cages, David Bowie and Catherine Deneuve. We saw it together when it came out in 1983, joked that he was Bowie's character, the doomed elegant vampire, and I was his violin student, Alice, the precocious gum-snapping teenager he must kill so that he can stay alive.

I had forgotten most things about the film. Bowie's anguished, accusing voice, for example, shouting across the ages: *Who's to keep you company when I'm gone?*

And the waiting room scene.

He's at the clinic, desperately trying to get the doctor's attention. *Yesterday I was thirty years old*, he says, showing Susan

Sarandon the liver spots on his hand, which have appeared overnight. *I'm a young man. Do you understand?*

She thinks he's nuts, tells him to take a seat in the waiting room, alerts building security. *Just let him sit there awhile and he'll probably get tired and leave.*

Hours pass, his hair turns white and falls out, his face sags into wrinkles, his eyes turn rheumy. By the time Susan Sarandon returns he's aged so much she doesn't recognize him, until he speaks. *You let me down. You didn't believe me. You just thought I was some ridiculous old crank.*

She understands, too late. *Please, wait!* she cries after him. *You can't leave!*

Too late, he's already pushed past her, out the clinic door, gone.

For a while, all movies hurt too much. Doesn't matter what genre, or if I've seen it a million times. *Poltergeist, Ghost World, Bad Timing, Being John Malkovich, The King of Comedy, Lost in Translation, Stranger Than Fiction, The Man Who Fell to Earth.*

Every movie is about Jim.

For a while I watch nothing but "making of" documentaries, the special featurettes on all my DVDs. Paul Schrader on *Taxi Driver,* Brian De Palma on *Carrie,* Peter Weir on *The Last Wave.*

Music is out of the question. My iPod takes on a treacherous look, like a Taser.

"Fire and Rain" is playing in every grocery store, every doctor's waiting room in town.

*   *   *

I can't get past #1 on the grief workbook's checklist, the Six Needs of Mourning: *Accept the reality of the death.* Whatever. I'll *pretend* to accept it—will that work?

But it's always been my tendency to lie to doctors, says the narrator of Denis Johnson's story "Car Crash While Hitchhiking," *as if good health consisted only of the ability to fool them.*

There has to be a way to get him back.

I start asking people: *If anyone had ever actually gotten someone back from the dead, we would know about it, right? I mean, not counting Jesus.*

Typing this essay on my computer, I read UNDO EDIT as UNDO DEATH.

About comedian John Belushi, the TV producer Norman Lear once said, *Whatever year I am destined to die, I have five years or ten years on top of that because those people who offered me that touch of madness gave me time, added to my life.*

But what if I don't want any extra life? Can't I transfer those years back to Jim, like frequent flier miles?

There has to be a way to get him back.

In my kitchen hangs the imported Roxy Music concert poster we bought together at Wax Trax in Chicago. Over my sofa, the wooden Mexican cross covered with *milagros*, tiny silver arms and legs and eyes and hearts, that I bought in Arizona when I was still planning to move there.

In my linen closet, the Ralph Lauren sheets he gave me for my dorm when I was going off to school for the first time—the most romantic gift I'd ever received, I thought.

On my coffee table, the kitschy square glass ashtray, circa

1963, printed with I LOVE YOU in twelve different languages: *Te amo, Ich liebe dich, Jeg elsker dig, Je t'aime,* half of a matched set Jim swiped from his mother's house in Scottsdale.

Looking at some twenty-year-old photos of Jim and me in Phoenix, I spot my cheap little black travel clock sitting atop the headboard on the hotel bed, where one of us had placed it for some reason, probably to remind us not to be late to something—the same seemingly indestructible clock that's followed me to each new place I live.

It sits across the room from me now, as I write this, ticking away more time.

It is 2008, and I'm watching late-night TV with Jim. I'm lying in bed, listening to his lazy Jack Nicholson drawl, nothing between us but my iPod headphones and twenty-one years and whatever separates the living from the dead. *I'm watching Rollerball,* he says in my ear, *and it's the dumbest movie I've ever watched in my life. I don't get it, I don't get any of it. Of course I keep dozing off, but I can't really sleep.*

He made me this one for Valentine's Day 1987, used the blank B side of an audition cassette he'd received in the mail. *On the other side of this tape is a real outstanding comedy routine some jag-off sent me,* he says. *I don't know if I'm going to erase it or not. But if I don't, go ahead and play it, I'm sure it's just brilliant.* People sent him tapes for months after his club closed; the floor of his apartment was littered with eight-by-ten glossy head shots and résumés. It was fun stepping on their hopeful, fatuous faces, all these people who wanted something from him, still, even as he applied for telemarketing jobs and food

stamps. Like the last line of "Car Crash While Hitchhiking":
And you, you ridiculous people, you expect me to help you.

There's nothing on, Jim says, flipping through the channels
on his TV, the old black-and-white portable with the broken
volume knob, stuck always at just a half-decibel too quiet, so
that you had to move gingerly, chew softly, slow your breath in
order to hear. *Even Ghost Stories, I already saw that one, the one
that's on tonight,* he says. *They always have that stupid fucking
trick ending.* I hear the metallic dink as he changes channels,
the static between channels. *Oh, this is a Bela Lugosi film where
they, like, turn these people into monkeys.* Dink. *Here's another
old movie. Everybody's, like, oh fuck, it's George Sanders.*

"I can see Nandji and I sitting there with the rain falling,"
says Peter Weir, recalling an aborigine tribal elder he directed
in the movie *The Last Wave,* "him telling me things that were
maybe from an unbroken continuity of fifty thousand years."
The tribe inhabited a remote island, did not share our easy
modern definitions of reality, of time as a straight line moving in one direction. *You're in trouble!* an aboriginal character
shouts at a white man in the film. *You don't know what dreams
are anymore!* Talking with that elder was like shortwave radio,
Weir says, "when you're tuning, you're dialing, and you're picking up a voice from thousands of miles away . . . he would say
a few things . . . and then I would lose him. I would lose that
frequency."

I don't know, Jim says, *this guy's about to get killed or something, he's a scuba diver, and this guy with a yachting cap on
is about to, like, shoot him with a harpoon. Probably thinks it's
a shark, I don't know. Oops, look out! He got the guy with the*

yacht cap first. Now they're shooting at him, but they'll never get him . . .

It is 2008 and Jim is dead. He laughs into my ear, close as ever, far away as ever.

This is fun, isn't it? he says. It's sort of just like being with me, isn't it? Only a lot more exciting.

About the Authors

Jami Attenberg is the author of *Instant Love* and *The Kept Man*. She has written about sex, technology, comic books, and urban life for *Jane*, *Print*, *Nerve*, *New York*, *Nylon*, *Salon*, and other publications. Her novel *The Melting Season* is forthcoming from Riverhead Books. Visit her online at whatever-whenever.net.

Lynda Barry has worked as a painter, cartoonist, writer, illustrator, playwright, editor, commentator, and teacher, and found they are very much alike. She is the inimitable creator behind the syndicated strip *Ernie Pook's Comeek* featuring the incomparable Marlys and Freddie, as well as the books *What It Is*, *One! Hundred! Demons!*, *Cruddy: An Illustrated Novel*, *The! Greatest! of! Marlys!*, and *Naked Ladies! Naked Ladies! Naked Ladies!* Drawn & Quarterly plans to publish a multivolume hardcover collection of *Ernie Pook's Comeek* starting in 2009 as well as her new book, *Nearsighted Monkey*. Her work has been widely praised, and her book *The Good Times Are Kill-*

ing Me—also adapted as an off-Broadway musical—won the Washington State Governor's Award. Barry currently offers her workshop, "Writing the Unthinkable," all over the place.

Wendy Brenner is the author of two books, *Phone Calls from the Dead* and *Large Animals in Everyday Life*. Her stories and essays have appeared in *Seventeen, Allure, Story, Plough-shares*, and other magazines and have been anthologized in *The Best American Magazine Writing* and *New Stories from the South*. She is a contributing writer for *Oxford American* magazine and teaches in the MFA program in creative writing at the University of North Carolina–Wilmington.

Kate Christensen's novel *The Great Man* won the 2008 PEN/Faulkner Award. Her fifth novel, *Trouble*, was published in June 2009 by Doubleday. She recently completed a new novel, *The Astral*. Her essays and reviews have appeared in various publications, including *Elle, Tin House, Salon, Real Simple*, the *Wall Street Journal*, and many anthologies. She lives in Brooklyn with her husband and their dog.

Brock Clarke is the author of two novels, *An Arsonist's Guide to Writers' Homes in New England* and *The Ordinary White Boy*, and two short story collections, *Carrying the Torch* and *What We Won't Do*. He has twice been a finalist for the National Magazine Award in fiction. His fiction and essays have appeared in the *Virginia Quarterly Review*, the *Believer, One Story, Southern Review, Georgia Review*, the *New York Times*, and *New England Review*; in the Pushcart Prize and *New Sto-*

ries from the South annual anthologies; and on NPR's *Selected Shorts*. He is a 2008 NEA fellow in fiction, and teaches at the University of Cincinnati.

Junot Díaz is the author of *The Brief Wondrous Life of Oscar Wao*, winner of the Pulitzer Prize for Fiction, the John Sargent Sr. First Novel Prize, and the National Book Critics Circle Award for Fiction, and *Drown*, winner of the PEN/Malamud Award. His fiction has appeared in the *New Yorker*, the *Paris Review*, and *The Best American Short Stories*. Born in the Dominican Republic and raised in New Jersey, Díaz lives in New York City and is a professor of writing at MIT.

Jennifer Finney Boylan is the author of ten books, including *I'm Looking Through You: Growing Up Haunted*. Her 2003 memoir, *She's Not There: A Life in Two Genders*, was the first best-selling work by a transgendered American. She has appeared on *The Oprah Winfrey Show*, *Larry King Live*, the *Today* show, and been the subject of documentaries on CBS News' *48 Hours* and on the History Channel. In 2007 she played herself on several episodes of ABC's *All My Children*. Jenny is professor of English at Colby College. She lives in Maine with her partner Deirdre and her sons Zach and Sean.

Emily Flake is an illustrator, cartoonist, and writer. Her work has appeared in such publications as *Forbes*, the *Nation*, and the *New York Times*. Her cartoon strip, *Lulu Eightball*, runs in alt-weeklies across the country. She is the author and illustrator of *These Things Ain't Gonna Smoke Themselves: A Love/*

Hate/Love/Hate/Love Letter to a Very Bad Habit. She makes her real home in Brooklyn, New York, and her Web home at www .eflakeagogo.com.

A journalist who lives in New York, **Michelle Green** has written for the *New York Times*, the *Wall Street Journal*, and the *Atlanta Journal-Constitution*. She is the author of *The Dream at the End of the World: Paul Bowles and the Literary Renegades in Tangier*.

Dan Kennedy is the author of the national bestseller *Rock On: An Office Power Ballad* and *Loser Goes First: My Thirty-Something Years of Dumb Luck and Minor Humiliation*, a regular contributor at *GQ*, and a long-standing writer at McSweeneys. net. He resides in New York City where he frequently performs onstage as part of the Moth storytelling collective. He is currently writing and developing the pilot of *Rock On* for HBO.

Josh Kilmer-Purcell is the author of the novel *Candy Everybody Wants* and the bestselling memoir *I Am Not Myself These Days*. He writes a monthly column for *Out* magazine. Kilmer-Purcell and his partner divide their time between Manhattan and a goat farm in upstate New York.

Pasha Malla is the author of *The Withdrawal Method* (stories) and *All our grandfathers are ghosts* (poems).

Wendy McClure is a columnist for *BUST* magazine and was a frequent contributor to the "True-Life Tales" feature in the *New York Times Magazine*. She is the author of the memoir

I'm Not the New Me and the humor book *The Amazing Mackerel Pudding Plan*, and her work has appeared in several anthologies, including *Sleepaway: Writings on Summer Camp*. She has an MFA in poetry from the Iowa Writers' Workshop and lives in Chicago, where she works as a children's book editor and maintains a Weblog at Poundy.com.

Maud Newton is a writer and blogger who grew up in Miami and now lives in a section of Brooklyn, New York, that has avoided gentrification into a hipster wonderland. Her essay, "Conversations You Have at Twenty," won second prize in the 2008 *StoryQuarterly/Narrative* Love Story Contest. Her essays and stories have also appeared in *Swink, Mr. Beller's Neighborhood, storySouth, Eyeshot, Maisonneuve, Pindeldyboz, Ducts,* and the anthology *When I Was a Loser,* and she has written for the *New York Times Book Review*, the *American Prospect*, the *Washington Post*, the *Boston Globe*, *Los Angeles Times*, *Newsday*, *Gawker*, VH1's Best Week Ever blog, and other publications and Web sites, including her own, MaudNewton.com. In 2004 the City College of New York chose her as the recipient of its Irwin and Alice Stark Short Fiction Award.

D. E. Rasso is a writer and editor whose work has appeared online at #1 Hit Song, Blottered, and Young Manhattanite, and in print at numerous quality literary journals and magazines with print runs of under thirty copies.

Margaret Sartor grew up in Monroe, Louisiana. Her most recent book is the *New York Times* best-selling memoir *Miss*

American Pie: A Diary of Love, Secrets, and Growing Up in the 1970s. As an editor, she has published three books, including *What Was True: The Photographs and Notebooks of William Gedney.* Her photographs have appeared in books and periodicals, including *DoubleTake, Esquire,* and the *New Yorker.* She has curated shows at the International Center of Photography in New York and the San Francisco Museum of Modern Art. She teaches at Duke University and lives with her husband and two children in Durham, North Carolina.

Saïd Sayrafiezadeh is the author of *When Skateboards Will Be Free,* a memoir about growing up communist in the United States. His essays and short stories have appeared in the *Paris Review, Granta,* and *Open City,* among others.

Gary Shteyngart is the author of *Absurdistan,* chosen as one of the ten best books of the year by the *New York Times Book Review* in 2006, and *The Russian Debutante's Handbook.* His fiction and essays have appeared in the *New Yorker, Granta, GQ, Esquire,* the *New York Times Magazine,* and many other publications. He lives in New York.

George Singleton has published four collections of stories and two novels: *These People Are Us, The Half-Mammals of Dixie, Why Dogs Chase Cars, Drowning in Gruel, Novel,* and *Work Shirts for Madmen.* His latest book—*Pep Talks, Warnings, and Screeds*—is a collection of aphorisms, analogies, and anecdotes that concern the fiction writer, illustrated by Daniel Wallace. More than one hundred of Singleton's short stories have appeared in *Glimmer Train*, the *Atlantic Monthly, Harper's, Playboy, Zoetrope: All-Story Georgia Review, Shenandoah*, and elsewhere. He's been anthologized in *New Stories from the South, Writers Harvest, They Write Among Us, Best Food Writing 2005, Behind the Short Story,* and *20 over 40*, among others. He lives happily in Dacusville, South Carolina, with ceramicist Glenda Guion, their collection of strays, and the two tattoos they got in Vegas, sober.

Amanda Stern is the author of the novel *The Long Haul*. Her nonfiction has been featured in the *New York Times*, the *New York Times Magazine*, the *East Hampton Star*, the *Believer*, and *Paste*. She's published fiction in the literary journals *Swink*, the *Saint Ann's Review, Hayden's Ferry Review, Spinning Jenny*, and *Five Chapters,* among other places. In 2003 she created the popular Happy Ending Music and Reading Series in New York City. She lives in Brooklyn and is at work on her second novel.

Michael Taeckens received his MFA from the Iowa Writers' Workshop. His writing has appeared in *Salon, Out,* the *Advocate*, and *River City*. He lives in Durham, North Carolina.

Patty Van Norman still considers herself a master of the breakup letter.

Dave White is the author of the memoir *Exile in Guyville* and writes about pop culture for MSNBC.com and the *Advocate*. His work has appeared in the *Village Voice* and *LA Weekly*. He lives in West Hollywood and can be found at imdavewhite .com.